THE TED
TRUEBLOOD
HUNTING
TREASURY

THE TED TRUEBLOOD HUNTING TREASURY

Ted Trueblood

DAVID McKAY COMPANY, INC.
New York

Library of Congress Cataloging in Publication Data

Trueblood, Ted Whitaker, 1913-
The Ted Trueblood hunting treasury.

Includes index.
1. Hunting.   I. Title.
SK33.T77   799.2′08   77-20845
ISBN 0-679-50802-3

10 9 8 7 6 5 4 3 2 1

Manufactured in the United States of America

Designed by C.R. Bloodgood

Contents

Acknowledgements

The author and publisher gratefully thank the editors of magazines in which much of this material originally appeared, for permission to reproduce in whole or in part the following articles from their pages: DON'T WAIT TOO LONG, Field & Stream, February, 1972, copyright © 1971 by Holt, Rinehart and Winston, Inc. THE OLD AND THE NEW, Field & Stream, November, 1970, copyright © 1970 by Holt, Rinehart and Winston, Inc. FUNDAMENTALS OF DEER HUNTING, Field & Stream, November, 1965, copyright © 1965 by Holt, Rinehart and Winston, Inc. I DON'T WANT TO KILL A DEER, Field & Stream, October, 1960, copyright © 1960 by Holt, Rinehart and Winston, Inc. WHAT TO DO AFTER YOU SHOOT IT, Field & Stream, October, 1971, copyright © 1971 by Holt, Rinehart and Winston, Inc. CARE OF WILD MEAT, Field & Stream, November, 1971, copyright © 1971 by Holt, Rinehart and Winston, Inc. SKILLET SKILL, Field & Stream, July, 1976, copyright © 1976 by CBS Publications. THE POT THAT DOES IT ALL, Field & Stream, April, 1971, copyright © 1971 by Holt, Rinehart and Winston, Inc. COOKING IN FOIL, Field & Stream, August, 1975, copyright © 1975 by CBS Publications. COOKING GAME, Field & Stream, December, 1966, copyright © 1966 by Holt, Rinehart and Winston, Inc. MATCHING WITS WITH ELK, Field & Stream, November, 1967, copyright © 1967 by Holt, Rinehart and Winston, Inc. REWARD FOR VIRTUE, Field & Stream, September, 1957, copyright © 1957 by Henry Holt and Company, Inc. ONE DAY, ONE ANTELOPE, Field & Stream, September, 1967, copyright © 1967 by Holt, Rinehart and Winston, Inc. THE FIVE-YEAR LION HUNT, Field & Stream, February, 1970, copyright © 1970 by Holt, Rinehart and Winston, Inc. TEST IT FIRST, Field & Stream, August, 1962, copyright © 1962 by Holt, Rinehart and Winston, Inc. OF BOYS AND GUNS, Field & Stream, December, 1971, copyright © 1971 by Holt, Rinehart and Winston, Inc. MY 6-OUNCE BENCH REST, Field & Stream, August, 1957, copyright © 1957 by Henry Holt and Company, Inc. BEWARE THE ONE-WIRE FENCE, Field & Stream, March, 1969, copyright © 1969 by Holt, Rinehart and Winston, Inc. THE WILD, FREE DAYS, Field & Stream, December, 1964, copyright © 1964 by Holt, Rinehart and Winston, Inc. MAKE SURE YOU MISSED, Field & Stream, September, 1956, copyright © 1956 by Henry Holt and Company, Inc. MAKE SURE YOU MISSED, Field & Stream, January, 1976, copyright © 1975 by CBS Publications. HUNTING CLOTHES, Field & Stream, September, 1965, copyright © 1965 by Holt, Rinehart and Winston, Inc. HUNTING IN THE SNOW, Field & Stream, December, 1963, copyright © 1963 by Holt, Rinehart and Winston, Inc. TENTS, Field & Stream, July, 1966, copyright © 1966 by Holt, Rinehart and Winston, Inc. KNIFE AND AX—YOUR INDISPENSABLE TOOLS, Field & Stream, June, 1959, copyright © 1959 by Henry Holt and Company, Inc. SHARPENING, Field & Stream, February, 1970, copyright © 1970 by Holt, Rinehart and Winston, Inc. WHAT GAME TRACKS REVEAL, Field & Stream, October, 1958, copyright © 1958 by Henry Holt and Company, Inc. FOILING GAME'S KEEN NOSE, Field & Stream, August, 1958, copyright © 1958 by Henry Holt and Company, Inc. HOW TO SIT STILL, Field

& Stream, September, 1960, copyright © 1960 by Holt, Rinehart and Winston, Inc. HOW NOT TO GET LOST, Field & Stream, September, 1974, copyright © 1974 by CBS Publications. LOST!, Field & Stream, October, 1974, copyright © 1975 by CBS Publications. HOW NOT TO TRAIN HUNTING DOGS, Field & Stream, December, 1961, copyright © 1961 by Holt, Rinehart and Winston, Inc. IS THAT SO?, Field & Stream, August, 1965, copyright © 1965 by Holt, Rinehart and Winston, Inc. THE GREAT DOVE GUN, Field & Stream, September, 1970, copyright © 1970 by Holt, Rinehart and Winston, Inc. A DAY ON FLUSTER FLAT, Field & Stream, September, 1960, copyright © 1960 by Holt, Rinehart and Winston, Inc. A HINT OF FALL, Field & Stream, August, 1969, copyright © 1969 by Holt, Rinehart and Winston, Inc. EDUCATION OF RUFF, Field & Stream, September, 1964, copyright © 1964 by Holt, Rinehart and Winston, Inc. THE SUCCESSFUL FAILURE, Field & Stream, May, 1974, copyright © 1974 by CBS Publications. SHOTGUN FITS, Field & Stream, September, 1971, copyright © 1971 by Holt, Rinehart and Winston, Inc. THE MYSTERIES OF LEAD, Field & Stream, November, 1974, copyright © 1974 by CBS Publications. YOU NEED A SCAPEGOAT, Field & Stream, September, 1962, copyright © 1962 by Holt, Rinehart and Winston, Inc. VERY EASY BIRDS TO MISS, Field & Stream, November, 1966, copyright © 1966 by Holt, Rinehart and Winston, Inc. COVEY BIRDS, Field & Stream, October, 1965, copyright © 1965 by Holt, Rinehart and Winston, Inc. MAKE THE DUCKS COME TO YOU, Field & Stream, November, 1956, copyright © 1956 by Henry Holt and Company, Inc. MYSTERIOUS JOURNEY, Field & Stream, January, 1971, copyright © 1970 by Holt, Rinehart and Winston, Inc. INVOLUNTARY BIRD WATCHING, Field & Stream, June, 1962, copyright © 1962 by Holt, Rinehart and Winston, Inc. OTHER VALUES, Field & Stream, December, 1962, copyright © 1962 by Holt, Rinehart and Winston, Inc. TED TRUEBLOOD TELLS HOW TO DEFEATHER, DRESS AND COOK WILD DUCKS SO THAT THEY ARE A DELICACY ON THE TABLE, Field & Stream, December, 1956, copyright © 1956 by Henry Holt and Company, Inc. DAYS ON BUNNY MOUNTAIN, Field & Stream, January, 1972, copyright © 1971 by Holt, Rinehart and Winston, Inc. A LETTER FROM THE FUTURE, Field & Stream, September, 1972, copyright © 1972 by CBS Publications. GIFTS THAT LAST A LIFETIME, Field & Stream, December, 1967, copyright © 1967 by Holt, Rinehart and Winston, Inc. TWO GREAT DAYS WITH DUCKS, Field & Stream, November, 1968, copyright © 1968 by Holt, Rinehart and Winston, Inc. OUTWIT-TING THE SNEAKY RINGNECK, Field & Stream, October, 1961, copyright © 1961 by Holt, Rinehart and Winston, Inc. THE ART OF FLIPPERY, Field & Stream, January, 1963, copyright © 1962 by Holt, Rinehart and Winston, Inc. CHUKAR TACTICS, Field & Stream, October, 1976, copyright © 1976 by CBS Publications. MAGNIFICENT MIDGETS, QUAIL ARE SPECIAL CHALLENGES TO ANY HUNGER, The Elks Magazine, October, 1953. SPELL OF THE HIGH COUNTRY, The Elks Magazine, October, 1958. TRUEBLOOD'S LAWS OF DUCK HUNTING, The Elks Magazine, December, 1958. WILD, WILD PHEASANT, The Elks Magazine, October, 1960. A DAY WITH HUNS, The Elks Magazine, October, 1961.

Preface

My first hunting license, which is framed and hangs above my desk, is dated 1927. My latest is in my billfold, and I have missed none in between. During my boyhood on the farm my father cleared and put into cultivation, there were always several guns behind the kitchen door. We used them frequently, on game in the fall and on pests during the off season. And since the entire neighborhood was young and there was abundant cover everywhere, we had no shortage of targets.

In my earlier years, I was merely eager to hunt. But as I matured I began to develop a philosophy toward the outdoors and nature and all things connected with them. The bag is now less important. I find pleasure in the simple things my ancestors did many centuries ago. I enjoy cutting wood, that munificent storehouse of the sun's energy, and making a campfire and cooking my dinner over its hot embers. Then I like to sit beside it and watch the twinkling stars emerge and listen to the wavering call of a coyote while the clean, sweet smoke rises like the wraith of some long-gone hunter to vanish in the darkening sky.

So this book is partly practical and, what I now think more important, partly philosophical. Some chapters are devoted to such subjects as making sourdough hotcakes, cooking in a Dutch oven, or hunting deer; in others I discuss the real, true things nature has to offer and the philosophy that has made hunting more rewarding with each passing season.

This is a selection from more than five hundred articles that have appeared in *Field & Stream* and *The Elks Magazine.* I am grateful to the publishers for their permission to present here those I consider the best on hunting, the camping associated with it, and the intangible riches bestowed by nature on all who visit the outdoors with open eyes and inquiring minds.

TED TRUEBLOOD

Nampa, Idaho, 1977

Foreword

Some years ago, while stuck for an idea for my "Exit Laughing" column in *Field & Stream,* and shortly after I'd returned from a delightful camping-cum-chukar-hunting expedition in southwestern Idaho with Ted and Ellen Trueblood, it occurred to me to reveal to the sporting public the fact that Ted Trueblood doesn't exist. I'm not sure whence came the idea, but it probably relates to the simple proposition, well known to several generations of outdoorsmen, that *Trueblood is too good to be true!* As indeed he is. (It might also relate to my having heard Hugh Grey, then editor of *Field & Stream,* telling a story about Trueblood and summing it up with the comment, "That guy is unreal!")

At any rate I wrote the following piece, turned it in, and went about my other chores. Here's the column as it appeared:

IS THERE REALLY
A TED TRUEBLOOD?

Usually this department is given over to the lighter side of outdoor sports, yet there comes a time when, in the interest of truth, we must speak out, simply because no one else dares. When what began—nearly twenty years ago—as a harmless practical joke on the readers of this magazine threatens to become a national scandal, it is time to make a clean breast of it.

And I must allow that some readers had begun to suspect the truth; even without this exposé, sooner or later America was bound to discover that *there is not—and never was—a Ted Trueblood!* "Ted Trueblood" is simply a creation of the collective imagination of *Field & Stream*'s editors. But before you condemn them too harshly, let me tell you how this famous (and fictitious) outdoor writer came into being.

It began one evening many years ago at the *Field & Stream* office when several of the editors were complaining that, although they worked for the world's leading outdoor magazine, they had almost no time, or not nearly enough, for hunting and fishing. "I wonder if anybody ever had the good fortune to do nothing but hunt and fish the year 'round," mused one editor. "Of course not," said another, "that just doesn't happen in real life." "But just imagine," said a third ink-stained wretch, "what a dream-life that would be!" "Maybe there really is such a guy, somewhere," said the gun editor. "Let's try to find him and do a story on him." "Not a chance," said the fishing editor. "There's no such critter. But I've got an idea—let's *invent* him!"

"It might make a good piece, at that," said the editor-in-chief. "But what would we call him? Let's make it Ted something, on account of Teddy Roosevelt being such a great outdoor guy." "How about Ted Trueblue?" said one of the editors. "Too corny," said another, "but what would you say to Ted Redblood?" "That's even cornier," said the editor-in-chief. "But let me propose a compromise—Ted Trueblood." "Fine," said the gun editor, "but what about a family? Is this bird married or single?" "How could he be married and do nothing but hunt and fish?" asked the article editor. "He's gotta be single. Otherwise he'd be too busy putting up screens or taking them down or carrying out the garbage to ever do any hunting and fishing."

"No," said the editor-in-chief, "let's have him married. To a blond, good-looking, All-American-type gal who hunts and fishes with him. And they've got a couple of All-American-type kids who hunt and fish too. If we're going to do this, let's do it right—shoot the works. Let's call the gal Alice or Ellen or something simple—Ellen's my choice—and the kids could be, oh, say Dan and Jack. And of course this guy has a faithful old bird dog named Joe or something."

By the time the meeting ended they'd decided to have "Ted Trueblood" live in Idaho, because it had both good shooting and fishing in great variety, and they'd even invented a town called "Nampa," which they arrived at by spelling Art Editor Al Apman's last name backwards.

"Look, this guy's worth more than one crummy article," said the boating editor. "Why not have him be a writer—maybe once a month or so he'd drop his fly rod or shotgun, grab a typewriter, and bat out an article for *Field & Stream?* We could make him an associate editor, even, and put his name on the masthead." "Okay," said the editor-in-chief, "let's do it." And thus began an editorial hoax that has lasted nearly two decades.

When I first learned of this some time ago I hurried into the city to confront Editor Hugh Grey and demand the truth, but on the way I bumped into Al McClane and stopped to have a quick serving of what my friend Sam Morgan used to call sour-mash soup at the Biltmore Bar, and by the time we had had several bowlfuls I couldn't remember what I'd come into town for, and went on back home. As a matter of fact, come to think about it, I'm not so damn sure there's really an Al McClane.

When the issue got out to subscribers and onto the newsstands, all hell, or a considerable portion of it, broke loose. Fourteen subscribers canceled their long-standing subscriptions in protest against having been deceived for all those years, and hundreds of others wrote indignant letters protesting the hoax. Several hundred other people wrote equally indignant letters saying there by God *was* a Ted Trueblood, and making interesting if biologically impossible conjectures about my parentage. After a reporter saw the stacks of telegrams, cablegrams, and pro-and-con mail on Hugh's desk, the *New York Times* ran a two-column story under the headline "No Trueblood? Take to the Hills, Men!" The Nampa, Idaho, Chamber of Commerce offered to punch my nose, and I heard that an Idaho sportsmen's group had put out a contract on me.

Even today, I occasionally meet someone who takes me aside and asks, with some embarrassment, if there really *is* a Ted Trueblood, and I assure them there isn't. (Trueblood himself refused to take sides in the controversy, but sent me a framed 8x10 photographic print, completely blank except for the lower right-hand corner, where he inscribed, "Best wishes from Ted Trueblood." All in all, it was good fun.

I don't know how many admirers Trueblood has, but it must run into the millions. And yet I'm sure that few of them are aware that Ted is not only a sportsman and outdoorsman of consummate skills, with a staggering store of knowledge and know-how, but is also one of the most energetic and effective workers for natural-resource conservation in the West. They don't know it because Trueblood doesn't write about his own important contributions to the future of wildlife and wild rivers and wilderness in America. But enough people have found out about some of his labors in the conservation vineyard that recently he was awarded the United States Department of the Interior's highest honor to a citizen-conservationist, was elected outdoorsman of the year for 1975 by the Outdoor Writers of America, received the Distinguished Service Award for 1976-77 from Trout Unlimited, and was named honorary national president of the Izaak Walton League of America for 1977-78, and despite what they say about prophets he has even been honored in his own country, Idaho.

And finally, here's a book about hunting, full of facts and wisdom and gentle humor and good writing, as further evidence that there really is a Ted Trueblood.

For which let us all give thanks.

Ed Zern

Part I

POINT OF VIEW

Chapter 1

Don't Wait Too Long

When my wife and I lived in Pleasantville, New York, the neighbor across the street retired one September. Other neighbors said he was worth a million dollars. I don't know about that. He would only say that he had worked hard and made some good investments and now he intended to enjoy life. In November, two months after he quit work, we had a heavy snow. He started to shovel it off his walk, had a heart attack, and died.

I immediately quit my job in the city, to which I had been commuting five days each week, and returned to the West, determined to hunt, fish, and write about it. Why work hard and save money and then die before I

If you wait until tomorrow, tomorrow may never come.

had a chance to enjoy the things for which I had been saving it? The very idea was insane.

Of course, nonwriters might assume that writing is work. Not so. We writers know better. On days when we're too tired to hunt or fish, play golf or go girl watching, we lie back in an easy chair with a scratch pad on our laps, doze, and stare at the ceiling. Occasionally we scribble down a few words for which editors pay us incredible sums, and when our wives or children disturb our daydreaming we run them the hell out and tell them we're working.

Those were the days! For twenty-five years, I did just that and I told my friends and eager editors that I refused to work—pardon me, write—for money I didn't need. Then I forgot the lesson I had learned in Pleasantville. I had one boy in college and one in high school and the same problems every man has. I got to working harder and harder and neglecting regular exercise. My diet wasn't all it should have been. I smoked and drank too much. But worst of all, I worried.

I was asking for it, and I got it—a heart attack, and a good one. And let me tell every man who is heading toward one by the same route, it will scare you as you have never been scared before.

I was lucky. My old fishing and duck-hunting buddy had one within days of mine and he didn't make it. We had both been working harder and relaxing less and we had hardly fished or hunted together at all during the past two seasons. "Next year," we'd say on the rare occasions when we got together.

They had Jim's funeral while I was still under oxygen and when I learned about it the shock was pretty bad. He was one of the strongest, toughest, most healthy-appearing men I ever knew. His death and my close call were another lesson, and I decided not to invite a third.

While I was laid up, I read all the books on diet I could find, tried to separate the wheat from the chaff, and passed the more convincing ones on to my wife. And she was eager to read them because she'd had her scare, too. As soon as I was able I started walking, on doctor's orders, gradually increasing it from less than half a block to four miles per day. I resolved to quit worrying. This was the most difficult part of all and I had to do it by myself. The reasoning that helped the most was this: "If I can't get something done that should be done, the hell with it. I couldn't do it if I were dead, either."

My coronary came in February and by July I was able to wade a trout stream; by October I was hunting chukars. That is the toughest hunting I know anything about because they inhabit very steep, rocky country. Of course, I didn't hunt as hard as I once had—or do now. When I began to feel tired I'd sit down and take five. I was happy merely to be there, appreciating the autumn scenery as I had never appreciated it before, and if I couldn't kill all the chukars on the mountain, the hell with them, too.

It has now been several years since I hit bottom and I know I'll never have any heart problems again. Thanks to a better diet, regular exercise, an after-lunch nap, holding my weight exactly where the doctor told me to, and not worrying, I feel better now than I ever did.

Only two things have bothered me physically: walking into a cold, hard wind and starting to climb too soon after eating. As anyone who has had a heart problem knows, you get a warning in plenty of time—if you only heed it. At the first pain I sit down on the ground with my back to the wind and rest. And only once did I have problems by starting up a mountain immediately after lunch. I just don't do that any more.

I have come to prefer doing all of the day's hunting in one session, even though I may be half-starved before I get back to the car. If we do make a morning hunt and then another in the afternoon, however, I stretch out on the ground for half an hour after lunch—and often go sound asleep—before starting out again.

I tell this story not to show how clever I was—I wasn't smart; I was scared—but to point up the futility of working full throttle for years on end with the hopes of stopping to enjoy life at some vague time in the future. Keep it up long enough and there probably won't be any future. Even if there is, you won't enjoy it. My father-in-law was a perfect example of that.

He was a salesman. When he was home on weekends, he did nothing but loaf. He had a pleasant personality and many friends, but he lacked both vice and hobby. I suppose you could have put his lifetime consumption of whiskey in any eyecup, and when my wife and I once talked him into going deer hunting with us he enjoyed it about as much as he would have enjoyed spending the weekend in a mortuary.

As his time for retirement approached, we tried to get him interested in something—anything—that would help to make the coming years enjoyable. One example:

We live in a geologically rich area where enthusiastic rock hounds, as people who hunt rocks are called, find fossils, agate, jasper, geodes, and other stones, some of which are both valuable and attractive. We knew retired couples who spent several days each week during the spring and fall—it gets too hot in the summer—hunting rocks. During the winter they cut and polished their finds and arranged them for display. Organized rockhound clubs held field trips in season, meetings, and displays during the cold months.

We took Dad out into the desert, to places we had discovered hunting, and showed him where and how to find agate and petrified wood. We got him to visit a local hobby shop and look at the equipment for cutting and polishing what he found. We gave him a good rock book.

It was all of no use. And this is not to say he didn't try. He did try, both this and other hobbies, but he had waited too long. He had forgotten completely how to play.

Meanwhile, Mom, who had always enjoyed a hundred things from playing the piano to fishing, went along enthusiastically, She liked to look for pretty rocks. She enjoyed cooking lunch over a little fire. She had a camera—Dad never took a picture in his life—and no matter what we proposed, she was ready.

At last, Dad retired. He and Mom took a few trips and then he sat down to watch television. He went downhill day by day and died ten years later. Mom is still going strong, playing pinochle with her friends and enjoying her music when she is alone in her apartment.

This is another reason for enjoying life as you go along. First, of course, you want to stay alive. Second, if you wait until retirement to start doing the things you've always wanted to do, it will be too late.

So don't wait until you retire to go fishing or hunting. Don't even wait until your annual vacation. Go at every opportunity. Things that appear more urgent at the moment may, in the long run, turn out to be far less so. And if fishing or hunting is out of the question, there are other activities that will restore you both mentally and physically.

What are good hobbies? Well, of course, everybody who will read this book hunts or fishes, or does both, and I don't have to sell anybody on these activities. Either will sustain a lifelong interest, but both have two drawbacks from a practical standpoint: First, in many regions they are seasonal. Second, in some of the great metropolitan areas getting to the spots where you can enjoy them is quite a struggle.

To be beneficial, exercise must be regular. An ideal hobby for the man who sits at a desk all day is one that requires physical effort; if your muscles get a workout during the day, some less strenuous activity is better. I had a friend who made a lifelong—and profitable—hobby of restoring antique clocks.

A hobby must have two qualities to give long satisfaction: it must be relaxing and it must provide a feeling of accomplishment. Photography does both. You take a hike through the park—thereby getting the exercise you need—and forget your weekday problems as you find and record on film the interesting pictures you see. Later, when you develop and print the negatives, you become engrossed in discovering how well you captured the scene, the mood, the feeling that caused you to snap the shutter in the first place.

No matter how amateurish you may be, you will experience a feeling of accomplishment. Better, you can take the same walk a week later, photograph the same things, and come up with finer pictures. And better yet, you can keep on doing this, each time realizing the glow of accomplishment, until you are no longer able to hobble around the paths or see through the viewfinder.

This is but one example. There are as many others as there are stars in the heavens or bugs struggling through the backyard grass—and believe it or not, many amateurs have not only found fascinating hobbies in these very subjects but have contributed to our store of scientific knowledge through their efforts.

And, since this is mostly a personal confession anyway, I'll give another personal example to prove the statement I just made. About twenty years ago, when my wife's hobby was photographing wildflowers, she became interested in mushrooms. She bought a book and learned the common edible species. Her interest grew. Soon she had more books and after a while a microscope and was learning how to identify all kinds of fungi. The flowers were all but forgotten.

The time came when she knew enough about mushrooms to begin collecting for one of the great universities, and to date she has made 6,370 collections. She now knows more than anybody else about the fungi of the high desert of northern Nevada, eastern Oregon, and southern Idaho. She has found many of the mushrooms that are well known in other parts of the country but had never been reported from this area. She has also found more than thirty new species never before found anywhere.

Now working with the aid of her second grant from one of the foundations that help to support scientific research, she will eventually produce a publication that will become a permanent addition to the store of human knowledge. And remember, it all started as a hobby. She had no special training; she didn't even go to college. She just dug in, and the more she learned the more fascinating the subject became—as is true of all good hobbies—and I am sure that fungi will sustain her interest as long as she may live.

So there is no limit to the number of interesting hobbies that anybody can take up—hobbies that are both relaxing and challenging. The important thing is: Don't wait too long. If you wait until tomorrow, tomorrow may never come.

Part II

DEER HUNTING BEATS ALL

Chapter 2

The Old and the New

Each autumn when the nights grow longer than the days and the aspens turn to gold on the hillsides, I am faced by an annual dilemma: Should we explore some new area or should we hunt once more in the old, familiar spot? There are strong inducements for both alternatives, and all deer hunters must answer the same question.

There are advantages in hunting country you know, but there might be more deer somewhere else. Besides, it is exciting to explore new territory. I will never forget the thrill of topping a ridge on my first deer hunt to look down into a mountain basin I had never seen before.

It's thrilling to pack into country you've never explored,
but the old, familiar spots also have their advantages.

After a long climb, the cool breeze in my face was as fresh as the Arctic.
It breathed a hint of the winter that was soon to come. I knew it couldn't be,
of course, but it was easy to imagine that my companion and I were the first
white men to cross this particular ridge at this particular point and so enjoy
this particular view of the granite-rimmed basin below.

There were alders along a trickle of water in the bottom. A stringer of
lodgepole pine, trunks as straight and slender as pickets in a fence, came up
along one side of the basin. Beneath them the grouseberry bushes had
taken on the blush of fall. Along the ridge on which Don Hill and I stood,
here and there on the slope below, and on the opposite slope were scattered
clumps of alpine fir. The hillsides were partly clothed by grass and low
brush, and partly by barren slides and jagged outcroppings of clean, gray
granite. A towering peak, still streaked with hard banks of last winter's
snow, jutted into the blue sky beyond.

It was a wild and free and thrilling sight, and before we had even caught
our breath Don said, "Boy! Look at that!"

At his words the biggest buck I have ever seen sprang from his bed in the shadow of some firs, not 20 yards below, and bounded into the open. I heard Don gulp. My heart leaped into my throat and by the time I could raise my rifle I was trembling like an aspen leaf. I could no more keep my dancing sights on the deer than I could fly. In desperation I fired shotgun style as they jerked across his chest. I imagine Don was equally unstrung, though naturally neither of us ever admitted to such boyish weakness.

The buck started around the hillside. We each fired several shots. By some miracle the buck went down. By an even greater miracle, there were two bullet holes in his rib cage—a fortunate thing since we were, it developed, to share both the venison and the glory. We saw no more deer that trip.

We dressed him where he fell, then strung him on a pole and tried to lift him. We couldn't do it, so we cut him in two, tied one half to the pole, and started to camp with it. When we came back for the second half we were so tired we decided to leave the head where it lay. We didn't even take the antlers. They were wide, heavy, and well shaped, with six points on one side and seven on the other, but we didn't realize what we had. Don was sixteen and I was seventeen years old.

So each fall when I must make the decision where to hunt I remember that first hunt—plus many others in new country since. Obviously, none of us in the 1970s can explore in the sense that Daniel Boone or Jim Bridger did, yet any hunter in an area he has never seen before is really exploring. Within its confines each bend of the stream and each view from a ridge top are as new to him as they were to the first pioneer who saw them.

Still-hunting in new country, watching carefully for sign to learn where the game is using, exploring each new vista, and finally succeeding offer real proof of hunting ability, provides a succession of thrills climaxed by well-deserved satisfaction. To breathe the clean air of the high places and glory in each new panorama, completely removed from any sight or sound of man, is in itself reward enough. Whatever game we may bag is an extra bonus.

Yet at the very time I am tempted by such thoughts I remember the familiar spot near home where my wife and I have camped and hunted for more than thirty years. I can smell the clean campfire smoke that drifts down the river bottom in the evening, mingling with the lush odor of overripe elderberries and the fresh smell of the pines. I can see the mountain maple ablaze on the hillsides and the billion diamonds of the frost when the sun first touches the meadow beyond our camp.

We have camped there, sometimes to hunt grouse, but more often deer, since before our sons were born. When they were tiny they played for hours with their little cars, building roads around a dirt bank near the tent and zooming the cars over them. When they were older, maybe ten or twelve, they built a platform in a nearby tree and perched on it to read while we hunted. The day came when they hunted with us. Now we go back alone.

Sentiment influences me, of course. The place has a thousand memories. But there is a practical reason for hunting here, too: We know the area surrounding it better than we do the town in which we live. We know every thicket where the sleek deer hide. We know every trail they follow and every saddle they pass through on migration. We know where they feed early and late and where they bed down during the day. We know the best time of the season to be here and the best time of the day to hunt each spot—and *how* to hunt each one. For example, Ellen's favorite hunt is a short one after dinner to the basin at the head of a long draw.

Our usual routine deer hunting is to leave camp before daylight and be where we expect to find game by the time it is light enough to shoot. We then still-hunt, sometimes together but more often separately, until 10 or 11 o'clock. (We hunt longer on snowy days because the deer don't brush up so early then.)

After our morning hunt we wander back to camp, have a bite to eat, and loaf or go fishing for a few hours. We eat dinner about 4 o'clock. After dinner we go out again and stay until it is too dark to see the sights.

Ellen likes to take her rifle and climb up to this basin, a steep half mile from camp. Once there, and if the wind is right, she sits quietly a few yards below the west rim and waits for the deer to come out to feed. (If she sat on top of the rim she would be silhouetted against the sky and easy to see.)

The basin is about 250 yards across and without trees, but it has an abundance of bitterbrush, snow brush, bitter cherry, and other choice deer food. Over the rim to the east there is a 100-acre thicket of Douglas fir, a safe retreat for deer during the day, but devoid of food. So at dusk any deer that may be there are likely to wander out into the basin to feed.

We have lost track of the number Ellen has killed by waiting patiently here as night descended, but I do remember her best shot. A young buck— three points on each side—came out of the timber but stopped on the opposite ridge and started nipping the leaves off some tall snow brush. Ellen could see only his head, and that only occasionally. It was nearly dark. She wouldn't be able to see the crosshairs in her scope much longer. She decided to try for a head shot, a small target at 250 yards.

At the crack of her rifle, however, the buck disappeared. She found him dead. She had to dress him and prop him open to cool before she could leave, and it was long after dark when she got back to camp.

This is an evening spot; we have never found deer here in the morning. Then they prefer to feed on the east-facing slope, on the other side of the timber, where the first rays of the rising sun drive away the chill—though they never linger in the open for long after the sun comes up.

There are other evening spots and others that are good in the morning.

We know them all and so we no longer make the hard, all-day hunts we once did. We kill our deer close to camp—and we don't have to work hard to do it.

This is the practical side. You may be sure that any deer using an area know it very well, and it gives a hunter a great advantage if he knows it as well as they do.

There is another reason for going back to the same deer camp year after year, preferably with the same companions. Every time you return you add to the store of memories that make each new hunt that much more rewarding. You recall the good times around the camp itself, the great meals, the funny things that happened on past hunts.

In the woods you remember the crossing where you caught the big buck dead to rights—and missed him clean. You recognize the spot where you made the best shot of your life.

So while I like to explore new country, I must admit that if I had only one more hunt to make I would surely go back to our old, familiar camp. And if I had to kill a deer, which, fortunately, I don't, I'd go there, too.

Chapter 3

Fundamentals of Deer Hunting

Although mule deer and whitetails are usually found in different surroundings—they do occur together in a few areas where their ranges overlap—
certain basic rules are fundamental to all deer hunting. Sound technique,
whether in Colorado or New York, produces more game. When I try to
remember all the things I didn't know on my first hunt—wow!

Right off, there's the problem of seeing deer. It's quite an art. Virtually all
youngsters who later become deer hunters see deer on summer fishing or
camping trips. In summer deer are "in the red," as old woodsmen put it.
Their coats are bright tan, and they contrast sharply with the green of their
surroundings.

Most young hunters go into the woods looking for a tan deer against a
green background. As long as the image persists they will be badly
handicapped because they're trying to see something that simply isn't there.
You don't see bright-tan deer in November. They are then gray, and they
blend softly into a background of gray brush and trees, and are infinitely
harder to see than in the summer.

With the changing of their pelage, deer also change their habits. Whether
you credit them with sensing the approach of another hunting season or
not, they become wilder and more secretive. They seldom venture onto the

Good bucks bed down for the day where they feel safe.
When you can get this close to one, without his
even suspecting anybody is near, you're a deer hunter.

open meadows during daylight. Instead, they stay in cover, usually with a good escape route handy, and venture out to feed only at night.

This means that you seldom see a *whole* deer unless it is already frightened and bounding away. You may see an ear or an antler of a deer standing behind a screen of brush watching you. If the brush is open underneath, you may see only the legs. So instead of the bright, fearless deer of summer, you must look for a gray deer in gray woods, nearly always in poor light, and usually partly screened by brush. The deer like it that way; it's one of the reasons why they're not extinct. You may be sure that a great many deer see, hear, or smell you without giving you even the faintest opportunity to see them.

Look for a shape that's out of place—the horizontal line of a deer's back or belly among the vertical lines of the saplings by which it is almost hidden. Look for the smooth, vertical legs close to the ground among the angular and twisted lower brush. Look for the rounded lines, a denser spot off the ground, an ear, or an antler.

Strangely, after you look and look and look and are on the verge of giving up and moving to another spot, then when you do see a deer, it will be so perfectly obvious you'll be amazed you didn't see it long before. You usually see game of all kinds this way.

Movement is another aid to seeing deer. Ordinarily, a deer that is aware of your presence but thinks you haven't seen it will hold perfectly still, but this isn't always so. A smart old buck will sometimes try to slip away. And in the case of at least two deer I can remember seeing in their beds, the thing that attracted my attention was the flick of an ear. One of them was a fine buck with four points on one antler and five on the other, and I shot him through the neck before he even got to his feet.

Next to seeing deer, the beginner's toughest job probably is controlling the overwhelming eagerness, or anxiety, that seizes him the very instant he does see one. He's afraid, of course, that if he doesn't shoot instantly it will get away. Consequently he takes a poor shot from a poor position and is far less likely to take home game than if he could restrain himself.

Four of us were starting out to hunt one morning, maybe half a mile from camp, when we saw five deer on the hillside across the valley. It had just come day and they were still feeding, but they were out of range, and we obviously would have to work out some strategy of approach if any of us was to get a shot.

While we were holding a whispered conference, the deer wandered into a small thicket, possibly 25 yards from the nearest point of heavy timber. The remainder of the slope was grassy with scattered low brush, and it was obvious that the deer would make a break for the big trees when we jumped them. But if we worked it right, some of us were sure to get shots before they were alarmed.

We decided the best plan was for two of us to drop back, cross the valley, and approach the cover from the point of timber. The other two could move in straight from where we stood, since the trees on our slope would conceal them until they reached the bottom, less than 100 yards from the deer. With a little luck they'd get even closer. The gentle breeze was straight down the valley and ideal for our strategy.

Jack and I volunteered to make the circuitous approach and told our companions to give us twenty minutes before starting theirs. We had scarcely been gone ten, however, when we heard two shots, then after a short pause three more. Wondering what had gone wrong, we abandoned the stealth with which we had been working toward the cover and hurried ahead. I got a flash of one deer racing down the valley through the trees.

We finally found our fellow hunters, shame-faced and empty-handed, in the bottom of the valley. Instead of waiting for us to walk around, as they had agreed to do, they had started their approach at once. On top of that, when they saw two deer lying down in the thicket they were unable to restrain themselves even until they were within range, much less for the allotted time. They had attempted to fire together at the bedded deer, then had shot again as the five bounded across the opening to the heavy timber.

Of course, as soon as it was over the culprits were ashamed of themselves. And well they should have been! They had violated one of the cardinal rules of hunting in their failure to adhere strictly to the previously agreed-upon plan. Furthermore, the failure of any of us to get a deer when we could easily have had two or three was due solely to our buddies' giving way to the foolish urge to shoot the instant they saw game.

Admittedly, there are times when you must shoot now or never. But far more often your chances of success are increased when you are deliberate. Unalarmed game is seldom in a hurry. There is nearly always time to look an animal over carefully—after all, you might not want that particular one—to let it move into position for a clean kill, and to get into the best possible position yourself. You'll shoot better prone than sitting if the terrain permits, and better sitting than offhand if you can't lie down. And obviously, if you can't get within decent range of your quarry, you shouldn't shoot at all.

When deer are driven, the stands are located along the edge of a clearing, abandoned road, or other opening whenever possible, so as to give the hunters on them a chance for a shot. No smart deer enters an opening without pausing to look it over first. If you happen to move at that moment, even to wipe the drop off the end of your nose, the buck that might have given you an easy shot will either bound across in a split second or else sneak around out of sight. The two prime rules are: First, never leave your stand until the appointed time and, second, never move while you're on it. Holding still is far from easy, but it pays off.

Beginning still-hunters walk through the woods looking for deer. Old-timers hunt. There's a world of difference. Although all deer are slow to recognize a man who doesn't move—I've had them walk by within 30 feet when I was standing in the open and never suspect a thing—they are quick to detect movement. And you never see a deer while you're watching where to take the next step. Put these two facts together, and it's obvious that the man who does a minimum of walking and a maximum of looking is the one who sees the most game. I like to hike right along until I reach the area I plan to hunt, but once I get there a sore-footed turtle could walk off and leave me.

Although the sharpness of deer's vision is debatable, there is no doubt about their hearing. I think a mule deer can hear a feather fall, and if he can do that, then a whitetail can hear a shadow. Quiet clothes—wool pants and jacket and soft shoes—are a tremendous help in still-hunting. Obviously, too, the fewer steps you take and the slower you take them, the less noise you will make. There is a wonderful satisfaction in surprising a good buck on his bed, but you'll never know it if you always hurry.

Feeding deer make some noise in the process. It is much easier to approach them than others that are standing still or lying down. This, coupled with the fact that they're likely to be in the open then, is one of the best reasons for hunting very early in the morning and as late in the evening as you can see to shoot. Deer feed early and late. Since they find more food along the edges, you have a better chance to see them, and since they are moving around browsing, it's easier to get in range.

A deer's sense of smell may be even better than its hearing. This could be a hard point to prove, because both senses are wonderfully acute, but don't ever hunt downwind and think, "Maybe they won't smell me." They will. If they happen to be close when they do, you'll see only running deer. If they get your scent while they're still out of sight, you won't see any deer at all.

Always hunt into or across the wind. If a good area lies downwind, make a detour to approach it properly, or else come back another time when the breeze is right. The scent of man is terrifying to nearly all wild creatures, and they make a real effort to avoid its source.

There is no problem in telling which way the wind is blowing when it's strong. A gentle breeze will warn your quarry just as surely, however, and it is much more difficult to detect. Dust, dry snow, the punk out of a rotten log, or a dry leaf crumbled up fine and allowed to trickle down from an upheld hand will show wind direction. Or moisten a finger in your mouth and hold it up. The side that feels cool first is upwind. A puff of smoke, of course, will show air movement if there is any at all.

The place to talk is in camp, not in the woods. Next to the human scent, the human voice saves the lives of more deer each fall than any other single thing.

A friend and I were sitting just beneath the top of a ridge late one afternoon watching the edge of the timber below, where we hoped some deer would soon come out, when we saw several other deer on the slope across the valley. They were far out of range—too far, in fact, to start a stalk in the limited time we had left—but they were not too far to watch.

Just downhill from the edge of a big cherry thicket where they apparently had spent the day, they fed unconcernedly for some time after we first saw them. Then they suddenly threw up their heads, milled around briefly, and bolted for the timber on the slope below us.

Puzzled, we looked everywhere for the cause of their alarm and finally saw two hunters come into view on the ridge above the thicket. We could hear them calling back and forth—and we were half a mile away! Undoubtedly, their voices had frightened the deer because the breeze was in the opposite direction.

Part of the art of deer hunting lies in learning to recognize the kind of spots they prefer at different times. The surest way to discover where game is using is to watch for tracks and droppings. Of course, when a lot of hunters are pushing the deer around, a lone track means only that one deer went by. But an abundance of fresh tracks, whether in an area where the deer have been feeding, in one where they have been bedding, or along their route between the two, is a sure sign of a spot to watch.

Whitetails are often hunted in cover so dense that getting a shot would be virtually impossible without driving. Those Yankees who condemn the use of hounds and buckshot obviously have never attempted to outwit a buck in the kind of stuff where a lot of Southern deer spend their entire lives. Nevertheless deer hunting to me is still-hunting.

I like the challenge. I like the feeling of being on a more or less even footing with the game. Against my advantages of better eyesight, a rifle, and—I hope—a better mind, the deer match their superior senses of smell and hearing, their intimate knowledge of the cover, and their wonderful alertness.

If I'm successful in this contest, it leaves me with a fine feeling of accomplishment. If I'm not, I need no alibi.

Chapter 4

I Don't Want to Kill a Deer

I don't want to kill a deer. I haven't really wanted to kill a deer for years. Yet I go deer hunting every fall and have, I suppose, shot about as many of them as most other men my age. If these statements constitute a paradox, bear with me.

Consider October, the hunter's moon. The heat of summer is over. The September rains have washed the haze of August from the air, and frosty nights have brought the first dusting of gold to the white-barked aspens. In all the arid West, from the Coast Range to the eastern slope of the Rockies, the shimmering, lovely days of Indian summer have laid their spell upon the land.

The early harvest is finished, but the orchards are still flecked with the rich red of late apples. The voice of the cornfield has changed from the whisper of summer to the dry rustle of autumn. The stubble, from which the grain had long since been taken, has the look of fall about it, and the young cock pheasants that it harbors are rapidly acquiring the full glory of their adult plumage.

Everywhere, especially in the cool of evening, the rich, ripe fruity odors of the season lie heavily upon the air. Late-curing hay; grapes hanging purple from the vine; the rich earth, disturbed to yield its treasures; melons, frost-sweetened and dead ripe—all these and many others add their savor.

Just being in deer country can be enough of a reward.
But if an opportunity like this presents itself, a hunter
might change his mind.

And always, somewhere in the distance, an eager householder, unable to
wait for the deluge of leaves that will come later, is burning the first
sprinkling. The smoke, thin and clean, drifts low across the countryside. It
adds spice to all the other mingled odors, seasoning them with the sure
proof that this is, indeed, October.

At this time we go hunting. It is a tradition. Our preparations are made
pleasant by memories of past trips and anticipation of the one ahead. We
are going to hunt deer, not merely to kill them. The reward is in the hunt,
but since there could be no hunting were there no deer, and since the
logical culmination of any hunt must lie in securing its object, we will no
doubt kill one.

Thus rifles and food and bedrolls and tent are loaded, and we drive away
from the rich, green valley into the brown foothills and through them,
winding always upward, into the home of the mule deer in October. Yellow
pines stand majestically alone on the south slopes, their trunks brick red in
the late sun. Aspens line the draws along the clear brooks that trickle down
and make bright splashes of yellow among the dark firs on the north
hillsides.

Camp is made, water carried from the little stream nearby, a fire kindled. Soon the heartening odors of good outdoor food and coffee mingle with the tang of the smoke that rises in a thin, straight column toward the earliest stars. We eat and loaf beside the embers and plan the morrow. This first evening, loaded with anticipation, is a real part of deer hunting, and we enjoy it to the fullest.

We will hunt a country we know well. It is always a challenge to explore a new area, but it is also rewarding to hunt where you know each ridge and valley, where every little bench and pocket holds its share of memories. Here beside this patch of timber I missed a big buck way back in 1936. With a forkhorn, two does, and two or three fawns he walked out of the thick cover just at sunset. He was very close, and I thought, "I'll shoot him in the neck," but, somehow, I missed. I saw the bullet kick up the dirt behind him, a little to one side, and before I could work the bolt he leaped back among the trees and disappeared.

And down the draw from this saddle is where another fine buck eluded us by running low along the bottom, screened by alders and aspens, until he was out of range. On this bench, several deer have fallen to our rifles during the years. And down the canyon below it, where alternate thickets vie with more open browse among the boulders on the hillsides, many fine bucks have rewarded us.

There are real, as well as sentimental, values in hunting a familiar country. You know where to look for deer that are trailing through on their annual migration from the high summer range to their lower wintering area. You know the pockets where they hide during the day. You know where to look for the resident deer that spent the summer here rather than higher in the mountains. And you have learned through experience the best way to approach all these places without alarming any game that might be in them.

The alarm rang at 4 o'clock. I crawled reluctantly out of the warm sleeping bag, touched a match to the fat-pine slivers in the little sheet-iron stove, lit the gasoline lantern, and dressed. Then I stepped outside. The snapping stars were so close I could almost touch them; not even the palest hint of gray showed in the east. There were slivers of ice in the water bucket. I slopped a little into the wash pan, and by the time I had applied it to face and hands no trace of sleepiness remained.

It is during these magic hours that a hunter has the best chance to see deer undisturbed in the open. In the early morning, usually not later than 8 o'clock, they gradually feed or wander into some tight and hard-to-approach thicket where they will spend the day. About sunset they emerge to feed again.

The grass was crisp underfoot as I walked along the bench east of camp. The mountain on my left loomed black against the northern sky, and since I couldn't possibly see a deer anyway, I hurried; I had about a mile to walk and I was chilly. I wore no coat because I knew it would be warm later, but now the air was sharp.

The eastern sky grew paler, and finally there was a hint of pink and saffron to give sure promise of approaching day. Individual trees became visible on the mountainside. I knew I'd soon be able to see a deer. I slowed down and attempted to walk quietly. The spot where I wanted to be at shooting time was just ahead.

Here a little stream came gurgling down out of the hills. Its drainage was a basin, perhaps a mile long and half that wide, divided into several draws and pockets, with steep ridges between. There were bare slopes and brushy ones, dense thickets and sparsely covered benches. It had everything—food, water, thick cover, and shade. During migration the deer—which followed a course generally parallel to the river in the bottom of the valley and did most of their traveling at night along the open slopes facing it—turned into this basin to spend the day. Here, finding things to their liking, they sometimes loitered for a week or more if the weather remained pleasant.

I paused at the mouth of the basin to test the wind. It was perfect, a steady, downstream breeze. I crossed the brook and started slowly up the game trail a few yards above it on the other side. It was now light enough to shoot. I took a few careful steps, paused to examine everything in sight, took a few more steps, and paused again. I tried not to make a sound.

Time was when I hunted mule deer from the ridges. I could watch a big area and cover more ground. Later—and wiser—I came to favor walking up a valley. I can't see so much country, but what I can see, I see better. I have to hunt more carefully, but any deer I see is usually in range.

I moved slowly along, alternately watching and walking. The predawn chill, which my brisk walk across the flat had overcome, caught up with me again. Shivering, I hung my rifle over my shoulder and put my hands into my pockets to warm my fingers. The light grew stronger, and at last the sun touched the highest tip of the high ridge on the west.

I was looking at it, anticipating its warmth—though the best of the hunting would be over by the time the sunlight reached the bottom of the valley—when I saw a movement halfway up the slope. It was in sparse brush along the point of a ridge that came straight down toward me from the peak. On the right, on the north slope of this ridge, was a dense stand of fir. On the left, extending toward the mouth of the little valley for several hundred yards, was a sparse stand of mixed snow brush, ninebark, and chokecherry, with clumps of bunch grass in the open spots.

The movement could have been made by a bird or a squirrel—or by the flick of an ear. I watched carefully but saw nothing more for several seconds. Then suddenly a deer stepped from behind a cherry bush. It was a long way up the slope. I raised my rifle slowly and looked at the animal through the scope. A doe. Does were not protected, but I had no desire to kill one, at least not this early in the hunt. Our best venison has always come from big bucks killed before the beginning of the rut.

I lowered my rifle and continued watching. Soon a second deer materialized, farther out in the brush. It was no bigger than the first, and I assumed that it was another doe or a small buck. Then, almost at the edge of the timber, a third deer stepped leisurely from behind a clump of ninebark, moving slowly toward the trees. Even before I could raise my rifle to look at him I knew he was the one I wanted. I could tell by his size and by the way he walked that he was a big buck. I got the scope up barely in time to get a glimpse of him before he disappeared. His rack was big; certainly each antler bore the four points of a mature mule-deer buck, and maybe more.

The chill was forgotten. I sat down in the game trail and watched the edge of the timber until the sunlight reached the bottom of the valley, hoping he would come out. He didn't. The two other deer, one a small buck, went in.

Thanks to having hunted here before, I didn't have to walk on up the valley and inspect that patch of timber to learn how big it was. I knew all about it. It covered 100 acres or so, from the top of the high ridge on the west to the creek in the bottom, and it ran from the crest of the hogback down into a ravine on the north. It was big enough to hide a hundred deer, and it would be impossible for a lone hunter to push any of them out—or get a shot if he did.

There were several things I might do. I could go on hunting and forget about the buck. I could continue up the creek and climb the hillside to inspect a bench north of the timber in the hope that the deer might have gone on through. I could, of course, work my way into the jungle and hope for the best.

None of these possibilities seemed very attractive. I felt sure that the little band of deer had gone into the timber to spend the day. When evening came they would emerge, and with luck I might be in the right spot waiting.

Back in camp by 9 o'clock, I cut some wood, started a stew that would be ready when my partner came, and looked around for any other odd jobs that needed doing. Twenty yards from the tent, the bench on which we were camped broke away sharply to the river bottom. I walked over and looked down at the river, sparkling among the cottonwoods. Its voice, muted by distance, rose and fell softly with the vagaries of the breeze.

The jobs didn't seem very important and the blanket of pine needles on the ground was soft. I decided to sit down in the mellow sunlight and look at things. I thought about the spots where the big buck was most likely to come out of the timber and wondered whether I should go fishing—the trout season was still open. And then I decided to sort of lie back on the needles for a minute or two and put my cap over my eyes.

My partner woke me when he came in. He had seen only tracks. We ate and discussed the possibility of getting a shot at the big buck in the evening. Two of us would have a better chance than one, since there were several spots where the three deer might emerge, either to feed or to continue their leisurely migration toward the winter range.

Northwest of the patch of timber was a low saddle over which deer often crossed into the drainage of the next creek. A hunter stationed here would also be able to watch the bench that bordered the timber on the north, a likely spot for them to feed in case they decided to loiter a few days in the little valley. If they intended to continue toward the winter range, however, they would be more likely to come out of the south side of the timber, probably near the spot where I had seen them in the morning, and swing around the points of the ridges that dropped sharply down toward the river.

The high point above the timber, where I had been looking at the sunlight when I first saw them, was the apex of several ridges. The good browse bordering the timber extended around to the river slope in the pockets between the heads of the ridges. It would be worthwhile to watch those pockets.

We left camp in late afternoon, not retracing my path of the morning but walking up the next creek to the west. This way we could reach our chosen stations without forewarning the deer, because the breeze regularly drifted up each valley in the evening. When we were a little beyond the saddle, we climbed the hillside nearly to it. Here we separated. My companion would find a position from which he could watch the hillside, the bench on the other side, and the northern and western edges of the timber.

Gradually climbing higher, I angled back toward the southern point of the ridge, staying on the west side, opposite the timber. Eventually I reached a spot from which I could watch a couple of brushy pockets, above and just around the corner from the southern edge of the cover. I couldn't see the cover—I was afraid to go around because the upcanyon breeze might drift my scent into it—but any deer that came out should eventually wander into my view.

I had barely settled myself down to begin my vigil when I heard a shot. Just one. It was back where I had come from. It could be nobody but my companion, since there were no other hunters in the area, and one shot usually means a dead deer.

Instantly I was torn by indecision. Had he killed the big buck? Should I go back to help dress it or should I stay here? Was there any chance of the buck's coming out now, assuming he was still alive? Well, if I returned I certainly would not get a shot, whereas if I stayed I might. So I leaned back against the hillside with my rifle across my lap and devoted my attention to the pockets below me. They were partly floored with grass and partly grown up to several varieties of browse. I searched them minutely and, satisfied they were vacant, allowed my attention to drift off across the valley.

This was the magic hour, when the night creatures begin to stir and game feeds in the long twilight. Instead of the keen anticipation that I should have felt, however, the ordeal of holding still bore heavily upon me. I was assailed by doubt. I sat there quietly while the sunset blushed and faded.

Imperceptibly the shadows grew thicker; it would soon be too dark to shoot. For the thousandth time I began a careful examination of the two pockets below me. And there, suddenly in full view and close, stood the buck of the morning! How he had arrived unseen was a mystery, but of his presence there could be no doubt. Nor did I have any question as to his identity. He was magnificent.

He was standing broadside, but his head was turned slightly away and he appeared to be looking at something farther down the little basin, perhaps at another deer that I couldn't see in the deep shadows. Slowly, quietly I raised my rifle and eased off the safety, holding it with thumb and finger so that there would be no click.

Twenty-four hours earlier I had harbored no particular desire to kill deer. I would hunt, yes, but I was not anxious to kill a deer. Twelve hours earlier I had seen this buck, and immediately, as though ordered by some remote ancestor whose very life depended upon the hunt, I had devoted every faculty to bringing about this very moment. Now, partly because my planning had been sound, but to a much greater degree because the buck had been unlucky enough to come into the open at this particular place and time, I was about to kill him. Without thought, without an instant's hesitation, I centered the crosshairs on his gray neck and squeezed the trigger.

Chapter 5

What to Do After You Shoot It

So you've killed a deer! Only 60 seconds ago you thought you'd never see one. Then, suddenly, there it was, standing alert and motionless in an opening among the trees. Now you're approaching it cautiously, rifle ready, half afraid it will get up and bound away. You're walking 3 feet above the ground.

But your buck is dead and it is really yours, your first. You realize your hands are trembling as reaction sets in, but you're too proud and happy to care. You stand and look at it and count the points and if you have your camera you take a picture. At last, you are brought back to earth by a dreadful thought: Somehow you've got to get what's inside out. You've got to dress your deer.

The thought is too much for some hunters—the ones who later discover they don't like venison. Every season deer are brought out of the woods bloated and sour, with everything inside right where it grew and perhaps gut shot to boot, with digestive juices and partly digested food oozing around through the body cavity. No men and few dogs can eat such an animal.

But if you are man enough to hunt deer—or any other big game—you are man enough to take proper care of it. If you do—with very rare exceptions— you will have delicious meat.

Now, what I am about to say may well seem adamant. This is not intended. I could tell you how to dress a deer without splitting the brisket and pelvis, for example, but space does not permit detailing more than one method. So I have chosen the one I have settled on as best.

The same thing applies to equipment. Many veteran hunters might not agree with me at all. Fine; the world is full of an infinite variety of equipment. The things I will suggest are those I now carry after many years of hunting.

Finally, since a deer is the first big-game animal for nearly all hunters, I will discuss deer only. All the others are put together the same way; elk and moose are more difficult to dress only because they are bigger.

You should have these things when you leave camp in the morning: Twenty feet of 3/16-inch nylon rope, a knife, a plastic bag, a hatchet, and, in fly weather, 10 yards of cheesecloth. You should also have the usual lunch, matches, and whatnot. This last includes your camera, a little extra food, and a tea can in case you don't make it back to camp that night. The easiest way to carry all this, plus your jacket after the day gets warm, is in a small red or fluorescent orange knapsack on your back. (The color is for safety's sake; otherwise, a Boy Scout knapsack would be fine.)

Custom dictates you should do two things first: Bleed your deer and remove the musk glands, which are marked by small patches of dark, oily hair on the lower hind legs. There are two on each, on opposite sides, and the chief reason for removing them is to prevent inadvertently touching them while dressing the deer and then touching the flesh. The musky oil would impart an unpleasant flavor.

Cut the hide about 4 inches up the leg from each gland. From this cut, start two others, angled out so they will pass safely around the oily hair. Being careful not to touch it with either knife or fingers, start pulling the patch of hide off the leg as you cut around the gland. When you are safely past it, angle your two cuts back together again. Pull and cut this patch of hide free and throw it away.

To bleed a deer, pull it around so the front legs are somewhat downhill with the animal on its side, then bend the neck up a bit. Use your rope to hold the head in this position, if necessary. Insert the blade of your knife full length right where the buck would tie his tie if he wore one. Reach back into the chest cavity, then cut toward the backbone. Bring the blade forward, edge toward the neck, and extend your entry cut about 2 inches forward.

If your deer was shot through the heart or lungs, no blood will come; it will all be in the chest cavity. Otherwise, keep probing until it starts gushing out. When it stops, proceed with the dressing.

Roll your deer onto its back and hold it there with your legs by standing straddle of it, facing the head. Use your rope if the slope is steep. Start at

In steep country, you'll use your rope to hold your deer in
position while you field-dress it.

the cut you made to bleed it and split the hide straight back, trying to follow
the exact center of the sternum (the plate down the bottom of the chest to
which the ribs are attached). Stop at the end of the sternum and turn to face
the other way.

Beginning here, you must be careful not to cut the membrane underneath the hide. If your knife went through, it would puncture the stomach
or intestines. Slit the hide to a point a few inches ahead of the penis. Then
start two cuts in a narrow V and continue them beyond the testicles until
even with the anus. Pull this strip of hide and the genitals back as you go.
Cut the penis free as necessary, but don't cut it off. When you have freed it
as far as it is exposed, drop the strip of hide to which the genitals are
attached behind the deer.

Use your hatchet to split the sternum from front to rear, but don't chop
farther. At this point carefully make a 1-inch cut, not deep, through the
membrane. Insert the first and second fingers of your left hand with the tips
pointed to the rear. Slip the tip of your knife blade between them, edge up,
and pointed in the same direction. Move fingers and blade along together,
clear to the solid bone of the pelvis. The fingers press the intestines down
out of the way as the knife slits the membrane and you avoid the most
common fault of the amateur butcher—cutting the entrails and spilling the
contents into the body cavity.

Lay your buck on one side with the feet downhill. Things will spill out.

Return to the front of the buck. If you don't intend to have his head
mounted, continue your first cut, the one with which you bled him, clear to
a spot between the corners of his jawbones. Cut through hide and flesh and
try to follow the exact bottom of the neck. Find the esophagus and

windpipe and sever them here. Pull them to the rear, cutting them free as necessary. This is one of the most important steps in dressing any big-game animal; if you neglect it the entire carcass will sour.

If you plan to mount the head, cut the esophagus and windpipe at the collarbone, go ahead and finish dressing the deer, then come back and proceed as follows: Make a vertical cut along the front of each shoulder from the V of the collarbone to the top of the back. Starting where these cuts join, make another cut straight forward, carefully following the very top of the neck, to the back of the buck's head. You can now work the neck hide down, around, and ahead until all the esophagus and windpipe can be removed. (This should be done in camp if you intend to take your deer in in one piece on the day you shoot it.)

All right. In either case we are now at the front of the chest cavity. Use a stick to prop it open. Continue pulling esophagus and windpipe to the rear and down. Heart and lungs will follow, though you will have to do a little cutting to free them. (The buck is still on his side with the opening downhill.)

Your progress will be halted by the diaphragm, the partition that divides the body cavity of all mammals. The heart and lungs lie ahead of it; the liver, stomach, and intestines, behind. Carefully cut all around the diaphragm, freeing it from the body wall. As soon as you get it loose, heart, lungs, liver, paunch, intestines, and kidneys will come clear of the body, though you may have to cut or break a few membranes attaching them to the back.

Separate heart and liver from the pile, cut them free, wipe them clean, and lay them on a log to drain and dry.

There is still the large intestine leading into the pelvis. Roll the buck onto his back again and hold the rear legs wide apart. Cut between the hams, following the center line carefully down to bone. There is a seam along the middle of the pelvis where the bones from each side join, and you will follow this seam to split it.

Now, be careful! The bladder lies within the pelvis and you don't want to cut it. Reach in from the front and gently press everything inside down away from the bone, breaking whatever membranes you encounter. With your hatchet, split the pelvis, striking cautious, horizontal blows toward the rear; not vertical ones that would break through into the bladder. Spread the back legs farther by standing between them and pushing them apart with your knees—or use your rope.

You will see that there is quite a tunnel through the pelvis. Working from the outside, cut the skin all around its edge until this cut joins the strip of hide with the genitals. You can avoid cutting into the colon by holding it up out of the way with your free hand as the blade passes under. Pick up the strip of hide and lift everything clear.

When you skin your game on the spot (the best system if
time allows), you can keep meat clean by working on
the hide. A hatchet is not only a better skinning tool
than a knife but also lets you split brisket, pelvis, and
backbone to halve the carcass. If you separate sides
between second and third ribs from rear, you'll have
quarters of about equal weight.

You're done! If the job seemed difficult, remember that it will be easier
next time. Eventually, you'll be able to do it in about ten minutes.

If your deer was gut-shot and water or snow is available, wash it out
carefully. If there is no water, wipe it as clean as possible with leaves, grass,
and part of your cheesecloth. Drain or splash out any puddles of blood.

What you should do next depends on circumstances. If there are a lot of
hunters in the woods you will probably take your deer to camp at once.
You will have better meat, however, if it is thoroughly chilled out before
you move it. I prefer to skin and quarter my game immediately, working on
the hide to keep the meat clean. Then I hang the quarters. I take the heart
and liver to camp in the plastic bag, along with my rifle and the head, if I
want it. Next day I come back with my packboard. It is much easier to
make two trips with a packboard than to carry or drag the entire deer down
in one.

If you don't want to do this and are not afraid to leave it overnight, get the carcass off the ground by hanging it, dragging it onto brush, or working poles under it. Animal heat is what spoils game. A deer will spoil as surely in December as it will in September, and the quicker you can chill it out, the better. With the body propped open by sticks and the air free to circulate underneath, a deer will cool out quite well, even in warm weather.

If it is raining or snowing, or looks as though it might, leave the carcass belly down on the brush or poles. Prop the body cavity open, but keep the rain out. On a sunny day, leave it in the shade.

Where I hunt, blowflies are active on warm days well into November. Use the cheesecloth to keep them out of the carcass or off the freshly cut or bloodshot parts of the quarters. Flies must have moisture to deposit their eggs, so clean-skinned or blood-glazed and dry parts are safe.

Aside from the work of two-legged thieves, I have never lost any game by leaving it in the woods for one night. Apparently there is enough man scent nearby to keep foxes and coyotes away. In every case bears took only the offal the first night.

The first thing to do when you arrive at camp is to hang your deer from a convenient limb or from a pole between two trees. Head up or tail up? I could start an argument by advocating either way. An animal skins easier and cleaner when you pull the hide down from front to rear. And, of course, you keep blood off the head and cape, which is desirable if you have a trophy. But if there is any blood left in the important hindquarters, it will drain out when they're up—this is the way they hang carcasses in a

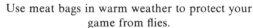

Use meat bags in warm weather to protect your
game from flies.

slaughterhouse—and the hams cool more quickly when they are separated.

This is done with a gambrel, which is a stick, about 2½ feet long for the average deer, maybe 2 inches in diameter, and pointed on each end. Tie a rope to the middle. Stick your knife through the hide and thin membrane at each hock, the backward-bending "knees" of the deer. Put one end of the gambrel through each slit and hang your prize.

Prop the body cavity open with sticks. If any additional washing out or cleaning up is called for, this is the time to do it. Then wipe the body cavity dry. If it is raining or snowing, put a piece of sheet plastic over the deer to keep the moisture off, but make sure there is a free circulation of air. If blowflies are still out, enclose the carcass in a meat bag.

To remove deer feet, you cut the front legs off at the knee, but not the back ones. Starting at the joint, cut a strip of hide off the front of the leg. Extend the cut down the bone until you find a fine, horizontal seam in it. Cut around the bone at this seam and break the leg off here. This way, you can still hang the quarters by the hock.

In some parts of the country, the weather remains hot during the deer season. In this case, keep your deer in the shade protected from flies, and then let it chill overnight. In the morning, before the sun reaches it, take it down and wrap it in anything available—extra blankets, canvas, even your sleeping bag. This will keep it cool during the day and you can hang it again after the sun sets and the flies go away. Provided the nights are cool, there is no danger in keeping a deer this way for a week, even though the days may be quite hot.

If you decide to quarter your deer, skin it, then split it down the middle of the backbone with saw or ax, and separate the front and rear quarters between the second and third ribs, counting from the rear. All quarters will then weigh approximately the same.

For the trip home, wrap the quarters individually in cheesecloth, muslin, or meat bags, then wrap all of them together in canvas. The object is to keep them cool, clean, and dry. The same rule applies to a whole carcass, though simply wrapping it in canvas is sufficient.

Most hunters leave the hide on and take their deer to commercial lockers or processing plants. Good enough. But if you do this, insist on proper aging in the cool room before the deer is cut up, wrapped, and frozen. Meat ages more rapidly in warm weather, so some judgment is required, but I usually hang a deer for about ten days from the time it was shot.

There are two other points on which you should also insist: First, the packages must be wrapped in good-quality, coated locker paper, such as Kordite, and sealed with freezer tape. (Double wrapping is worth whatever more it may cost.) Second, they must be quick-frozen.

This is essential for upland birds, waterfowl, and fish, as well as for big game. Slow freezing permits the formation of big ice crystals that break

In wrapping game for freezer (these are venison chops), use coated freezer paper.

Use the so-called drugstore wrap, folding the seams twice. If meat might remain long in the freezer, wrap doubly.

down the tissues and result in the loss of the flavorsome juices when the food is thawed to cook. In the case of fish, these crystals burst the oil-retaining cells and this, in turn, allows the oil to permeate the flesh and degrade the flavor.

If you decide to prepare your deer for freezing at home yourself, don't hesitate because you may not know the standard cuts. It really doesn't matter. I have a friend who is a graduate of a meat cutter's school, and once when I was helping him cut up an elk I apologized for my crude work. He asked, "Do you know what butchers learn at school?"

I admitted that I actually didn't but surmised that they must surely learn the proper way to cut up a carcass. He said, "Yeah—and that's how to hide the biggest bone with the least meat!"

Ruffed grouse, which may have been eating skunk cabbage, and sage hens, which are almost certain to have been eating sagebrush leaves during the hunting season, should be drawn immediately after they are killed. Failure to do so will result in disagreeable-tasting flesh in case the birds' crops happened to be filled with these foods when they were shot.

Occasionally other upland birds also eat things that would give them an unpleasant flavor. Where they occur, wild onions are seasonal favorites of both Hungarian and chukar partridge, which scratch out the bulbs and eat them. When they are doing this, any birds bagged should be drawn at once.

Hot weather may also make it necessary to draw birds immediately. We start hunting chukars in September, when the sweat runs down our faces and soaks our caps, and then we take extra care to get the birds home in good shape. We draw them at once, then lay them in the shade to air and cool each time we sit down to rest and again as soon as we get back to the car. We put them on ice before we start home.

Here is a quick and easy way to draw an upland bird: Pluck a few feathers from the front of the breast. Slit the skin and remove the crop. Next, pull out the feathers near the vent and cut around it. Then reach in with your fingers or a stick and pull out the innards.

I should mention that we never field-dress doves or quail. They're so small that they cool quickly without it, though we do spread them out in the shade at every opportunity and then put them on ice as soon as possible when the weather is warm.

We prefer to pluck our upland birds, even though it is much slower than skinning them. If you pick birds dry, two times are best—shortly after they are killed and again when they are stone cold. The feathers seem to set up and are hard to remove without tearing the skin while the birds are cooling.

Any upland bird can be dipped in hot water the same as a domestic chicken to make the feathers come out easier. (You can't do this if you draw them first, of course.) The water should be about 180 degrees. Hold the bird by the feet and dip it briefly, sloshing it up and down. Yank out a few feathers. If they come easily lay that bird aside and turn to the next. If not, dip it again.

Be careful not to overdo the immersion in hot water. You'll lose the skin as well as the feathers if you do, and quail are so tender that the briefest possible dipping is usually enough. In fact, we pick ours dry like doves; the feathers come out almost as easily.

There is a controversy of long standing over the hanging of upland birds—ducks, too, for that matter—and if you prefer a "gamy" flavor, have at it. Hang your game in a cool place with the entrails in for as long as you like. We prefer to clean our birds the day we kill them, but we do age them in the refrigerator for several days before we eat or freeze them.

The packaging to use for the game you freeze depends on how long you intend to keep it. For a few days, you can put birds in plastic bags or wrap them in ordinary waxed paper. Coated freezer wrap, such as you use for venison, will keep them longer. If they might be in the freezer for a month or more, however, they need more protection to prevent the drying out that is called locker burn.

Possibly because more surface inside and out is exposed, upland birds and ducks are more vulnerable to locker burn than any kind of red meat. After considerable experimenting, we decided that the best way to freeze all of them is in water. And we use milk cartons which, being square, are economical of freezer space, and which come in a choice of sizes to match the contents.

A half-gallon carton is just right for one mallard, sage hen, blue grouse, or pheasant. There is little wasted space in it with two chukars or ruffed grouse, three Huns, six quail, or a dozen doves. And completely surrounded by ice, they last forever. We occasionally find an odd carton in our freezer with, say, a couple of chukars, and the date on the top may reveal that they are three or four years old. They're as good as the day we froze them.

If you roast pheasants or other upland birds, you should freeze them dressed whole like chickens. Since we broil most of ours, we prepare them for broiling. We split doves and quail down the back, but leave the breast intact. All the others are split along the center of the back and the breastbone—and poultry shears are a great help in this job. If we should

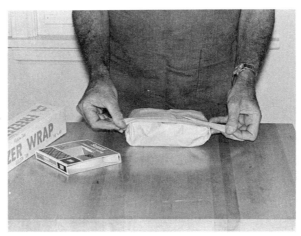

Seal each package well with freezer tape. Mark boldly on each package: what's in it and date it goes into freezer.

decide to fry any of the larger birds, it's no trick to disjoint them after they have thawed. We cut up cottontails, then freeze them in water the same as birds, and we freeze ducks whole for roasting.

A word of caution: Never, but never, put a package in your freezer without identifying and dating it, even though you may expect to eat the contents within the week. Something will happen to change your mind and you'll eventually wind up with a lot of mysterious bundles floating around.

It is also a good idea to keep a pad and pencil near the freezer, then list food as you put it in and cross it off when you take it out. That way, when you want to give guests grouse for dinner you can tell whether you have them without rummaging through the entire box.

Part III

COOKING ON HUNTING TRIPS AND AT HOME

Chapter 6

Skillet Skill

Like that of many simple tools, the product of the skillet depends upon the skill of the user. Give me a brush and a can of paint and I'd be lucky to spread a uniform coat over a doghouse, yet Charlie Russell, using the same simple tool, captured the very spirit of the Old West and made it live forever.

"Live by the skillet, die by the skillet" was not said entirely in jest. The crimes against food that have been committed with the aid of a simple frying pan—or spider, as it was called in pioneer times—are as the legions of the dead. I have committed my share of them.

The fat in your skillet should be very hot before you put
in any kind of meat. Here Ted is using the Dutch oven
as a warmer for meat already cooked.

My boyhood camp-cooking utensils were a skillet and a coffeepot. Only
coffee—at least, we called it that—came from the coffeepot. Everything else
that required more than warming suffered the indignity of the skillet. It was
years before I boiled, broiled, or baked anything. I well remember how
delicious bread and butter tasted after eating my half-scorched, half-raw
fried potatoes and trout. And how good was a can of pork and beans,
opened and set beside the fire to warm!

They were good because I didn't touch them. Now, thousands of
campfires later, I regularly improve upon them. Dice four slices of bacon
and an onion the size of a tennis ball. Brown in a skillet over medium heat—
brown, mind you, not scorch. The onion will still show mostly white when
done. Drain off nearly all the grease. Leave the skillet beside the fire. Dump
in two level tablespoonfuls of sugar and four of vinegar, plus a few shakes
of salt and pepper, then add the contents of a 21-ounce can of pork and
beans. Put the skillet back on the fire and stir occasionally until the beans

are hot, which they will reveal by bubbling. They're ready. This is supposed to be enough for four people, but two hungry hunters will lick it up.

My early skillets were all of sheet steel. They were inexpensive and light, though the handles sticking out at an angle were a nuisance in packing. Their worst feature was the thin metal from which they were made. Because of it, they heated instantly and cooled as fast, and I had to watch the contents like a hawk. Potatoes would scorch while I looked away to set the coffeepot back from the fire. I still have several sheet-steel skillets, but seldom use them.

Without going into my reasons—which might be construed as arguments and I really don't care whether you agree with me or not—I'll simply say that I don't like nonstick-coated cooking utensils of any kind and don't use them. That leaves stainless steel, aluminum, and old-fashioned cast iron. I like the last by far the best for skillets, griddles, and Dutch ovens for all campfire or camp-stove cooking—and at home, too, for that matter. Cast iron's drawback is its weight; obviously, nobody is going to carry a 5-pound cast-iron skillet on a backpacking trip.

Aside from weight, the cast-iron skillet's only disadvantage is the short handle, which soon gets too hot to touch with a bare hand. (Wooden handles don't last long on camp skillets.) I can't cook over a campfire without three aids my wife never uses at home: a pair of thick cotton gloves, pliers, and a shovel. Between gloves and pliers I can handle a hot skillet. But there is another solution:

Ralph Preuss of Mason City, Iowa, sent me a handle extension. It was simply a rectangular tube of fairly heavy (16-gauge) sheet metal, 1⅜x⅜ inches, inside measurement, with a ³⁄₁₆-inch-wide slot full length of one of the wide sides. This slot permits spreading the extension or pushing the sides together, a good feature since not all skillet handles are the same size. He made it long enough so I could trim it to equal the width of my skillet plus the length of the handle for ease in packing. It can be any length you like. It slides on and off the handle easily, but won't drop the skillet, and any sheet-metal shop can make one for you in a few minutes.

Skillets come in various shapes: rectangular, oblong, and round. For no good reason, I prefer the conventional round shape and have given away others I've tried. Suit yourself.

My wife and I keep a cooking kit packed and ready to go. I put it together for two people, but can easily cook for four with it. There are two skillets. One is cast-iron, 2½ inches deep with an inside bottom diameter of 8½ inches. The other is aluminum, 2¼x7½, with a detachable handle so it will fit inside the iron skillet. One of the kettle lids fits the aluminum skillet; I don't carry a lid for the iron skillet because of weight and bulk. When I need a lid, I press down a piece of aluminum foil to a tight fit all around the rim.

Nearly all frying is done in the iron skillet, but the other serves many purposes. For example, I make a corn-and-oyster dish in it that is not only quick and easy, but also very good. The ingredients are a 1-pound can of cream-style corn, an 8-ounce can of oysters, and about a dozen 2-inch-square soda crackers, poked into the well-mixed corn and oysters to take up excess liquid, which should not be poured off. I heat it until it is bubbling, preferably in an oven but often on a camp stove or over a fire, and it is ready to serve. I have yet to try it on anyone who didn't ask for a second helping.

Both skillet and frying earned bad reputations among dietitians because of wrong technique. I saw the best (or worst) example in New Zealand. Four of us came in late, dead tired, and hungry as wolves, from a long, hard hunt to a shack in the back reaches of the station (ranch) that belonged to our host. He started a fire in the stove, then picked up the skillet in which he had fried mutton chops for breakfast. The grease was still in it. Into this cold grease he dropped fat mutton chops. Then he set the skillet on the still-cool stove and turned his attention to other food.

The tallow melted slowly and the chops absorbed it. When they had browned, we ate them. I still can't look a sheep in the face.

Any kind of meat, from chicken to beef, should be seared quickly in very hot fat. This forms a crust that seals in the flavorful juices and seals out the grease. Then reduce the heat and finish the cooking process slowly for such meats as chicken or chicken-fried steak. Half an inch of fat is superior to a layer that barely covers the bottom of the skillet. Vegetable oil is better from a dietary standpoint than hydrogenated oil or animal fat, but nothing equals bacon grease for flavor, particularly for fish.

When your chicken or chicken-fried steak is done, take it up and pour off all but about two tablespoonfuls of the fat. Dump in half a teaspoonful of salt, then add as much flour as the fat will absorb to make a thick, dry, crumbly paste. You'll need to turn up the heat a bit at this point. Keep stirring and working the paste over the bottom of the skillet until the flour cooks and becomes a light-brown color.

When the paste has browned, pour in about a pint of milk or water, or about ½ pint of canned milk and ½ pint of water—if you boiled potatoes use the water off them—and continue stirring, frequently scraping the bottom of the skillet. If your heat is right, the entire surface of the gravy will soon be bubbling. Let it cook down to about two-thirds its original volume, but stop when it still is a bit on the thin side. It will thicken more as it cools.

I suppose I've cooked a thousand steaks on a cast-iron skillet without any grease at all. It's called pan broiling and it's the way to go when you have good steak, get to camp late, and don't want to wait for wood to burn down to coals for broiling, or for charcoal—or don't have either.

Get your skillet smoking hot on the camp stove or fire and spread about a tablespoonful of salt over the bottom. Make sure the steak is dry and flop it into the skillet. The smoke will fly as the suet scorches, but don't worry about it; you get smoke when it drips onto charcoal, too. Just don't get your skillet so hot it starts to flame.

When a color change has crept about a third of the way up the sides of the steak, turn it. When it has crept as far up the second side, take it up. This steak will be rare. If you want it medium, or if it's extra thick, reduce the heat after the first searing and cook it longer. A well-done steak requires longer cooking with still less heat after the initial searing.

A small, wild trout, like a ruffed grouse, is such a delicacy that it ordinarily should have no seasoning but a little salt. After eating trout for breakfast several mornings in a row, however, you might try this: Brown your trout quickly, preferably in bacon grease, and take care not to cook them through. Reduce the heat and pour a cup of dry sherry into the skillet. Let them simmer, not boil, for five minutes. Peter Barrett taught me this and I immediately elected him trout cook; it's great.

For subsequent skilletfuls—Pete and I can easily polish off a dozen 10-inchers—omit the browning and merely put the trout into the goop in the skillet. You may have to add a bit more sherry from time to time as it evaporates. Take care not to overcook; it's the most common fault.

Sherry gives a different and delightful flavor to any kind of bird, from chicken to chukar, that you might cook in a skillet. First, disjoint your bird, salt and pepper the pieces, and drop them into a paper or plastic bag with half a cup of flour. Shake well to coat each piece uniformly with flour.

Brown the bird in bacon grease or vegetable oil over brisk heat—and you can cook enough for four hungry hunters in a deep 10-inch skillet if you keep turning and shifting the pieces to brown all sides of each. Don't cook it until it's done; just brown it.

Now, drain off nearly all the oil and pour in a cup of dry sherry. Reduce the heat so it will barely simmer and cover the skillet tightly with lid or foil. Let it simmer 15 or 20 minutes, never until completely dry, and take out the bird.

Dump the remaining flour from your shaking bag into the skillet and make gravy, as previously described. You can't brown the flour in the sherry goop, of course, so the gravy will be cream-colored when done. But grown men will plead like children for a second helping on their mashed potatoes.

Far from being an ulcer maker, the oft-maligned skillet is a versatile camp-cooking utensil, its uses limited only by the cook's inventiveness. More than forty years ago, my brother Burtt and I made a six-weeks' backpack trip in the high-mountain country, where we didn't see another person from the time we left one road until we came out on another. Along toward the end, we were starving for sweets.

One afternoon after we had established a campsite by the simple expedient of leaning our packs against a tree, we set out to catch trout for dinner. We had gone only a little way, however, when we came to a patch of wild gooseberries, ripe, tart, and good. Impulsively, I said, "If you'll pick enough, I'll make a pie."

They weren't very big and they were scattered, but he leaned his fly rod against a tree and went to work, dropping the berries into his hat as he picked them. I went back to camp, started a fire, and made a piecrust. I had no flat surface save the bottom of our inverted gold pan, which served well enough when lightly floured. And I had nothing with which to roll the dough, so I simply beat and pushed it into the required thickness with the heels of my hands. When it looked about right, I inverted the gold pan over our lightly oiled skillet and the crust dropped into place. I then made a second crust for the top of the bravely promised pie.

Burtt got back with his hat full of berries and I poured them into the skillet. Next, I sprinkled on most, maybe all, of our remaining sugar and pinched the top crust to the lower one around the edges. I made a few cuts in it, as I had seen my mother do, and set the skillet on a thin bed of coals scraped from the fire.

Burtt went back to the creek to catch trout for dinner while I concentrated on the pie. I propped our gold pan at an angle so it would reflect heat from the fire onto the top crust, kept the flames up by adding fuel as necessary, and from time to time scraped a few more coals under the skillet.

My brother got back with enough trout and we boiled them, since we had only one skillet. By the time we had eaten the trout, we decided the pie was done. We divided it equally on our two plates and went to work. We licked up every crumb.

With night upon us, Burtt drank the last of his tea, groaned softly, and keeled over beside the fire. I followed suit.

We woke up about midnight, I suppose—we didn't have a watch—with only a few glowing embers left to mark the fire. We were numb with cold. There would be a white frost in the morning. We revived the fire, warmed up, shook out our blankets, rolled up in them, and soon were asleep again.

Chapter 7

Two Foolproof Methods of Camp Cooking

In the West, where all the women are beautiful and all the men are brave, and the bartender couldn't mix a martini to save his soul because he has never even heard of it, the one indispensable item of camp gear is the Dutch oven.

It was named for the celebrated frontiersman Dutch O'Leary, who had to camp out for a week with no equipment save the two cast-iron skillets his squaw hurled at him as he dodged out of the tepee. But he soon discovered that by putting one upside down over the other he could cook anything from buffalo tongue to lemon chiffon pie.

For a time he considered naming his invention the O'Leary Oven, but since he was a modest man, he picked the more self-effacing name. (A fortunate choice, it developed, since the Netherlands government immediately gave him an honorarium of 5,000 guilders per year and he was able to devote all his time to chasing squaws instead of wasting half of it chasing the buffalo he had previously been forced to pursue for food.)

As with many of the other great strides in the slow process of evolution, the Dutch oven didn't come all at once. A little-known genius named Beaver Charlie made a trip to Pittsburgh to have an oven cast with the bottom part twice as deep and the top merely a lid. This was an improvement.

But it remained for a trapper called Steeljaws Newhouse to add the final touch. He got tired of eating the apple pie that was scorched on the bottom but raw on top and set off to Pittsburgh to have a Dutch oven made with an upturned rim around the lid. "You can always have a hot bottom," he reasoned, "but you can't heat the top. Hot coals there would do it."

The only trouble was that during the three years it took Steeljaws to make the trip from Jackson Hole to Pittsburgh his compass reading was thrown off by the Iron Mountains in Michigan and he wound up in Tennessee. Walking up to a Lodge on the bank of what he assumed to be the Allegheny River, Steeljaws asked, "Is this Pittsburgh?"

Mr. Lodge replied, "Why not? I been trying to think of a name for this pesky place since I got here. Pittsburgh it is. Only maybe we ought to call it South Pittsburgh. My Uncle Alf, the traveling man, tells me there's a town in Pennsylvania called Pittsburgh. I wouldn't want to copycat after them damn Yankees."

Since he had nothing better to do at the moment, the original Tennessee Lodge heated up his foundry and made a cast-iron Dutch oven for Steeljaws. The legs were a fortunate accident; Lodge poured a little too much iron and it filled the vent holes in the mold. Steeljaws hurried West with his treasure and I, through great good fortune, eventually fell heir to it. I must add, too, that the Lodge Manufacturing Company, of South Pittsburgh, Tennessee, makes Dutch ovens to this day.

The traditional Dutch oven of the trapper, miner, sheepherder, and cowboy was a heavy, flat-bottomed, cast-iron pot with a tight-fitting cast-iron cover and three short legs. The cover, only slightly domed, fitted down inside the rim of the pot about ⅜ of an inch, then extended across the flat-topped rim. This made a good seal to keep steam in; dirt and ashes out. Around the outer edge of the cover there was a turned-up flange and in the center a handle with a notch in the middle.

This notch is important. It marks the balance point of the lid. When you lift it covered with hot coals to inspect the cooking food, feel out the notch with your hook and the lid won't tip to spill ashes into the contents of the pot.

The pot of my old Dutch oven has an inside depth of 4⅜ inches and an inside diameter of 10⅝. The modern trend is to make them somewhat shallower in relation to width. This is better for frying, but probably not quite so good for baking, stewing, or roasting.

Regardless of exact dimensions, the Dutch oven is the greatest piece of outdoor cooking equipment I have ever used. Naturally, I don't carry mine on backpacking trips because it weighs 18½ pounds, but when weight is no problem it always goes along. It serves as both pot and skillet, besides baking anything from biscuits to pies to beef. When the wind blows, it keeps the ashes out of the food and maintains its uniform heat. It keeps food hot after it is done. And when dinner is over it can sit outside the tent, even through a sandstorm, without one speck of grit finding its way under the tight-fitting lid.

The legs are a real help in campfire cooking and they don't hurt a thing when you set the Dutch oven on a gasoline camp stove or on a grill over the fire. They stick down between the bars. If you would use your oven on a conventional stove, however, then you must have one without legs and, of course, the flanged lid serves no useful purpose, either. My advice is to buy an original-type Dutch oven for camping and use a covered cast-iron skillet at home.

One of the reasons why the Dutch oven has always been so popular with men who work outdoors and do their own cooking is that they can leave it unattended all day and still have a good meal piping hot and ready to eat when they get back to camp in the evening. One of our favorites, which we enjoy on both hunting and fishing trips, is pot roast, and here's how to prepare it:

Before breakfast, I build a big fire in a pit approximately 2 feet wide and 2 feet deep. Any kind of wood will do. With lodgepole pine, which is not noted for its hot coals, I heap the fuel up. We eat breakfast and prepare the vegetables while the fire burns down. We use onions, potatoes, carrots, cabbage, celery, turnips—whatever is available in camp, including a 1-pound can of tomatoes. The next step is to put a little oil in the pot and brown the beef quickly on both sides, leaving the lid off.

We salt and pepper the meat, put the vegetables in on top of it, filling the oven nearly to the lid, and sprinkle salt and pepper on them. Water is unnecessary since the vegetables provide more than enough moisture.

When the fire has burned down to coals, I shovel out four-fifths of them, heap them beside the pit, and set the covered Dutch oven level on the remainder. This job requires a hook with a handle about 30 inches long. It can either be cut on the spot from a convenient alder or made from heavy wire and carried with the camp outfit.

Next, holding the oven's bail up with the hook, I shovel all the coals back into the pit, surrounding the oven completely and heaping them up on the lid. The final step is to cover the whole kaboodle with a 6-inch layer of soil.

Dinner is now on the way. We can hunt all day with the comforting knowledge that hot, tasty food will be waiting for us when we return to camp.

Dutch oven stew is prepared in much the same way. Some cooks brown their chunks of stew meat, but I prefer not to. I simply put them on the bottom of the pot, add seasoning, and either a cup of cold water or a can of consommé. The vegetables, including a No. 2½ can of tomatoes, come next.

We don't care for thickening in stew, but if you prefer it, mix a heaping tablespoon of flour with enough cold water to achieve the consistency of cream and pour it in. The cooking procedure is the same as for pot roast.

Some of our greatest camp meals have been centered on game birds—sage hens, grouse, chukars, quail—cooked in the Dutch oven. During the spring and summer we prepare chicken in the same way. Quail, split down the back, can be cooked whole; the larger birds should be cut into pieces.

Salt and pepper the birds, then flour them by shaking four or five pieces at a time in a big paper bag containing half a cup of flour (we prefer whole-wheat).

Your Dutch oven, on a grill over the campfire or a gasoline stove, should be hot by now, with about two-thirds of a cup of salad oil on the bottom. Brown the pieces on all sides.

When they are nicely browned, reduce the heat, pour in two cups of sherry, shake in the flour left in the paper bag, and put the lid on the oven. Simmer slowly for half an hour, then turn all the pieces and simmer for another 30 minutes.

The simmering is important; avoid a rapid boil. When you think your birds are done, taste the liquid. If it is bitter, simmer some more with the lid ajar. This dish, to paraphrase Walton, is too good for any but hunters and very honest men, and a few mushrooms, diced and then browned with the birds, make it even better. The goop left in the kettle when the birds come out is the most delicious gravy I have ever eaten.

Big bread, so called because the loaf fits the Dutch oven, is the favorite of sheepherders who must be away from camp all day tending their woolly charges. Using either yeast or sourdough, they put the well-kneaded loaf in the greased oven, let it rise, put the lid on, and bury it in the coals the same as with a pot roast. The wood for this must be very well burned down, otherwise the bread will scorch.

Few campers, save in a wilderness, bother to bake bread, but it can also be baked aboveground in a conventional bread pan set inside the Dutch oven. You bake pie in a pie tin, the same way. Biscuits are baked in the Dutch oven without a separate pan and since they are quick and easy and more likely to tempt the camp cook, let's go into the technique.

The first step, as with all aboveground baking, is to preheat the oven. Shovel a mound of coals from your campfire. Lay the lid on the coals and set the pot on the lid. (Since heat rises, you want the lid hotter than the bottom when you start baking.) Prepare your dough while they are heating.

Since you probably won't have a rolling pin, bread board, and biscuit cutter, make the dough a little softer than usual—just firm enough so you can handle it with well-floured hands without its sticking. Make balls of dough about the size of eggs and lay them on the bottom of the hot, well-greased kettle. Let them touch each other, but don't pack them in tightly.

In a Dutch oven you can cook not only just about anything you could cook in a skillet but a lot of things the skillet can't handle. Here's the start of a batch of biscuits.

When fire has burned down to coals, shovel most of them aside and set onto remaining coals the three-legged Dutch oven with its tight-fitting lid. Then shovel onto the lipped lid the coals you just shoveled aside.

With a little practice in judging baking time, you'll be greeted with a sight like this when you check on your biscuits.

Set the kettle on the coals, which will have cooled somewhat by now. If they are still red, sprinkle dirt or ashes over them. Then put the lid on and heap it with hot coals from the fire. Look at the biscuits in 15 minutes. They should be done, but you can check this by running a toothpick or sliver into one. If the tops are not nicely browned, remove the cooled coals from the lid and replace them with hot ones from the fire.

All Dutch-oven baking above ground is done this way. Bread and pie take longer than biscuits, of course, so you may have to replenish the coals several times. Beef or venison roasts, chickens or game birds, are roasted by this same method. With any of them, as with biscuits, you need more heat on the lid than under the bottom.

The Dutch oven has two disadvantages: It is heavy and it requires a lot of fuel. But you can cook virtually anything in it and the food so prepared is always delicious. Furthermore, it is virtually foolproof, thanks to the thick cast iron.

If the lid of a new oven doesn't seat well, smear valve grinding compound on the rim of the pot and the edge of the lid and rotate it until you have a fit like a bank vault door.

Food may stick at first. Cover the bottom with ½ inch of bacon grease or lard and keep it smoking hot for 2 hours. Then never wash it with detergent. After use simply wipe it out or, if necessary, pour in water, bring it to a boil, put the lid on, and let it steam a few minutes. Pour the water out and wipe it dry while still hot. This cleans and sterilizes both lid and pot and won't cause the food you cook next to stick.

Second only to the Dutch oven, aluminum foil is the most versatile camp-cooking "utensil" there is. In addition, foil weighs next to nothing. I have used aluminum foil for camp cooking ever since it became available shortly after World War II. It has many advantages—in addition to the fact that you don't have a lot of messy pots and pans to clean up after every meal. You can cook just about anything in it, including most kinds of vegetables, apples and pears, and all kinds of meat, game, and fish. But most important of all, foil cookery is almost foolproof.

Properly wrapped, each bundle becomes a virtual pressure cooker. The confined steam retains flavor and prevents scorching. I'll admit you can scorch food in foil, but you really have to try, barring one thing: a hole in the wrapping. In this case the steam escapes and food will scorch in heat that would otherwise be perfectly safe.

The standard, 12-inch foil your wife uses in the kitchen is about half as thick as the paper on which this is printed, yet I prefer it for most camp cooking and habitually keep a 200-foot roll in my grub box. Only when I make a larger-than-usual bundle, as for a pheasant or chicken, do I prefer the 18-inch width. It is twice as thick and so a single wrap should be sufficient to do the job.

I have found, however, that a double wrap of the lighter foil has three advantages: First, it is less likely to leak steam, no matter how carefully you roll your seams of the single heavier wrap. Second, when I remove food from the fire I shuck off the outer wrap, thereby getting rid of the ashes, and

Before wrapping potatoes in foil for baking, smear each with about this much butter. Two layers of standard-weight foil are better than a single layer of the heavy. Ted carries his butter in a jar to keep dirt and bugs out.

Just about any vegetable can be cooked in foil. Here Ted has cut the tip end out of a cabbage and put salt, pepper, and butter into the hole before wrapping in foil.

put the food on the table in the inner wrap. This keeps it hot. Third, I have discovered that, somehow, I'm more likely to break or tear the single wrap, thereby allowing steam to escape, than to puncture both layers of the lighter foil.

It's hard to give precise times for campfire cooking since you can't set the temperature control to maintain the desired heat as you can on your oven at home. You develop judgment with practice, but cooking in foil is so nearly foolproof that timing is not nearly as critical as you might fear. And you do have a simple method of checking: squeeze the bundle. When it's soft the vegetable inside is done.

On the average, an 8-ounce baking potato will require from 45 minutes to an hour, longer than most other vegetables. I start a fire when we get to camp, coat the potatoes with vegetable oil, wrap them, and line them up around the base of the fire. The second vegetable, perhaps a head of cabbage, quartered, smeared with margarine, and sprinkled with salt and pepper on both cut sides goes on next, also lined up around the base of the fire. As it burns down I move the bundles closer, turning them in the process so all sides get equal exposure to the heat.

Core apples, fill the holes with sugar, cinnamon, and butter, and bake like potatoes. Split pears lengthwise, cut out the cores, and fill with the same mixture—about half butter, ⅜ sugar, and ⅛ cinnamon. Bake in foil until they're soft.

You need three things for campfire cooking in foil: a shovel to shift fire and coals, a blunt stick about 2½ feet long to use with the shovel for moving and turning bundles, and a pair of gloves. You'll use them for testing softness and for peeling off the outer layer of foil. Lacking the shovel, two sticks will do, but it's always a good idea to have a shovel near an outdoor fire, anyway.

Most root vegetables can be cooked in foil just like potatoes, but with slight variations. You can cut the ends off an onion, preferably about 3 inches in diameter, leave the outer husks on, wrap it, and set it beside the fire. The dry outer skin may scorch a bit, but the inside layers won't. When done, split the onion and add salt, pepper, and butter or margarine. Or, you can split the onion first, put salt, pepper, and butter between the halves, push them together, and wrap. Either way, you'll find this vegetable entirely different from onions cooked any other way—with a flavor that we like better.

Cook turnips just like potatoes. Small turnips, like small potatoes, can be wrapped two to the package. You can bundle from three to six carrots together, depending on how big they are. Add salt, pepper, and butter or margarine.

A stalk of celery, split in two, seasoned lightly, and buttered on the inside, will be tender and delicious when properly cooked in foil. Pieces of squash are improved by a dab of butter on top. Don't remove the rind. Roasting ears require nothing but wrapping and cooking.

There are several ways to cook fish in foil. Rich-fleshed fish, such as salmon, steelhead, and fat trout, need only a sprinkle of salt and pepper before wrapping and cooking over coals. Sometimes we add a few drops of lemon juice, though to my taste nothing improves the natural flavor of these fish.

Dry-fleshed fish can be improved by a different treatment. Alternate thin strips of bacon and fillets, perhaps four or five, depending on size, in your bundle. This thicker package won't cook through so quickly. Consequently, you need a milder heat to get the middle done without scorching the outside. We have found it works very well to bury them in the ashes of our breakfast campfire, heap the ashes over them, and then sprinkle a 1-inch layer of earth over the whole thing.

Obviously, the ashes of some kinds of wood retain heat better than others. If your bundles are cool by the time you dig them up for lunch, heat them thoroughly, but not too rapidly, before you open them.

And this is perhaps as good a place as any to mention that charcoal serves perfectly where you can't find suitable wood. We usually take it along on the desert, where the biggest stick in sight is often about the size of your finger. And you don't need to lug along a charcoal broiler or hibachi; charcoal burns well right on the ground. If you intend to broil steaks, fish, or other food on a grill above it, however, spread a sheet of foil on the earth first. It will reflect all the heat up toward the food.

One fall my wife and I camped for several days with Barney and Doris Wilkerson to hunt chukars and fish for bass and, even though we had been using foil a long time, Barney taught us something new. First, he spread a strip of foil on the ground, then dumped on some charcoal and lit it. As soon as it was going well, long before it had burned down to the uniform gray most charcoal cooks use, he put four steaks on a light wire grill about 8 inches above the charcoal.

Next, using the heavy, 18-inch foil, he made a sort of little tent completely around the grill and above the steaks. He peaked the roof so the foil didn't touch them, and double-folded the edges to keep the smoke in. The result was out of this world—nicely browned, rare, and with a delightful smoky flavor. The same system worked the following evening with chukars, cut in half lengthwise through breast and back, and broiled precisely the same as the steaks. He turned both one time.

We do a lot of our upland bird hunting in areas too remote to drive home each evening, so we camp—we enjoy camping anyway—and while we usually take steak for the first evening we depend on our guns thereafter. I guess we've cooked birds just about every way they can be cooked—boiled, broiled, fried, baked (reflector oven or camp-stove oven), browned and simmered in sherry in a Dutch oven, and in foil. The last method results in birds that are different from any others and has an advantage over broiling where only resinous wood is available: the foil keeps out the smoke that might give the flesh an unpleasant flavor.

Chukars and ruffed grouse are about the same size and any hungry hunter can eat one. Twelve-inch foil wraps them properly. Young sage hens and blue grouse, about the size of cock pheasants, weigh twice as much as chukars, and one bird will serve two people. You need 18-inch foil to bundle them well.

Pluck and draw your bird and save the heart, liver and gizzard. (Don't hunt for the gizzard in a sage hen; they have none.) In camp you use anything available for stuffing, but the one that follows turned out to be so good that we've often had it at home since I first tried it.

I cut an orange, rind and all, into half-inch cubes, then dice an onion of similar size. A stick (not stalk) of celery, leaves and all, gets the same treatment. Finally, I dice the giblets, add salt, pepper, about a tablespoon of Worcestershire or A-1 sauce, and mix well. This will stuff one blue or two ruffed grouse (or a roaster chicken) with a bit left over.

I rub the bird with vegetable oil, sprinkle with salt and pepper, and wrap it in foil. Placed near the edge of a hot fire and turned frequently to expose all sides equally to the heat, a 2½-pound bird will be cooked through in an hour—about the time your foil-wrapped potatoes are done. A ruffed grouse or chukar requires half as long.

At this point, though the bird is edible, it won't be nicely browned. Your fire should be burned down to coals by now. Lay the bird, or birds, right on them and listen. If you hear sizzling inside the foil, the birds are browning. Turn frequently and take them off in 10 minutes. They should be nicely browned, tender, juicy, and flavorful.

Don't attempt to economize by using foil twice. It is almost certain to have holes through which, even though they might be minute, the steam will escape and result in scorching the food inside.

If you wad foil up, it will last as long as aluminum beverage cans, but if you spread it flat over a modest fire or hot coals, it will burn. For years, when camping in remote places, we buried our garbage, but coons or bears sometimes dug it up. We now make a practice of burning everything that will burn and bringing the remainder home in plastic bags. If everyone did this, the outdoors would not be gradually filling up with litter.

Chapter 8

Hints on
Cooking Game at Home

Once when Dave Newell was editor of *Field & Stream* somebody sent him about 10 pounds of bighorn sheep.

It came packed in dry ice, frozen hard as a rock, and Dave invited all of us on the editorial staff to help eat it.

We were delighted at the prospect. Among men who've eaten them all, bighorn is considered the finest of North American big game. We took Dave's sheep to a restaurant near the office where we often ate and asked the cook to prepare it for our lunch next day.

He really put his heart into the job, but the result, from all we could tell by tasting it, might have been moose, mutton, beef, or bear. It had been marinated in wine, then loaded with spices. Whatever distinguishing flavor the bighorn may have had was sacrificed to the cook's determination to do his very best. We had to tell him it was great—he had probably worked all night—but we were lying. That wasn't our idea of the way to cook game, nor is it mine yet.

My game recipes are simple. They're based on the premise that game is good; that cooking should preserve its distinguishing flavor. Consider pheasant. Our family thinks pheasants are wonderful eating, far better than chicken. Yet we have friends who like chicken better. I think I know why.

First, they skin their pheasants. This stems from laziness because it is easier to tear the skin off any bird than to pluck it. But did you ever buy a skinned chicken? When you remove the skin, the fat and flavor go with it. Furthermore, a skinned bird tends to dry out during the cooking process.

Second, most of these non-pheasant-liking friends soak their birds overnight in salt water. They should try this on a steak! And still a third cardinal sin is cooking game—any and all game—far too done. Many, perhaps most, women somehow feel that because it's game it should cook longer than its domestic counterpart. I can think of but one exception to the rule that the longer you cook meat the drier, tougher, and more tasteless it becomes. The exception is stew. And here, of course, you want the flavor to leave the meat and penetrate the vegetables cooking with it.

I'm not one who favors hanging upland game or waterfowl prior to drawing them. In cool weather we pick and dress our birds the evening of the day we kill them. After our game is cleaned, however, we like to leave it in the refrigerator several days before cooking or freezing it. And we feel all upland birds and waterfowl should be frozen in water to prevent the drying out called locker burn.

But back to cooking. Anybody who can fry chicken can fry any upland birds or small game. The process is exactly the same—and don't cook it any longer than you would chicken.

Maybe I'm old-fashioned, but I still think the best utensil for this job is a heavy cast-iron skillet with a tight-fitting lid. With ¼ inch of hot grease in the skillet, brown all pieces on both sides over sharp heat, then turn the burner down, put the lid on, and let them fry slowly for 15 minutes. The last thing, pour in half a cup of water, replace the lid, and let your pheasant steam for 5 minutes—but be sure to take it up before the last of the water boils away. Drying out the meat makes it tough.

Now, what's left in the skillet makes the best gravy in this world or the next. Pour out part of the grease, leaving about 3 tablespoonfuls and all the goodies. Put in two heaping tablespoonfuls of flour. Rub it around with your pancake turner until it starts to brown. Add some salt and pepper. Pour in a quart of fresh milk, or some of the water you boiled the potatoes in and half a big can of evaporated milk. Keep stirring while the gravy boils down to the proper consistency and call one of the kids to mash the potatoes.

Rabbit, squirrel, pheasant, grouse, chukar, quail—any upland game—is even better than the traditional fried chicken. But to preserve the utmost of the delicate game flavor we think broiling can't be beat. There's only one drawback to broiling—no gravy.

The best source of heat for broiling is hardwood coals or charcoal. Pheasant broiled over charcoal is helped in the same way that steak is—by the faint hint of smoke and the crusty edges. And the older and tougher the bird, the better broiling is as a cooking method. An old rooster with spurs like a Mexican cowboy will be tender after broiling quickly.

Split the bird in half lengthwise, salt and pepper, and treat the two halves just as you would steak. For the best flavor and the most tender flesh, the outside should be golden brown, the inside pink and juicy. If the broiling bird appears dry, brush it with salad oil or melted butter.

Of course, you can't always broil game over coals or charcoal, but your gas or electric oven will do a beautiful job. Again, the process is like broiling steak. You have to establish the proper times for various birds in your own oven by experimenting. The broiler unit is hotter in some than in others; also, the distance of the broiler rack from the unit varies.

You can broil any kind of game in your electric or gas oven just as you would steak.

For a change, try this: salt and pepper your game birds and then marinate them in a mixture of vegetable oil and A-1 Sauce.

We split quail down the back but don't cut the breast, spread them out, and give them 5 minutes on each side in our electric oven. We split pheasants, grouse, and chukars completely through lengthwise. Pheasant halves get 8 minutes to the side; chukar halves, 5. Doves split down the back and spread out like quail take 3 minutes on each side—and if you don't care for doves, try broiling them quickly. You're likely to change your mind.

Finally, for variety, here's a broiling trick you really should try: Get your birds or small game ready to cook an hour ahead of time. Put ½ cup of vegetable oil in a pan and add five tablespoonfuls of A-1 Sauce. Put your salted and peppered pieces in this mixture and shuffle them around occasionally. They'll broil to a beautiful brown with a mouth-watering flavor.

On many subjects, I'm open to reason—I think. But there is only one way to cook a duck. Have your birds clean, dry, and at room temperature. Stuff them with diced green pepper, celery, and onion, flavored with a little sage, salt, and pepper. Preheat your oven to its highest temperature, about 500 degrees on most electric stoves. Pop your ducks in, and if they're big ones—fat mallards, say—give them 20 minutes, no more. Let green-winged teal have 12, and judge the others accordingly.

As soon as you take them from the oven, dig the stuffing out into a wooden bowl. It will still be crisp and take the place of salad. Then split each duck lengthwise with knife and poultry shears and serve half a mallard or a whole teal to each person. They'll beg for more.

Bull moose and elk, buck deer, and the males of all our other horned and antlered game quit eating and lose weight rapidly when they go into the rut. They shouldn't be killed for food at this time. If you have to hunt then and want to kill a male, look for one either too young or too old to be a lover. And if you wind up with a mature buck, his neck swollen and no fat on his back, have him made into salami, jerky, or hamburger, and add a pound of beef fat to 5 pounds of venison for the last. Even the salami, jerky, or hamburger won't be very good, but it's the best you can do.

The tastiest big game we ever had came from mature bucks or bulls killed early in the season when they were rolling with fat. Given proper care in the field, a buck killed then—or a fat doe at any time—doesn't need special preparation. We cook all kinds of big game just the same as corresponding cuts of their domestic counterparts. Broiled venison chops are delicious. A big roast of elk or moose is as good as any beef roast you can buy. Here again, don't get carried away and cook it to a cinder just because it's game. The inside should be pink and juicy, the outside crisp.

This covers almost everything but bear. One fall I shot a two-year-old bear that had been living on berries, and we've never had better meat. But a bear would just as soon eat carrion as berries—in fact, maybe he'd rather. I killed another bear one time that smelled so bad I could hardly skin it, and I doubt that I could have eaten a bite of the meat if I'd been starving. And unlike a possum, which also loves carrion, you can't put a bear in a cage and fatten it on clean food before you eat it.

We love all other kinds of game at our house, from rabbit to moose and from dove to duck. But when it comes to bear, I confess my feelings are a little like the hillbilly's. Asked if he'd ever eaten bear, he thought, then answered, "Well, I've tried!"

Part IV
HUNTING OTHER BIG GAME

Chapter 9

Matching Wits with Elk

A herd of elk was feeding on the big, southern slope west of camp. It fed there every night. The tracks revealed that there were about a dozen animals—cows, calves, a mature bull, and probably a spike or two hanging around the outskirts.

My wife and I were camped by the spring at the very head of Pup Creek and these elk were close, just over the low ridge that separated Pup Creek from the east fork of Dog Creek. This was unusual. Unlike deer, elk simply won't stick around where they can hear the sounds that reveal the presence of their mortal enemy, man. Chopping wood, rattling pans, conversation—

These bull elk are on their winter range in Yellowstone
National Park.

any of these typical man-made noises can cause a herd of elk to move to a
new and safer location.

In this case, however, the elk were grazing the grassy slope at night when
our camp was quiet. Early each morning they crossed the ridge at its crest
and went on farther north to spend the day in a typical "elk jungle," a big
pocket of dense spruce strewn with fallen trees and dotted with bogholes.
This was about a mile from the feeding area and two miles from our camp.
Being on the other side of the long, high, east-and-west ridge, the elk were
unable to hear the noise we made during the daytime. And at night our
scent and smoke drifted down into the Pup Creek drainage with the
lowering air.

We had scouted the area thoroughly and we knew exactly what the elk
were doing. The problem was to get within range of them when it was light
enough to shoot. So long as the weather remained calm and sunny, we
knew we could depend on the evening breeze flowing downhill into the
Dog Creek drainage from the slope where the elk were feeding. If we were

Bark stripped from the trunk of this little lodgepole pine
shows that a bull elk polished his antlers here. He
may or may not still be nearby.

concealed low on the slope when they came over the top, they would never suspect our presence. We decided to try this first.

We left camp at sunset and walked out around the sidehill for three-quarters of a mile. Here we found a spot where we could sit comfortably near the edge of a little thicket and watch the big area of grass and low brush where the elk fed. Above it, along the crest of the ridge, was the edge of the lodgepole timber from which we expected them to emerge.

It was a long wait. We didn't say a word. We didn't move. I didn't smoke, and I managed to choke back the occasional cough caused by that pleasant vice. A flock of blue grouse, which had walked up the slope feeding during the day, sailed from the ridge down to a grove of big yellow pines where they would spend the night.

A chipmunk raced along a log, rustled through the fallen leaves in front of us, and began gathering seeds from a clump of ripe grass not ten feet away. Bending down each stalk in turn, he quickly stripped it of its treasures and stuffed them into his cheek pouches. When they were bulging full he hurried away over the route by which he had come, hid the seeds in some secret spot, and hurried back again. He made five round trips before dusk, but because we didn't move he never suspected our presence.

At last it became so dark that we could no longer see the crosshairs in our scopes against the dark background of a tree trunk. It was too late to shoot. And then the elk came out! First a cow, then two cows and a calf, then the bull appeared near the edge of the timber 300 yards away. More followed. They gradually worked down the slope toward us and we were able to count fourteen.

It was easy to see their dark forms against the light background of the pale-yellow grass, but there wasn't a thing we could do about it. You can't shoot at a fine game animal and hope to hit it just anywhere. You have to place your shot, and this was now impossible. We watched until we could no longer see them, then cautiously worked our way back to camp.

The next morning we started in the dark and were back in our hiding spot before it was light enough to shoot. The elk were already gone. Obviously, they had wandered into the timber at the approach of dawn. We left and spent the day hunting in a different area—unsuccessfully.

It was no use trying to stalk the herd in its daytime retreat. I had already tried that. Approaching cautiously from the downwind side, I had actually crawled into the jungle far enough to see the legs of several elk below the low-sweeping branches of the spruce trees. But getting a clear shot was something else again. And, of course, if I shot and missed or startled the elk by my presence they would leave and probably not take up residence again until they had put several miles between themselves and the cause of their alarm.

The best chance—in fact, the only chance now—was to intercept them somewhere between their daytime retreat and their nighttime feeding area. This could be difficult. Once off the long south slope, where the regular air movement was a gentle flow downhill from shortly after sunset until sunrise, the breeze might be tricky. And though most of the timber between the spruce jungle and the ridge was open lodgepole pine, visibility would still be limited. We would have to be in just the right spot at just the right time—with the wind from the right direction.

Next morning we left camp before daylight, climbed the slope to the top of the east-west ridge, and walked out along it until we approached the area where the elk had been crossing. We then angled northwest until we decided we were near the route the elk would take. Luckily, there was no air movement here at all. The only light was from the stars. There was nothing to do but wait. Leaving my wife sitting with her back against a tree, I went on 200 yards before I sat down. Being separated would improve the odds.

I watched the stars fade out and the sky grow pale in the east. It was chilly. I shivered and wished I had worn more clothes. Even though it was September, the elevation was about 6,000 feet and we had a white frost every morning.

A pine squirrel woke and saluted the new day with a long outburst of staccato chattering. Far away to the south I heard the raucous voice of a Canada jay. It was making a great fuss over something.

At last the light improved to the point where I could see the crosshairs against a tree trunk. Now I could shoot. Waiting became more difficult. Would the elk come within range? Had they passed our chosen spot? Perhaps they were already approaching the jungle. I strained my ears and eyes and forced myself to sit quietly although the chill was biting into the very marrow of my bones. I wished I had chosen a better spot. Small fir trees, which I had been unable to see earlier, were scattered among the pines ahead of me, limiting my vision to about 80 yards in that direction. Fortunately, the area through which I had come was quite open; I could see Ellen sitting against her tree and for some distance beyond. If the elk came between us we'd be okay.

Then I heard a branch snap. It was in front of me, behind the firs. Was it an elk? I heard another sound. It had to be. My heart began to race. Very cautiously, I eased the bolt back and chambered a cartridge in my .270.

I could hear footfalls. Or could I? Maybe my imagination was playing tricks. It seemed as though I could hear many heavy animals walking past, out of sight beyond the firs. It couldn't be imagination. I heard the snap of another fallen branch. The elk were there. We had stopped 200 yards too soon. Now I was positive that I heard several elk moving beyond the fir trees. I felt sick; they might as well be miles away.

They were moving carelessly, wandering in loose formation, totally unaware of the enemies that were waiting. I could hear them plainly now. Gradually resignation replaced my first disappointment. There was still no breeeze. The elk would pass unalarmed and we could try again.

My mind turned to thinking about elk generally. How adept they are at taking care of themselves! Of course they would walk among the little firs where they were less likely to be seen. What else could I expect? This was habit with them.

Suddenly a shot broke the dawn silence. It startled me. I nearly left the ground. Ellen had pivoted around to face the other way. She was lowering her rifle. Considering our planning and preparations, I knew that she would shoot only at an elk, but I could see nothing. She got slowly up. I heard the elk behind the fir trees pounding away.

I started to my feet. Maybe if I ran after them I could see one. There was bound to be a laggard. Then I gasped and sat back down. A bull, maybe not the herd bull, but a bull, was running almost directly toward me. I didn't move. He was coming from perhaps 200 yards straight south of Ellen, running at an angle to intercept the herd behind the trees.

I wondered if Ellen had shot at him. No, her rifle had been pointed toward the east. I glanced in her direction. She was walking straight away from me, looking ahead. She didn't even see the bull.

I'd have to take him on the run, but he'd be close. It looked as though he'd pass within 50 feet. I didn't bat an eye. When he was nearly to me, I pushed the safety off. Believe it or not, he heard it! He must have heard the click! He slid to a halt. He was in shotgun range, looking wildly for the new danger ahead.

I raised my rifle. He saw me and wheeled on two legs, showing the broadside of his chest. I shot before his front feet touched the ground, at an all but stationary target. The crosshairs were at the point of his "elbow," low against his chest, and I knew the hold was good.

The bull came down running, but I didn't attempt to shoot again. A heart shot is never instantly fatal. He ran about 75 yards, then dropped.

No need for quiet now. I called to Ellen and asked if she got one. She said she had a spike bull. He had been following the herd, but staying at a safe distance, and probably the bull I shot had fallen back to run him still farther away.

I rough-dressed my bull as quickly as I could, then hurried to help Ellen finish hers. Our hunt was over; our strategy had worked.

We walked to camp and ate a second breakfast, then returned with our block and tackle, ax, and eight meat bags, one for each quarter of the two elk. And while we were skinning and quartering them and hanging the quarters above the reach of bears, the woods grew ominously quiet. Before we finished, a wind came whipping through the trees, and on its heels, snow. Sweeping in with the swift intensity that storms in the high country often have, it coated the windward side of the lodgepole trunks with a wet, white blanket and hid the brown pine needles underfoot.

At last we were done and we walked back to our snug camp and built a cheerful fire in the little stove. Then, safe and warm and dry, we sat and listened to the snowflakes hissing down the taut canvas overhead. Our outfitter would be along with his pack string in a few days to pick up our game and take it, and us, back to the landing strip, where a plane would pick us up. In the meantime we could loaf and hunt deer and enjoy the freshness of the mountains after this early storm. The pressure was off.

Chapter 10

Reward for Virtue

As I keep telling my boys, if you do right, you'll be rewarded. Take the fall when I didn't really want to go elk hunting. I went for just two reasons: my family needed meat, and my wife needed a vacation. It turned out to be the best hunt I ever had, and that undoubtedly was my reward for being so unselfish.

We flew from McCall, Idaho, to Chamberlain Basin. It's a big chunk of country south of the main Salmon River, west of the Middle Fork and east of the South Fork, and so far it has never been blighted by a road. Our old friend Slim Horn met Ellen and me at the landing strip with his pack string. He took us, our food, and our camp outfit to the head of Pup Creek and left us there.

Seeing Pup Creek again was like meeting another old friend. We've camped there many times and killed a pile of game down the creek or back over the ridge at the heads of Deer Creek and Dog Creek. The spot stirred pleasant memories. The same, familiar, white-trunked aspens were dropping the last of their yellow leaves around the tent. The old lodgepole slopes and ridges, mellowed by the low-slanting October sun, beckoned us. The recently rain-washed air, pine-scented and crystal-clear, was good to breathe. The little spring just a few yards behind the tent—the very head of Pup Creek—was gurgling softly, as it always had when we camped there.

But this time Pup Creek let us down—or we let it down. There were lots of elk and some deer around when we started hunting, but we muffed our chances. We did things wrong a time or two, and elk allow only one mistake. Then it started to snow and the game left and we moved camp farther down the basin, to the edge of the winter range. But there was one good day at Pup Creek that I want to tell you about, because we took the time to do something I've always wanted to do on a big-game hunt—but never before did.

We left camp half an hour before dawn, and at 10 o'clock were holding a whispered debate about which of four elk, lying on the point of a blow-down jack-pine ridge 75 yards away, we should kill. Meat hunting is not the helter-skelter, kill-any-of-'em thing that some folks imagine. This was late in October, and the elk were through their rut. A mature bull would not be fit to eat. We wanted dry cows, spikes, or two-year-old bulls. We had also decided to shoot a couple of fat four-point buck deer.

Now, the four elk we were watching provided something of a problem. There were three cows and a calf. Obviously, two of the cows were dry and should be fat. But we didn't want to kill the cow with the calf, or the calf itself, of course. Unfortunately, we spent too long in trying to make up our minds. We had just about decided to kill the big dark cow lying farthest from the calf when one of those damnable little midmorning breezes went sneaking around the side of the hill and told the elk that they were not alone. We soon were. They leaped up and disappeared over the ridge. You don't take any desperation shots when you have plenty of time in a country like Chamberlain. We didn't shoot.

But this is really what I want to tell you about. Noon found us walking across a lovely meadow at the head of Deer Creek. Up here, Deer Creek is a little stream that doesn't look very promising, but it is the home of countless little native cutthroat trout jeweled with black, lavender, and scarlet, arrow-swift, fat and shy as a marten. Right in the forks there is a lone lodgepole standing and some dead lodgepoles down, and a green-clothed banquet table in the V of the little stream. We stopped there to eat our lunch.

I had a scrap of line and a snelled fly carefully coiled in my billfold against this very moment. A slender alder from the stream, a few minutes of crawling cautiously along its banks, and we had trout to supplement our menu.

We built a little fire and made our coffee. Then we propped our sandwiches up with sticks to toast, and while they were being altered from white to golden brown we broiled our little trout over the glowing coals. Sprinkled lightly with salt, flavored subtly by the green willow twigs on which we'd skewered them, and seasoned by six hours of hard walking, no fish were ever half so good.

Loafing afterward in the mellow autumn sunlight for a couple of hours, we finished our coffee, made some more, and finished that, too. This was one of those rare times that are just right in every way. When the shadows began to lengthen noticeably toward the east, we reluctantly turned our steps toward camp.

It was fortunate that we enjoyed the sun during this very special nooning because we were to see it no more for many days thereafter. Snow began to fall that night. With it the woods changed. No longer mellow and friendly, they became bleak, mysterious. And with their change, the game left the high country. We followed a few days later, riding out the long trail through falling snow to camp at Quaking Aspen Springs.

Things happened here. The snow continued to fall, day after day, until it piled up nearly knee-deep on the ridge where Slim had set up our camp. Elk by the hundred trailed past along the south slope, 1,000 feet below. The deer were moving too, working down to their winter range, where the snow was not so deep. Other creatures were also on the prowl, no doubt sensing the cold days ahead.

Slim stayed a day to hunt with us. We were now the last people in Chamberlain, and he, too, wanted an elk for winter meat. He drove his horses down the slope half a mile below camp and left them there in the belief that they could paw grass out of the snow to fill their bellies.

Next day's dawn came—dull, white, snowy, lifeless—while Slim and I walked out the trail from camp. Half an hour later, still walking the ridge trail, we saw some elk. Six of them, all cows, were feeding up out of a draw a quarter of a mile away. The wind was fortunately in our favor.

We stepped back behind some trees and advanced under their cover as far as we could. Then we dropped down and bellied out to the point of a ridge that overlooked the slope on which we had last seen the elk. They were still there, moving slowly up the roof-steep mountain as they pawed the snow away from clumps of grass and ate. We were as close as we could get.

I wished we could cut the range in half, but there was no way to do it. We checked the muzzles of our rifles to make sure that they were free of snow, then cleared off the scopes. Slim insisted that I shoot first. I picked the fattest cow, centered the crosshairs 3 inches below the butt of her ear, and squeezed the trigger. She shot down the mountain, sliding, tumbling, hurtling in a cloud of snow.

At the report, the five others wheeled and lunged, quartering, up the slope directly away from us. Then out of the draw below, into which we had been unable to see, came more elk. Elk upon elk, dozens of elk, at least forty in all, poured up out of the draw and followed the leaders across the snowy slope.

Slim waited. It seemed that he would never shoot, but at last the elk stopped. Plainly they were unsure of the direction of the shot. They were 350, maybe 400 yards away, but at the crack of his '06 a big, dark, heavy cow collapsed and started tumbling and sliding down the mountain, just as mine had done. We watched her out of sight.

We found mine first. It had slid 250 yards and hung up on a clump of chokecherry bushes. We started to dress it. Then it occurred to me that I might as well go and dress Slim's so as to get both done as quickly as possible. I felt my way around the sidehill until I came to the chute in the snow that it had made sliding down. I followed cautiously—I had no desire to make a similar path to the bottom of the mountain.

No brush had arrested the course of Slim's cow. She had slid clear to the bottom and finally come to rest in a steep, rocky ravine. I've no idea how far she slid, but I do know that it took me three-quarters of an hour to get there. When I did, she was gone. The outline of her body, where she had lain stretched out full length in the snow, was plain, but her tracks led off around the mountain. (I later discovered that Slim had hit her in the shoulders, just above the backbone. This shot petrifies animals, but they always get up and go away unless finished off with a second shot.)

I took her trail and followed it. She had gone out of the ravine, around the point of a ridge, into another draw, and out of it and had started across a flat. Here she passed through a little clump of firs. As I walked rapidly along through them I saw where her tracks had been joined by those of a second animal. A big cougar—his footprints were 5 inches across—was following her.

My pulse quickened. The cougar was undoubtedly between me and the elk—assuming he hadn't already caught her—and with luck I'd get a shot at him. No doubt the occasional drop of blood she was losing made him choose the particular track in preference to all the hundreds of others that were everywhere on the mountain. Or maybe he'd seen her moving slowly along, head down and obviously hurt. I quickened my pace.

The tracks went on for maybe half a mile, over a ridge and onto another, larger flat. Here I faced a dilemma. The cow had skirted one side of a thicket of Christmas trees. The cougar had left her trail. He had doubled back and gone the other way. What to do? I puzzled over it several minutes. Finally I decided that it was my duty as a sportsman to follow the cow and put her out of her misery as quickly as possible. Besides, if the cougar had given up—as he apparently had—the chance of seeing him without the aid of dogs was only one in a million.

The cow's tracks led me around the copse. At the far point I found her. She was dead. Almost instantly I realized that I had made a blunder. Backtracking confirmed my suspicions. The cougar, evidently close behind the cow, had left her when she neared the thicket. He had bounded around the other side and ambushed her as she passed the point. The ensuing struggle was plainly recorded in the snow over a course of 60 feet. He'd had her down three times, and the third time she stayed. There were claw marks 2 inches long on her face, and her neck was broken. Big, bloody tracks, 15 feet apart, led to the closest cover, 100 yards away.

When I elected to follow the cow's tracks, I'd taken a course that was straight downwind. Following it for two or three minutes in that direction, before I could see the cow, had given the cougar ample time to scent me and bound away. If I had followed his trail around the other side of the thicket, I'd have approached across the breeze and undoubtedly would have got a shot at him—at a range of 60 feet. The cow's muscles were still twitching when I started dressing her.

When I was almost done, I heard a snort. A fat four-point mule-deer buck, walking across the flat 100 yards below, had winded me and stopped. My rifle was leaning against a tree 6 feet away. I moved toward it, slowly and cautiously, but the buck saw me and bounded ahead. He went behind the trunks of two massive, close-growing yellow pines.

My fingers closed on the gun. I wrapped the sling around my arm and sat down by the dead cow. Thirty seconds later, the buck's nose emerged. Then I could see one eye. It wasn't enough to shoot at. I pushed the safety off and waited. We both waited. When he couldn't stand it any longer, he came out head up, and trotted in the direction he had been going originally. I put the crosshairs on his neck. Too jerky, too uncertain at that range. I dropped them down and back to his heart and sent the 130-grain bullet on its way.

He went on as though unhurt for 63 yards—I stepped it off later—and then he fell, and he didn't have any heart left at all. After I had dressed him, I went back and finished cleaning out the cow. I quartered both carcasses and dragged the quarters onto poles to get them off the ground, then covered them with brush to keep the ravens off. Realizing I was tired, I split some pitch off the roots of a wind-downed fir, built a fire, and made some tea from snow water. I ate. It was good to sit, leaning against a tree, with one foot on each side of the little fire, and feed chips of pitch into the blaze. The snow was falling gently.

My watch said it was 4 o'clock; it would be dark in an hour. I was far from camp, and every foot of the way was uphill. Reluctantly I left the cheering influence of the fire, shouldered my pack and rifle, and began the long climb. Three hundred yards above, I came upon the smoking-fresh tracks of a bear. They were big. I followed them a little way to the massive trunk of a fallen pine. Here I saw where he had walked back and forth behind it, undoubtedly watching while I finished my work with the game and ate my lunch. Fresh tracks, with no snow in them, led off into a thicket of young firs. He had left only when he saw me start toward him, up the hill.

Another dilemma. Although the cougar was unlikely to return after my frightening him off his kill, the bear most certainly would be back. A hungry bear has the capacity of twenty starving men, and a bear getting ready to hibernate, as this one should be, sometimes makes an indescribable mess of whatever he is unable to eat.

I could build a fire and sit beside the elk all night, but I couldn't watch the buck at the same time. He was too far away and around the corner of a patch of firs. It wasn't particularly cold, but it was snowing and I was damp from wallowing through the stuff all day. I decided to take a chance and go to camp. I'd come back as soon as daylight permitted. Maybe I could catch the scoundrel at his thievery.

I sat on the log and watched the flat below as long as I dared, but the bear didn't return. (No doubt he was watching *me* from some safe hiding spot.) The white glow of the lantern through the tent looked good as I approached it long after dark.

I learned from Ellen that Slim had taken his horses back to his base camp at the landing strip. He'd come in after them to get the elk we'd shot, but when he went to round them up he discovered that they'd been unable to feed. The snow was too deep. He'd found them standing disconsolately under some giant firs, pawing out the little sustenance that grew there.

I'd told him several times we were in no hurry. I said I could take care of any game we killed, that we had plenty of grub and liked the country. So his parting words had been, "I'll be back when the storm breaks."

It would have been fine, except for the bear. It was warm in the tent. There was plenty of wood in the corner. Snowflakes hissed against the stovepipe. The food was doubly good. There is no place so snug on a snowy night as a good tent, far out in the wilds.

I wanted Ellen to go with me next morning; she could help hang out of reach of the bear whatever was left of the elk and the deer. Because of her, I was delayed. It had just come full daylight and we were maybe a mile from camp when I saw the head of an elk, apparently lying on a log in a blowdown. I paused and said, "Look at that! Do you suppose some joker propped that head up on a log to fool people?"

At the words, the head arose. It was connected, in the conventional way, to a perfectly healthy elk. He was a four-pointer and fat as butter. He'd be good. I said, "Shoot him in the eye."

There's nothing like having an obedient wife. The young bull was looking at us, at a range of about 75 feet. She raised her rifle and fired instantly, and he disappeared among the logs. When we got there, we discovered that she didn't quite hit his eye, but she missed it by only an inch or so.

I had to dress him out and get him off the ground, of course, and that delayed us. When we got to the cougar-killed cow and my buck, the bear had come and gone. But we'd been lucky, far luckier than I'd expected. Bruin had gorged himself on the offal of the elk, and the meat was

Ellen Trueblood looks over the young bull elk that Ted
told her to shoot in the eye.

untouched. We finally got it all up in the air and ate our lunch. About that
time the snow stopped falling for the first time all day. We started back to
camp. On the way we saw a big buck, considerably bigger than mine. Ellen
made another excellent shot. She blew his liver all to pieces. I congratulated
her as soon as I discovered this. I hate liver. She said if he hadn't been so
far—he was about 400 yards—she certainly wouldn't have shot him that
way. I don't doubt it, either.

Again we got to camp after dark, and again it was good to be there,
because the snow had begun to fall once more shortly after she'd killed her
buck. We now had my buck and Slim's elk hung out of the reach of the
bear, but there were three other animals he could get at—and no doubt
would find sooner or later. These were her elk and buck and my elk. The
snow showed no sign of stopping.

At daylight next morning, after a cautious stalk, I discovered that the
bear had been at his dirty work and left. Apparently standing on a fallen
tree, he'd batted down one quarter of my dear. Slim's elk was too high for
him. He'd cleaned up the remainder of the offal and carried away the head
and hide of my deer. I spent most of the day, working alone and without
the aid of my blocks, moving the rest of my buck and getting it higher, and
hanging Ellen's buck, which was closer than any of our other game.

Late in the afternoon I met Ellen on the trail. She'd inspected her elk

Slim Horn leads his packstring down a mountain on way
to get elk and deer.

first, then gone on to look at mine. Both were all right. On the way to camp
we ran the bear away from hers, but we didn't get a shot at him. He'd come
as soon as she'd left—probably watched her go, in fact—cleaned up the
heart, lungs, and liver, and started on one loin.

There was nothing to do but hang that elk. Ellen went on to camp for the
necessary equipment while I quartered him and cut some poles. We
finished the job at dark. It was still snowing.

The first thing in the morning we got my elk safely out of the bear's
reach. Our meat was safe, but by now I was determined to kill that bear if it
took all winter. We had five baits, widely separated, and fifteen inches of
snow on the ground. All we had to do was guess which one he'd visit next
and watch it from the downwind side until he showed up.

I hate to confess it, but he licked us on every turn. It finally stopped
snowing and Slim came back, this time with his mules loaded with baled
hay and oats. Slim and I brought in the game, and next day packed up and
rode back to the landing strip.

Ellen and I hated to leave. We'd never caught a glimpse of the bear,
although the snow showed that he was still making the rounds, but we had
seen many other interesting things while we were watching for him. We'd

Slim's packstring comes back with the meat. In steep
mountain country, trailwise horses and mules—
especially mules—will pick a better route
than you would.

seen fox and coyote, ravens, magpies and jays, several eagles, and I've no
idea how many deer and elk.

But it really was time to go. When we got home, we discovered that there
had been stories in the papers about snowbound hunters, marooned in the
desolate wilds. Our relatives were worried, and our baby sitter was beside
herself. We were welcomed as if we'd come back from the moon. The bird
season was open and the two pointers in the back yard were especially glad
to see us; they were raring to go. Even our two boys were genuinely glad.
When we walked in, they turned off the television.

Chapter 11

One Day, One Antelope

The eastern sky was blushing with the promise of another dawn when I started a sagebrush fire and filled the coffeepot. Then, huddling over the growing flames because the air was sharp—there was white frost on the grass—I looked around. We were camped on a tiny meadow at the head of a dry wash in rolling country typical of the high, Northern desert. No tree nor house nor fence, nor any other camp, broke the monotony of the gray sage that stretched endlessly to the horizon in all directions.

At first I could see only the skyline, but as the fire grew and the stars faded I could pick up other details. By the time the coffee boiled and the grounds had settled and I—after a wait that seemed like years—finally sat back with a cup of the precious stuff, I could see fairly well.

As my eyes swept over a gradual slope about a mile northeast of camp, they picked up several white spots that seemed strangely out of place on the drab hillside. Could it be? This was the opening day of the antelope season that year. Could these be antelope, within sight of camp at dawn the first morning?

I hurried the few yards to the car and got the binoculars, then, resting my elbows on the hood, looked at the spots again. They were antelope! I counted them—an even dozen!

I got out the bacon and eggs and started the other breakfast preparations,

In a sprint, antelope can hit 50 miles per hour. At 35 or
40 miles per hour, they can keep running indefinitely.

pausing occasionally to look through the glasses at the antelope. They were
ignoring me. Good! Perhaps I could figure out a way to stalk them.

My wife and I ate breakfast. I uncased my rifle, stuffed some cartridges in
the magazine and put a few in my pocket, then tucked a can of tomato juice
inside my shirt above my belt. The day would be hot later and there was no
water within miles. I made sure I had my knife and a big white
handkerchief and hung the binoculars around my neck.

Meanwhile, I kept studying the terrain, trying to work out an approach to
the antelope, which were still grazing unconcernedly within a block or so of
the spot where I had seen them first. It would not be easy. Most of the
sagebrush was a scant 10 inches high, though there were a few widely
scattered clumps of big sage about 3 feet tall. Here and there small areas of
grass provided no better cover than the low brush.

Down the dry wash, about half a mile north of camp, there was a little,
rocky butte, perhaps 50 feet high and three times as wide across the base.
Since there was no possible way to approach the antelope unseen starting
directly from camp, I decided that looking the country over from the butte
might be worthwhile. I asked my wife, who had no antelope permit, to walk
back and forth in front of the camp for fifteen minutes so the antelope
would continue to watch her. Then I went around behind the car and lay

down in a shallow depression that ran through our tiny meadow into the dry wash. I bellied down the depression to the wash, then crawled down it for 100 yards. At this point it became deep enough so I could walk in a bent-over position. The wash, which passed the butte on the west side, would take me to its shelter.

I was scarcely halfway there, however, when I approached the end of a low ridge that ran parallel to the wash and which had concealed part of a basin that lay west and north of camp. Purely from habit, I peered over the end of the ridge through the low sage without exposing myself. More antelope! Ten of them, and only half as far away as the first bunch.

The breeze, coming straight from the north, was equally favorable for a stalk in either direction. But there was one other factor to consider. The antelope to the northeast had watched my wife and me in camp. They would be alert. The others were unaware that there was a man within forty miles and they were close enough so I could see one good buck with the 6X glasses. I decided to try for them.

First, I eased back up the wash a few yards, then crawled up the ridge into a clump of big sagebrush on its crest. I got into the middle of the brush unseen, yet by peering out through it I could see the antelope quite well. I tied the white handkerchief to my rifle barrel, like a flag, and waved it slowly back and forth above the brush. The antelope saw it instantly. I waved my flag for about five minutes, then lowered it into the brush and waited.

As soon as I lowered my handkerchief, the antelope lowered their heads and resumed grazing. One or two lay down. I devoted my time to studying the intervening basin. It was about half a mile from my position to the antelope and there was no possible way to cross it without being seen. If their curiosity didn't bring them into range, the only way to get a shot would be to wait until they crossed the western ridge out of sight, then follow.

I continued flagging them for the greater part of an hour. Each time I raised the white handkerchief above the tops of the brush, their heads came up instantly. But they showed no inclination whatever of approaching. Finally, I gave up. I would wait them out.

The ten antelope were working gradually toward the ridge at the western edge of the basin. Once they crossed it, I could start after them. They were in no hurry. They grazed a while, lay down, got up and grazed some more, then lay down again. It must have taken them two hours to move a quarter mile. But, of course, it was still early because I had left camp before sunup.

Once the last antelope was out of sight, I made quick time across the basin and up the slope on the far side. I crawled the last few yards and came to the ridge top behind a clump of bunch grass. Peering through it, I saw the ten antelope—but they were already out of range. They were wandering away to the west, alternately feeding and resting, and there was no way to get closer. The country was wide open.

This was the luck of hunting. They could have bedded down just over the crest and I would have been within range when I came to the top. But I suppose if game made a practice of lying down within rifle range of a ridge it would be extinct.

I eased back down the ridge and walked just under its top to the north. Eventually I crossed another ridge, at right angles to this one, and looked down into a wide valley. Careful glassing revealed two more bunches of antelope, but both were so far away that I couldn't even see them with the naked eye.

About this time, the breeze made a complete reversal and started blowing from the south. I hurried west for half a mile, then headed south hoping to intercept the ten antelope. They were nowhere in sight.

I walked south, angling some to the west, for perhaps five miles. This entailed crossing many valleys, where there was no chance of seeing game, and crawling carefully to the crest of many ridges to inspect the next basin without being seen. Along the way, I drank my can of tomato juice, smoked my pipe, and rested for half an hour. Finally, I turned east in order to make a big circle around camp.

The long process of crossing barren valleys and stalking ridges continued. At last, I realized that I was now southeast of camp. The sun was getting low in the west. I had completed three-quarters of a circle. I was tired. I decided to go on in.

It was the longest walk, but I got there. I was beat. My wife was sitting at the camp table reading a magazine. I had a long, long drink of water and sat down opposite her and pulled off my shoes to cool my feet and lit my pipe and she said, "Look."

The same antelope that I had seen at dawn were still on the same slope a mile northeast of camp. They hadn't moved a quarter mile all day. She said, "They've been there all the time. I thought maybe you were stalking them. I was afraid to slam a car door or light a fire or anything. Where have you been?"

I told her while I smoked my pipe and my feet cooled off and as I sat there resting I watched the unattainable antelope. It was hopeless. I was back exactly where I had started at dawn.

But as the sun dropped toward the western ridge—it was quite close now, big and red as a pumpkin—the antelope got up. They nibbled here and there, then started trailing away toward the west. I looked through the glasses. There were eleven. I couldn't see the twelfth, though I was sure there had been a dozen in the morning.

The slope on which they had spent the day and across which they were now moving was about a mile from camp. The rocky butte was halfway to it. If the antelope went far enough to pass behind the butte, I could cut the distance to them in half. Was it worth a chance? Who could tell? Whatever happened, I didn't have much time.

The antelope went on, moving quite briskly. Then four turned and trotted off across the horizon to the north. That left seven. They were walking steadily toward the point where they would be hidden behind the little butte. I put my shoes back on and got my rifle off the hood of the car where I had laid it when I got to camp. I checked the breeze with a puff of smoke. There was none now.

At last, the seven antelope walked behind the butte. I started toward it at a trot. I reached it unseen, climbed it quickly, and dropped to my hands and knees just under the crest. The top was a jumble of broken rock. I peered over between two of them, through a crack no wider than my hand.

Oh, miracle of miracles! The seven antelope had turned toward the butte. They were only 300 yards away. They were grazing without a fear in the world. But when I put the glasses on them, still peering through the crack between the two big rocks, I saw that they were all does and fawns.

I had no desire to kill a doe, much less a fawn, though both were legal on my "any antelope" permit. What to do? Should I go back to camp? My wife was getting dinner and I was very hungry. It had been a long day. I was lying on a mass of brick-size, sharp-cornered rocks. They hurt. Still, I hated to give up.

The sun was now but half a pumpkin, bisected by the same ridge over which I had followed the ten antelope some ten hours before. Undecided, I didn't move. And while I lay there suffering the agonies of indecision and sharp rocks, the seven antelope lay down. They had fed enough for a while; now they would rest.

My .270 was sighted for 250 yards. I could kill one of them. No, the hell with it. You don't kill an antelope just for meat. Ernest Thompson Seton estimated that there were 40 million antelope in the United States in primitive times. Forty million! This dropped to a low of 17,000 in 1908. They have made a wonderful comeback now. But, still, I couldn't kill a doe antelope as I would a doe deer where they were overusing their range and would eventually starve anyway.

While I watched and the sun dropped out of sight and the sharp rocks bit further and further into me, one of the does raised her head and looked off toward the east, the direction from which she and her companions had come.

Other does raised their heads, all looking intently toward the east. I looked. Another antelope was walking slowly through the sage. It was a buck. He was coming toward the does and fawns.

I drew back the bolt and eased a cartridge into the chamber. The buck was still too far away. I didn't dare to move. He came on and on. He stopped to nibble at some weeds, then came on again. At last, he reached the does and fawns. He turned square away from me and stopped, his white rump gleaming. I couldn't shoot.

Finally, he turned. I put the crosshairs high on his shoulder. I inhaled deeply, exhaled half a breath, and squeezed off my shot.

Gently, the buck folded and lay down. The seven does and fawns leaped up, stared wildly in all directions, then raced off into the glow of the sunset.

I stood on the rocky butte and yelled and waved my cap and when I saw my wife getting into the car I started walking toward my buck. It was 256 yards, not 300, and the bullet had struck exactly where I aimed.

We have a four-wheel-drive car that goes where you tell it to and Ellen drove it to me, where I was dressing my antelope, and I laid the lovely little buck on the tailgate and we drove back to camp.

Chapter 12

Moose Are Too Big

Irvin S. Cobb once wrote a very funny story called "The Plural of Moose is Mise." Maybe so, but I don't think moose need any plural. Moose are too big. One is enough.

I went moose hunting one time—sort of against my will—and I must concede that one adventure on that trip was unforgettable. Period. You can't qualify the word; I'll remember if I live to be a hundred. It earned me a singular distinction, too.

But I'm still not a moose hunter. I'm a bird hunter. Now you take quail. There is game of the proper size. You kill one and you can put it in your pocket and go on looking for another. Nobody puts a moose in his pocket.

I was in Alaska one summer before the human population exploded, and time got away as it always does when you're fishing, and before I knew it the time came for my brother Burtt to lay in his winter's supply of moose meat. He said, "Come along. We need a couple. I don't care if I never shoot another moose, but Ted [my nephew, Burtt's son, who was fourteen then] has never shot a moose either."

I thought Burtt put a little too much emphasis on that *either.* I said, "I haven't lost any moose. But if there are some grouse around, and maybe some fish, I'll go along. We can have some fun whether I shoot a moose or not."

"There are grouse," Burtt said. "I'll take my shotgun for you. But you'd better take a rifle. You might change your mind."

I walked downtown in Anchorage and rented a .30-'06. When the man said $3 a day I nearly fell through the floor. I said, "Why, I've worked many a day for $3!"

"Not in Alaska, you haven't."

We loaded Burtt's 20-foot canoe into his truck, along with sleeping bags, a tent, an ax, food, and other essentials and drove out of town. The scenery would take your breath. September in Alaska is like October in New England. Framed by dark spruce, the popple streaked the hillsides. It looked as though some giant had splashed golden paint wildly in all directions.

We stopped at a river and transferred our load from truck to canoe. Ted sat in the middle. Burtt put me in the bow with a paddle, but I wasn't much help. I had never run a glacial river before and I soon discovered that it was an entirely different ball game from running a clear stream. You can't see into the milky water at all. You can only read the surface to locate rocks, snags, and other hazards. It's a knack I didn't master.

I suppose the river bar was half a mile wide, a gray expanse of sand and stones between the edges of the timber on either side. The river, low now, meandered through the bar. We came to a finger of spruce extending farther out onto the barren bar than others we had seen. "That's where we camp," Burtt said. "There's a clear-water stream flowing down through the spruce. It comes from a lake about a quarter of a mile back in the woods."

We lined the canoe up the clear stream to the edge of the timber. It was the kind of setting for a camp that artists paint. The spruce was open underneath with a luxuriant carpet of bright-green moss that looked like a well-kept lawn. It was soft as a feather bed—and it was dry. That, alone, is something for Alaska! The brook, just big enough to get your feet wet crossing if you weren't careful, chuckled down over the rocks, 30 feet from the spot where we would have our tent and fire. Across the river bar a mountain with shoulders like a buffalo rolled up and up in strips of black and gold.

I picked up the ax and started looking for a dead spruce. Burtt said, "Wait. This strip of timber between the lake and bar is only a quarter of a mile wide. About three-quarters long. I think we ought to hunt it first. Could be moose in it. If so, we'll never kill one in a better spot.

"I'll walk over near the lake and then turn east parallel to it. Ted [the boy], you come about halfway and wait for me to get to the lake before you start. And you," he said to me, "give us twenty minutes. Then stay just far enough in the timber so you can get a glimpse of the bar once in a while."

I looked at my watch, sat down on a bedroll, and lit my pipe. So this was moose hunting! Well, I didn't have to kill one. And it was a lovely spot. I was anxious to see the lake. Burtt had said there were Dolly Vardens in it and I had the equipment to remove some of them.

I loaded my $3-a-day rifle. We had stopped along the road to check the sights and it was dead-on for me at 100 yards. In fact, I had hit a six-ounce milk can with it. A moose is a big target compared to a milk can.

The time came for me to start. Walking on the lush moss was like walking on a cloud; I could move without a sound. The woods were mostly open. The lower branches of the spruce hung down about to my shirt pockets so by stooping I could see well for 100 yards or so, both ahead and to the sides. There were a few thick clumps of young spruce into which I couldn't see, and a few small patches of brush.

I was approaching one of them when I saw something black. It was big. It was horizontal and on the ground. I dropped to my knees and saw another, a little farther away. Moose! Two moose, lying down!

I'll admit that for a man who didn't want to kill a moose a strange thrill shot through me. They were only 40 yards away, but I couldn't see their heads because of the brush. I crawled to one side until I could. They were a cow and calf. I got up and started ahead and they wandered away.

Burtt and Ted didn't see any. We walked back to camp and when we got there Burtt said, "There's a trapper's cabin over by the lake and I saw a covey of sharptails in the clearing near it. You take my shotgun and go shoot two or three. They'll be good. Ted and I will make camp."

I said, "Won't shooting run all the moose out of the country?"

"I don't think so," he told me. "There aren't any on this side of the lake, anyway."

So I took his gun and started for the cabin. Now, this gun is a trap-grade Model 12. It's too straight for me. I can hit a rising bird with it if I remember what I'm doing, but I shoot high if I don't. I put it to my shoulder a time or two as I walked along and thought, "Now remember, you've got to see daylight under the bird."

I found the cabin and tramped around in the clearing, but I didn't flush any grouse. There was a little clump of young spruce trees, shoulder high and thick as the hair on a dog, about 30 feet from the corner of the cabin. It was the only cover in the clearing.

I was standing at the corner wondering what to do next when a bull moose rose in all his awesome majesty from that little clump of trees! He was facing me. He blinked his beady eyes.

My first thought was the most profane word I know. After hunting the area with rifles—Burtt must have walked within yards of this idiot—and not seeing any game, now here I was looking into the face of a bull moose. And I had a shotgun!

Then I had another thought: "At 30 feet a shotgun is a cannon. It will petrify him. I will shoot him between the eyes."

Then I swung the gun up, forgetting my wise thoughts of a few minutes before, forgetting everything. I even forgot I didn't want to kill a moose. I swung the gun up and pulled the trigger instinctively, just like I'd shoot at a grouse rocketing away through the woods.

The moose flew. He flew 20 feet the first jump and after that he took off. For an instant I was tempted to try him on the wing as he went by, but I didn't have much time. He passed at 5 yards before I could decide.

I ran to camp. I said, "I just missed a moose."

Ted said, in a rising crescendo so that the last word was almost a shriek, "With a shotgun?"

"Well, it was all I had."

We grabbed our rifles and ran back. First, we looked carefully where the moose had been standing. There was not one clipped hair or a single drop of blood. I had shot over the top of his head. If a moose is capable of a headache, that bull must have had a world-beater.

Next we trailed him for about a quarter of a mile. His tracks indicated he was unhurt and leaving the country.

There was a strained silence in camp when we got back and started fixing dinner. My relatives didn't say anything. I think they were embarrassed. Finally, to break the ice, I said, "Well, I now have a unique distinction. I've got to be the only living human who ever missed a moose with a shotgun."

The ice was more than broken; it was shattered. My brother and his redheaded boy shrieked and howled and choked and tears ran down their cheeks. They rolled on the ground. They held their sides and got red in the face. I didn't think it was *that* funny.

After dinner, I helped Burtt put the canoe on the lake—we had to heist it over a beaver dam—and Ted got in the bow with his rifle. Burtt paddled away. We had half an hour of rifle-shooting time left.

I was washing the dishes when I heard a shot. In twenty minutes, they were back. Ted had killed a moose. We took the lantern, ax, block and tackle, ropes, knives, whetstone, some lunch, and the coffeepot back to where a very dead moose lay on a gentle slope above the lake.

Ted built a fire and kept the coffeepot going while Burtt and I worked. By midnight I knew beyond the shadow of a doubt that moose are too big. It was midnight when we finished—and we're not exactly beginners when it comes to taking care of game. But at last we had it skinned, dressed, cu into six pieces, and hung from a pole between two trees. We slept late th next morning.

Ted with his small moose. "The smallest moose you can
find," he says, "is still too big."

It was another perfect day—chilly early, then short-sleeve weather with the mountains all green and black and gold and the Arctic cotton shimmering on the higher bars.

Ted loafed in camp and fished. Burtt and I walked up a side stream farther than we'd thought we could the midnight before. We saw tracks of wolves, grizzlies, and moose, but luckily didn't see any of the animals that made them. Luckily, I say, because we were too far and moose are too big. That evening I shot a moose with a rifle. We saw it, a young bull, from ~ss the lake and Burtt paddled straight to it while I sat in the bow. You 'n't do that to a whitetail deer or an elk. At 60 yards, Burtt quit ~g. One shot, dead moose, hard work until midnight again.

ose was only about 40 feet from the water, Ted's a bit farther. We ~. Here's how you get to your feet with a sixth of a moose:
~ tie it to a pack board. Then you set the board upright. Next,
~ to the shoulder straps. You're now sitting flat on the ground
~truggle to your feet. But you can't. So the boy comes around
~ a mighty push and, lo! you're walking.
~ to the canoe a sixth at a time, loaded both, and paddled
~ had to carry them down the creek to the river, too,
~ enough water to float such a load. This reconfirmed

Burtt ferried Ted and me across, along with our camp outfit. We carried it up to the road and while Ted waited with it I walked back and brought the truck. Burtt floated the two moose—a dangerous load for even his big anoe—down the river to the next spot where the road touched. We were waiting for him there.

It was a good trip and I know for sure about moose now. But I wonder where those sharptails went.

Chapter 13

Spell of
the High Country

You are sitting on a ridge when it hits you. You have been studying the grass patches and the shale slides of the mountain across the canyon, and after a while you lower your binoculars and just look, and then it hits you. And you will never forget.

You came 1500 miles by plane and you were tired when you started because you had done a month's work in advance. When you finally got off the plane, you stowed your duffel bag and bedroll and your precious rifle in the back of a pickup truck and then rode for endless, jolting miles. You stopped long after dark, and you were barely conscious of the odors of lodgepole pine and horses and the outline of the ranch buildings against the blue-black sky and snapping stars. You ate a bite, maybe, and hung your suit over the back of a chair and laid out your hunting clothes with a great feeling of relief and fell into bed.

You were up next morning while the frost still lay white on the grass. You watched the golden sunlight slide down the westerly peaks as the horses were loaded, and at last you were on one of them. Your guide made a final adjustment of the stirrups and hung your rifle on the saddle by some mysterious arrangement of straps and thongs and handed you the reins, and the procession started. There was a flurry of excitement as a packhorse bit the one ahead and pulled back in mute protest of his lot, but at last

On the way to high country, far beyond the end
of the road.

guide and wrangler got the string lined out across the frosty meadow and
you fell in behind.

The Western saddle felt wonderful. It fit comfortably and the low cantle
gave just the right support. You rode through the pasture bars with scarcely
a backward glance at the ranch buildings clustered in their little basin
among the peaks, a thin, white wisp of smoke curling slowly up into the
sunlight above the trees. You rode through slender lodgepole and past
white-barked aspens with their trembling leaves and saw, when the early
sun sent its first slanting rays among them, that wildflowers were still
blooming on the forest floor.

On and on you rode, through the trees and across wild meadows of knee-
high grass, and around boggy spots grown thick with scrub alders and
willows. You forded streams and trailed around steep slopes, wondering at
the ease with which your horse kept his footing among the rolling stones.
Through swales and along ridges you rode, and always your course was up.

And finally your saddle, which had been so comfortable as you left the meadow, became a rack of pain.

Under the churning hoofs of the horses, the dust rolled up to clog your nostrils and coat your face. You pulled your jacket off and tied it behind because the same sun that you had welcomed so eagerly a few hours before now beat down mercilessly upon your back. Your horse, whose gait had been like a rocking chair at sunrise, now seemed, with diabolical cunning, to jar and jolt you deliberately at every step. And always the miserable saddle, bruising and rubbing at every movement of the plodding horse! Your legs ached from their unaccustomed position, but when you tried to rest them by taking your feet out of the stirrups, the pounding of your hip joints against the leather was even more unbearable.

You had an all-too-brief pause for lunch. Then you were mounted again, and the long afternoon wore on in an endless monotony of creaking leather and rolling dust and the constant agony of the saddle. At last, at long last, hours after you had ceased to count the weary miles or even to wonder whether you would ever walk again, your guide stopped the horses and swung down.

You were vaguely conscious of a different kind of country. You were at the edge of a high meadow with great, rolling, grass-streaked ridges sweeping back, and towering peaks above. There was a clean, sharp freshness in the air, different, even, from the dawn freshness you had noticed at the ranch. There was no more lodgepole or aspen, but a thick clump of alpine fir, near which you would camp. A clear rivulet bubbled from the base of the granite slide nearby to wander down and join the brook meandering through the meadow.

By sheer will power, you managed to lift yourself from the saddle and half fall off your horse. You untied your rifle and leaned it, still cased, against a tree. Then, stumbling and sore, you tried to help guide and wrangler as they unpacked and set up camp and cooked. But you discovered that your efforts were hopelessly inept compared to their swift efficiency. You finally compromised by rolling out your bed and inflating your air mattress and bringing in a few sticks of wood.

Then they fed you and you crawled away into your bed and died. You awoke to the odors of bacon and steaming coffee and the sound of hotcakes sizzling as they hit the pan, and things were better.

You started out, and it was good to be walking again—after the first few tentative yards proved that you could walk. You pumped the frost-charged air into your lungs and your blood began to circulate and you felt almost like a boy once more. You were tempted to stretch out and show this quiet fellow beside you that you could *really* walk; but, on second thought, you decided merely to hold the easy pace he'd set. At the head of the meadow, scarcely half a mile from camp, you were glad of this decision.

Your guide turned up a ridge, still holding the same easy pace, but after a few hundred yards it seemed much faster. After an hour, it was racing. No longer were you conscious of towering peaks and rolling ridges and snow-white clouds against a velvet sky. The air, which had charged you with fresh vigor when you left the camp, now was thin and unsatisfying. You couldn't possibly get enough of it.

Another hour. The sun was full on you. You could feel the sweat roll inside your hatband when you tipped your head. It trickled down across your face and got into your eyes. Your mouth was dry. Your rifle sling ate into your shoulder. The gun weighed twenty pounds. All of the saddle-weariness of the day before possessed you, and your legs were rubber. You could see nothing but the guide's back, ten feet ahead, always swinging upward in that tireless pace of his.

Occasionally, he stopped, and when he did you stopped, too, instantly, gasping for breath. But the pauses were always too short and the course was always up. You wondered dumbly why you had ever talked yourself into such a venture. You wished, with the hopeless feeling of wishing too late, that you had done some hiking to get into better condition before you started.

Finally, your guide sat down. He actually sat down! You managed to raise your head enough to look around and see that you were on the crest of a high ridge, with a great canyon immediately before you and another, higher, ridge beyond. Your guide had hooked his elbows around his knees and was looking through his binoculars. You managed to lay your rifle to one side and then, unashamed, fell to the earth and attempted to press yourself into it. No spring-filled mattress ever felt so good to you.

Maybe you slept a little—or came awfully close to it—because you were by now utterly relaxed as well as utterly exhausted. You were here. You were in sheep country. The long journey by plane and car and horse and, finally, on foot was over.

After a while, you managed to sit up and, lo! you had miraculously recovered. Your guide was still looking, still silent. You raised your binoculars and began to glass the opposite slope, too. But you saw nothing and if your guide saw anything he didn't say, and presently you lowered the glasses again and just looked. And then it hit you.

Like the blast of fresh air when you leave a stuffy, smoke-filled room and step out into the winter street; like the clean, cold, invigorating water when you plunge into a pool, this new feeling swept over you.

Suddenly you were as wild and free as the eagle circling above a distant peak. You were as different from the harassed creature that stepped off the plane forty-eight hours earlier as was the eagle from the marmot he watched.

Slowly you turn your head in all directions, looking. For the first time, you are fully conscious of your surroundings. They are breath-taking. Slope upon slope, ridge upon ridge, peak upon peak, mile after mile, they stretch

Sheep hunting is mostly looking. And then if you should
spot a sheep in the far end of a basin like this, you've
got to start walking.

away into the haze of distance. Could there be another man but you and
your companion in these wild mountains? If so, he certainly left no sign.
There is no house, no road, not even a wisp of smoke.

As you look, exultant but also awed, you gradually become conscious of

Next to looking, the most time-consuming part of sheep
hunting is the climbing. If you happen to be hunting
in a September snow high in the Rockies, your efforts
will be particularly tiring.

something else. At first you can't define it. You sense it, but it is so strange, so new, so different, that your brain refuses to recognize it. Then, suddenly, you know. It is silence! It is the perfect, utter, absolute quiet of the far, wild places above the trees when the wind is still and there is no sound whatever. How long has it been since your nerves were not assailed by the jarring of some man-made noise! Years, probably—you can't remember.

So in the solitude of this vast country you sit flat on the earth and its soothing strength flows into you, and you are warm in the sun and yet cool in the dry air. And though you feel strong and very good, you somehow feel very tiny, too. You are a minute speck of life in a great, silent wilderness of rock and sky.

You know now that the long hours of extra work, the planning and preparing, the exhausting journey, were all worthwhile. Even if you don't find the ram you want so badly, they were worthwhile. You have fallen under the spell of the high, wild country. You are a sheep hunter.

Each morning you will leave camp before the sun melts the frost from the meadow and you will climb until you think that you can climb no farther. Then you will stop and look, searching every slide and bench and tiny pocket with your glasses—because sheep hunting is two-thirds looking—and after that you will go on to a new vantage point and look some more. And each evening you will return to camp utterly weary, your legs shaking, the soles of your feet on fire from walking rapidly downhill. But each day you will go a little farther, because you'll be getting tougher.

You will see ewes and lambs and yearling rams and occasionally a goat or elk or bear, if you're in the right kind of country. You'll see blue grouse and ptarmigan, because they are at home on the high ridges, and you'll listen to the *eeeep* of the conies and watch them storing hay for winter in the rock slides.

At last, you'll see a ram, or several rams. You'll study them intently and say softly to your guide, "What do you think?"

He'll study them some more and say sadly, "Well, they're rams."

Then you'll be faced with that same, awful decision that all sheep hunters from the beginning have had to make. Should you kill one and be sure? Or should you wait? Your time is getting short. There are only a few more days. Would it be better to take one of them or to continue hunting for the trophy of your dreams?

Ram hunter, I hope you answer right. If you do, and the gods smile and the weather holds and your time does not run out too soon, there will come a morning when you go farther and faster than you have ever gone before. And you will top a new ridge and look into a new basin and there, magnificent in his solitude, will be the ram of all rams.

You will test the wind and pray for it to hold. Then you will withdraw carefully and plan the stalk, and once committed to it you will move with stealth and endurance that you never knew you had. You will walk, on legs like steel springs, as far as you can walk. Then you will crawl, and the cuts that you'll find on your hands later will always be a mystery because you'll never feel them now.

At last, you'll be as close as you can get and the ram will still be there, undisturbed. You'll ease a cartridge into the chamber of your rifle quietly, loading it for the first time in all these many days. Then, if you are normal, you'll make a terrible discovery.

You will suddenly be a quivering, spineless mass of blubber! Your legs, so strong only a few minutes before, will now be putty. Your hands will shake uncontrollably. Your lungs will labor. Your heart will pound until you wonder if the ram won't hear it. You will only be able to half see.

Lie down, hunter, and put your head on your forearm and breathe deeply. Let the shakes run their course. The ram has not left yet; he'll stay a few minutes longer. Now, wrap the sling beneath your arm and squirm around until the crosshairs hang low behind his shoulder. Then take a deep breath and exhale most of it and then gently, oh so gently, squeeze the trigger.

Your guide will shake your hand. He will be jubilant because he, too, will be tired, and for all those weary miles he was haunted by the fear that maybe you couldn't shoot. The two of you will hurry to your ram, sprinting across the grass, scrambling over the slides, and you will pause beside it.

In silent admiration your eyes will run over the great curled horns, the deep chest, the short, strong legs, the sure hoofs. You will be elated, but you will also feel regret. You played it fair and you worked hard and there is the trophy you have always wanted—one of the greatest of them all. But you have also taken the life of one of God's most magnificent creatures. This ram, now still and lifeless, was, only minutes before, the very embodiment of all that is free and wild in his magnificent, high country.

As you kneel beside him to measure the outside curl and basal circumference of his massive horns, you will realize that he was getting old. Some winter before too long he would have perished in a snowslide, or fallen to his death as he threaded his way across the ice-shrouded face of a cliff, or become food for cougar or coyote. You know there is no gentle death in nature, and your bullet was more merciful than any of these.

But logic does not help. You have come to love this grand country. In it, the hardest hunt you ever made was by far the greatest. You can think of no place where you would rather spend the golden days of autumn, every year. And you are proud, of course. But even as you measure you know, deep in your heart, that you will never kill another ram.

The spell of the high, wild, silent places will always be your master.

Ted with the trophy of his dreams. Big ram's horns
measured 41 inches around the outside curl and
16½ inches around the base.

Part V

SKILLS OF THE SEASONED HUNTER

Chapter 14

Test It First

I like old things. Old clothes and old equipment become more and more valuable with the passage of time. I wouldn't trade my prewar rifle for a new one of the same model and caliber if I had a chance. I wear my boots until they practically fall off my feet, and my most treasured fly rod is now about twenty-five years old.

I am not alone in this feeling; it is widespread among men who like to hunt and fish. Recently on a trip with Bruce Bowler I observed that his jacket was in tatters, and one evening when his flashlight fell out through a hole in the pocket I said, "Bowler, you're about due for a new coat."

When you're forty miles from the nearest road and get an
October storm that leaves a foot of snow, followed
by subzero temperatures, all your gear must be right.
Pretesting is the way to make sure.

"Yes," he agreed, "and I hate to get it. This has been a wonderful coat.
I've worn it on a dozen elk hunts. I wore it fishing in Canada. I've seen
some wonderful country and been through some tough storms wearing this
coat. It never let me down."

Undoubtedly, Bruce's feeling toward his old red-wool hunting coat was
partly sentimental. We get attached to old equipment because each item
brings back pleasant memories, and probably some subconscious yearning
for the good old days. There is hardly a sportsman who doesn't wish things
were the way they used to be. We see a stream that once was great ruined
by pollution, a grouse cover turned into a housing development, a duck
marsh drained in the name of progress. We get so we resent change, and
our attachment to the old things is probably an expression of this feeling.

But there is also a very practical reason for the loyalty. I have absolute
confidence in my old rifle; like Bowler's coat, it has never let me down. I
know that it will do its part if I do mine. Other items that have served me

well in the past are taken on each new trip with confidence because I know that they will serve me well again. The comfort of old shoes is proverbial—and comfort is the first consideration with all outdoor clothing. Style means nothing in the woods.

As a matter of fact, the practical reasons for clinging to old equipment are even stronger than the sentimental ones. An item that we know is good, that has proved itself in service, is not to be discarded lightly. Nevertheless, we do have to buy new things occasionally, whether we want to or not. When we do, there is only one safe procedure: each item should be tested thoroughly before being put into use.

This was impressed on me forcibly (for maybe the hundredth time!) when I bought a new air mattress. My old one had developed a slow leak that I couldn't find. I'd inflate it in the evening just before going to bed and about 3 o'clock in the morning I'd be lying on the rocks and sticks. So I bought a new one and made plans to test it, but as usual I kept procrastinating. Finally I started on a trip, and instead of taking time to inflate the new mattress at home, I rolled it with my sleeping bag and took off.

That evening in camp I discovered that I couldn't blow the mattress up. I puffed and puffed and still it stayed flat. Eventually I got to looking and discovered that the seam along one edge had not been fully cemented at the factory; it was wide open for about two feet. Of course, I had no patching material and I probably couldn't have fixed a leak so big anyway. There was nothing to do but to sleep on the ground for the duration of the outing.

Admittedly, an air mattress isn't so important. Its lack didn't spoil the trip, as the failure of some more vital item of equipment might have done, but each night it caused me to resolve *never* to trust anything, on any expedition, without thoroughly pretesting it at home.

Very likely the failure to test rifles carefully ahead of time has resulted in more disappointment than any other single thing—and by testing I mean being considerably more thorough than giving them a casual sighting-in. A man can easily spend a thousand dollars on a once-in-a-lifetime big-game hunt, and on that hunt he may get a chance at a once-in-a-lifetime trophy. If his rifle shoots off, his trip is spoiled. I've seen it happen.

Sighting-in should be done at targets on a range. It requires liberal quantities of both time and ammunition—and nobody else can do it for you. A bench rest or sandbag helps to make sure your hold is right, but after a few preliminary three-shot groups—making sight adjustments on the basis of one shot is a waste of time—I like to use the same positions I will use in hunting. These include sitting and prone with the sling, and, finally, offhand. This last is a humbling experience and invariably convinces me that I should always get as close as I can and into the best possible position before touching off a shot at any game animal.

In hunting, the first shot is nearly always the best, yet some rifles have a tendency to climb (shoot higher and higher) as the barrel warms up. For this reason, a man should concentrate on getting his group where he wants it, at the desired range, from a cold barrel. This takes time. It is also worthwhile to shoot a few rapid-fire ten-shot groups to determine whether the rifle holds its zero as the barrel gets hot. If it doesn't, a competent gunsmith can probably help, but even without his aid you will know what to expect.

The arms companies put out trajectory tables, and using one with the rifle, make of ammunition, and bullet you intend to use hunting will make the job of sighting-in easier. It will enable you to do your preliminary shooting at 100 yards and have your shots hit about where you want them to at longer ranges. But there are a number of valid reasons why you should also shoot at these ranges before you quit testing.

When you finish, you should wind up with a trajectory table similar to the one I worked out for my .270 and carried in my billfold until I'd memorized it. It discloses that the bullet first crosses the line of sight at 30 yards, is 1 inch high at 50, 2½ high at 100, 3 high at 150, 2 high at 200, on the nose at 250, 3½ inches low at 300, 8 low at 350, and 15 low at 400.

Such a table, verified by actual shooting, provides a lot of useful information. For example, I have occasionally surprised a hunting companion by shooting the heads off grouse for camp meat. A lot of hunters are still amazed that anybody can shoot a big-game rifle as well at close range as he shoots a .22. The secret lies in knowing the precise distance at which the bullet first crosses the line of sight—a factor that varies, depending on the height of the line of sight above the bore. Once you know it for your rifle, however, accurate close-range shooting is a cinch. In my own case, I know that the bullet will never be off more than an inch at a range of up to 50 yards. It will be low to 30, then exactly on, then gradually higher as the range increases.

I also know, of course, that I don't have to worry about evaluation until the target is at about 300 yards' range—and I can't remember when I've fired a shot at game that far away, though I have the necessary information on how to hold in case it should ever be necessary. (My feeling on this matter is that the mark of a good hunter is to get close and kill clean. Making a long shot should be cause for embarrassment, rather than pride.)

After a rifle is thoroughly sighted-in and the trajectory established, there is one more thing to think about. If the humidity is high when you do your sighting-in, and if you then hunt in the Southwest, where every day is hot and dry, your rifle may be off. Same thing if it is dry when you sight in and humid or rainy when you hunt. That's because the stock can warp enough to change the bedding of the barrel, thus throwing your bullets off. This is not a common hazard, but I have seen it happen. I took the barrel and action out of my .270 and soaked the inside of the stock with linseed oil.

The outside had been protected by an oil finish, of course, but the wood inside was raw.

After going through all this, it is no wonder that I wouldn't trade my old rifle for a new one. I know it is right and that it will stay right, no matter what the weather. I also know that it will shoot the same, whether the barrel is hot or cold. I no longer need go through the elaborate procedure outlined above. I simply fire a few groups at 200 yards to make sure nobody has tampered with the sights, then go hunting with the sure knowledge that if I miss it will be my own fault.

Shoes need pretesting even more urgently. After a man has suffered through one siege of blisters, he will never again wear a new pair on a hunting trip. They should always be thoroughly broken in and molded to your feet first, and you should hike far enough in them to reveal any treacherous seam or tight spot that might give trouble later. The same rule obviously applies to all clothing, but shoes are the most important because they are the one thing that can completely ruin a trip. If you can't walk, you can't hunt.

Bedrolls—both sleeping bags and air mattresses—should be pretested carefully. Being unable to sleep properly can be a disaster, for you can't hunt hard every day unless you rest well at night. I'll admit that I don't know how to test a sleeping bag in August to see if it's warm enough for use in October when the temperature may hit zero, but a man can at least make sure it's big enough.

Cameras and exposure meters should always be checked carefully before an important trip. Professional photographers are forever testing their equipment, and would no more start out with an untried camera than they would start to Labrador barefoot. Admittedly, it would be worse to miss the biggest moose in the world than to fail to get a picture of him, but the latter could be quite a disappointment, too.

If you buy a new camera or a meter, or take out old equipment that hasn't been used for some time, you should expose at least one roll of film—several would be better—as a test. Shoot in both bright light and dim, because conditions won't always be ideal. Use various *f* stops and shutter speeds. Focus critically. Follow carefully the exposures indicated by the meter, making sure that you're using the correct ASA film rating, then have the film processed, and check the results. If you don't feel that they're all they should be, your dealer or an experienced photographer can advise you as to what correction may be necessary.

This may seem like a lot of bother about something that really isn't very important, anyway. But I know a man who bought a complete new outfit—camera, telephoto lens, meter, and filters—and took it to Africa untested. He shot hundreds of pictures and could hardly wait to see them when he got home. Imagine his disappointment when he discovered that all were

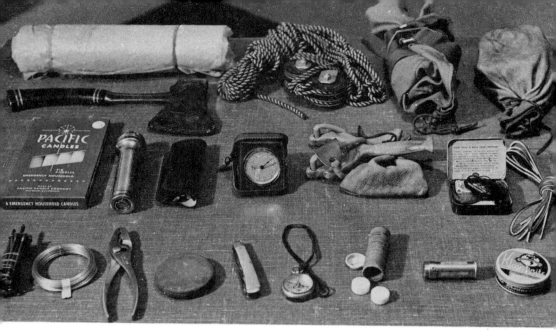

Some good gear to have along on a hunting trip, after pretesting all of it you possibly can: Top row, left to right, sheet plastic (if you pack it in, pack it out) and hatchet, block and tackle with 100 feet of 1,000-pound-test nylon cord, day pack, ditty bag with razor, toothbrush, and so on; middle row, candles, flashlight, spare eyeglasses, alarm clock, flipper (slingshot) and ammunition, gun-care kit, spare bootlaces; bottom row, nails, wire, pliers, whetstone, spare knife, compass, fire-starting tabs, waterproof matchsafe, fishing tackle in typewriter-ribbon box.

blanks! He insists that he took the lens cap off, so either the shutter failed to open or he had loaded the film improperly and it didn't feed through the camera. In either case, the disaster could have been avoided by shooting a few rolls ahead of time.

Another source of trouble—and I'm especially prone to err in this respect because I like to travel light—is not to take enough of the essential things. A complete change of clothes, extra socks and heavy underwear, a second pair of shoes, and a few more rolls of film don't add much weight to your duffel, but the time can come on any trip when having them will be mighty important.

Most of us are busy; sometimes I wonder how anybody could be busier than I am unless he's twins. But there are some things nobody can do for us. The time we take now to check and test and make sure that we have enough proven equipment for the hunt we plan a month from now is time that we will never begrudge spending.

Chapter 15

Of Boys and Guns

Half the reason for owning a gun is the romance of it. Most of my friends have more guns than they need. They like to look at them and handle them and are stirred by the memories of past hunts and the dreams of hunts to come. And though we may not consciously think of such legendary heroes as Daniel Boone, Davy Crockett, and Buffalo Bill, the association is there, just the same.

Boys are especially susceptible to the romance of guns. I have never known a boy who wasn't fascinated by them. Some boys outgrow this feeling; others never do. When I was a little boy I used to beg to take my father's old, long-barreled .30-30 to bed with me, and if I had been good he'd let me. I still have it, and from time to time I enjoy taking it out of the cabinet, putting it to my shoulder a few times, then rubbing it with an oily rag and setting it away again. It reminds me of my first deer, which I shot with it, and of my father, and boyhood days on the homestead.

Early one morning when I was five or six my father started out to feed the stock, then slipped quietly back into the house again. He took his rifle from its usual spot in the corner behind the kitchen door and filled the magazine with cartridges from a box on the shelf nearby. I was barely out of bed, but instantly I was wide awake and bursting with curiosity. In answer to my question he said, "Two coyotes trying to get the chickens. You can come, but don't slam the door."

He quietly levered a cartridge into the chamber as he slipped around the corner of the house. I followed, barefoot and shivering with both cold and excitement.

Our chickens were confined at night to a pen of 5-foot woven wire about 50 years behind the house. One coyote was sitting looking at the fence as though puzzled. The other was sniffing along the lower edge, evidently hunting for a hole. My father raised his .30-30 deliberately and fired at the sitting coyote. He missed. The dust flew from beside its front feet.

At the report, both coyotes leaped to full speed. They fairly flew around the corner of the hen yard, then tore away across an open field. My father fired at them three or four more times and every time I could tell the bullet struck low by the dust it kicked up.

He unloaded his rifle and we went in and my mother asked whether he got one. He answered simply, "No. They got away."

I was puzzled. I knew he was an excellent shot; I had seen him hit targets much more difficult than a sitting coyote at 50 yards. Now, I realize why he missed. He had no intention of killing them. He liked to hear them sing in the evening as well as I do now. All he intended to do was to scare them so badly they would never visit our chicken pen again. In that, he succeeded.

That old rifle is one gun I would never sell, and my feeling is by no means unique. Such attachment for a firearm is common among men who love guns and hunting. Most of my friends have at least one gun they wouldn't part with for any price. And not surprisingly, this gun is often an old, beat-up, single-shot .22 or a single-barrel shotgun. It is usually the owner's first gun and more than likely a gift. Not long ago a middle-aged friend showed me his first gun, a silvery .22, with the bluing long worn off, and told me his father gave it to him.

I suspect that if you want to give your son a Christmas present he'll keep all of his life and remember you by long after you are gone, you could make no better choice than a gun. I gave my sons identical .22's for Christmas when they were twelve and ten years old. Jack, the younger, has become an enthusiastic hunter who loads his own ammunition and can shoot a tight group on the range. Dan, mature now, cares little for hunting and seldom does. But both boys still have the .22's I gave them and when I suggested to Jack recently that he trade his in on a better one he just smiled.

There are parents, I'm sure, who don't hunt but yet would like to give a gun to a son for Christmas. This could pose somewhat of a problem because any youngster learning to handle firearms needs adult guidance, preferably from his father. Fortunately, the National Shooting Sports Foundation, 1075 Post Road, Riverside, Connecticut 06878, has an answer to this very situation in an excellent little book called *What Every Parent Should Know . . . When a Boy or Girl Wants a Gun*. It's free.

I think no other gift makes a boy feel grown up so suddenly. With a gun goes responsibility and if a boy is mature enough to own a gun, then he will be responsible with it. The Ten Commandments of Safety which, I believe, are packaged with every new gun, should be learned by every boy with his first. And one of them, "Never point a gun at anything you do not want to shoot," is especially important. I got an unforgettable lesson on it when I was thirteen, long before the Ten Commandments of Safety were written.

My first shotgun, a 20-gauge double, had a rather tricky safety. The safe position was in the middle. If you pushed the button ahead to shoot, it automatically returned to safe when you broke the gun to reload. But if you drew the button to the rear it stayed in that off position until manually returned to safe. I developed a habit of glancing at it after loading, then pulling a trigger to be doubly sure. It was a good habit, but one evening after school when I was hurrying out pheasant hunting, I loaded my gun as I walked across the back yard, then checked the safety as I went along the side of the garden. Only I didn't point the muzzle up in the air as I should have done. There was an old white hen in the garden, busily picking up seeds. I pointed at her and pulled the trigger. The feathers flew and she was instantly a very dead chicken.

It was a dreadful shock. But I learned a lesson I'll never forget and, no doubt partly as the result of it, I have been extremely careful with guns ever since. Furthermore, I refuse to hunt with anybody who isn't. If I am out with someone who puts a loaded gun into the car or boat or carries his gun in the field so the muzzle swings past my dog or me—or commits any of the other common gun-handling faults—we never go together again. I am determined to enjoy a lot more hunting seasons.

My father had a good rule during my first two or three years of hunting. I could hunt with him or another adult or by myself, but I was not allowed to hunt with other boys. He used to say, "One boy, whole boy; two boys, half a boy; three boys, no boy at all."

I was six years older than my brother so the rule for him was a little different. He could hunt with me, but not with boys his own age. I had received enough coaching from my father by that time so he felt it was safe for me to teach my little brother.

With my two sons being only two years apart, I could hardly work it that way. I gave them BB guns for Christmas when they were seven and five. They were well indoctrinated with the rules of safe gun handling by the time pellet guns followed at ages ten and eight. And by the Christmas when they got their .22's, I felt it was safe for them to hunt together without me.

No matter how much coaching he may have, there is one thing nobody can explain to a boy and that is the overwhelming excitement he'll feel at the first sight of game. He may have seen a thousand rabbits but when, gun in hand, he sees the first rabbit he can shoot, his hands will tremble, his throat will go dry, and his heart will pound. This is one of the reasons why

Ted's sons started with BB guns when they were nine and
seven years old. Can you guess from the haircuts
when that was?

it's a good idea for a boy to hunt alone or with an adult at first. And this excitement will return with each new hunting experience, such as the first deer.

You give a boy lasting pleasure when you give him a gun. Let him have a 40-acre wood lot with a few squirrels in the trees and some cottontails in the briar patches and he has everything he needs for months of exploration and adventure. And if there is a brook meandering through the woods, so much the better, because brooks have a particular magic of their own.

A gun subtly leads a boy to a love of nature and an appreciation of all the wonders of the out-of-doors. With his gun—and a little imagination—he will tread silently in the footprints of the Mountain Men, brave as they were brave, alert to anything that moves in the shadows of the mysterious woods. And what matter if his game is a squirrel or a cottontail rather than a buffalo or an elk? What matter if his happy hunting ground is a wood lot rather than the entire Rockies? Not a thing.

Hunting will develop alertness, patience, and his powers of observation, and these desirable qualities will stay with him all of his life, even though when he becomes a man circumstances may force him, as they have forced many others, to give up his boyhood pleasures.

Chapter 16

My Six-Ounce
Bench Rest

The four rams were 250 yards away. They were on their feet, milling—alarmed but not yet running. The sheep knew something was wrong, but they hadn't winded us and we were half screened by the last of the dwarf spruce at timber line. Alvin Guinn was watching them through the glasses. "That big one on the left," he whispered, "you'll never get a better head. Not if you hunt for twenty years. Take him before he starts to run." He lowered the binoculars, then raised them again as the ram turned. "Don't let that big sonofagun get away!"

To say that I was excited is a drab understatement. I was like an overwound clock spring. And no wonder. For twenty years my heart had been set on a good bighorn ram. It was the only trophy I'd ever really wanted. Now there it was. The ram was big and beautiful and wild—magnificent, the very embodiment of the wild Alberta country. But he was 250 yards away, up a mountain that was steeper than a scared cat's back. I would have liked to cut the range in half, but there was no way to do it. If we went a yard farther, we'd be past the spruce. There was no more cover.

Unhooking the short strap of my rifle sling and letting it hang, I put my left arm through the loop formed by the long strap as far as it would go. Then I pushed the keepers back tight. I was already on my knees; so I dropped down into the standard military prone position on a spot of grass among the rocks and wiggled around until I had an unobstructed view of the rams under the branches of the spruce, and until the rifle muzzle hung naturally in the right position.

This took time. Alvin was squirming with apprehension—kept telling me to hurry, that they were about to run. And of course I wanted to shoot. I had wanted to shoot the instant I saw them. But I also wanted the ram. Thirty-five years of hunting with a rifle had taught me that the first shot is *always* the best shot. I knew I could kill that ram from a prone position with the aid of the sling if I waited until my lungs stopped heaving from the climb we had just made, waited until my heart stopped pounding and my hands quit shaking. I doubted that I could hit him at all shooting offhand. And the sitting position is difficult when your target is uphill. My gamble was whether the rams would stay there long enough. If they did, I'd win. If they didn't, I might lose, but even at that, I would gladly trade 50 yards of range for the benefit of the sling and the prone position.

At last, after what seemed like years of forced deep breathing, I felt that I was ready. I quietly eased the bolt back and pushed it forward again, chambering a cartridge. The big ram was facing me. I don't like a head-on shot because I've seldom made a clean kill when I've tried it. So I waited some more until he took a few steps to the left and stopped broadside. I took a deep breath, exhaled half of it, centered the crosshairs just above his "elbow" and squeezed the trigger. He tumbled 30 yards down the mountain and came to rest against a boulder. The hunt was over.

By the time I got home I had driven 2,000 miles, ridden 50, walked 100— and fired one shot. The ram's head is on my wall. It is a dandy, too, far better than I had hoped for. The trip was a great success. It might easily have been a failure, however, but for the insignificant-looking strap attached to the underside of my rifle.

A sling provides a good way to carry a rifle. I use mine for that purpose about two-thirds of the time when I'm hunting. A gun is not so heavy on a sling over your shoulder, and sometimes in rough country you need both hands.

But if I had to make a choice between a sling for carrying and a sling for shooting—that is, if it could serve only one purpose or the other, not both— I'd certainly take the shooting sling. I would much rather carry my rifle in my hand for ten hours than do without the sling during that vital ten seconds when I'm trying to get off the all-important first shot. A sling is the greatest aid to marksmanship a hunter can carry. I have occasionally referred to mine as my six-ounce bench rest, and the exaggeration is actually not very great.

In my opinion, the best sling is the standard military type, though mine is only an inch wide and of somewhat lighter leather than the Army uses. It has the same two sets of claw hooks, however, and the same two leather

Shown here rigged for carrying the rifle is the standard
military sling, a tremendous aid in shooting a rifle
accurately from all the standard positions.

bands, or keepers, to tighten the long loop on my arm when the opportunity
arises to shoot prone.

To get into it, I unhook the short strap and slide both keepers up the long
loop. Next I give it a half turn to the left so that the strap will lie flat over
my left hand. Then I put my arm through, all the way. I slide the keepers
back down, tight against my arm. My left hand holds the fore-end, back of
the sling swivel, and the sling passes over the back of the hand.

The length of the long loop has to be adjusted to the individual shooter
by hooking the claw into the proper pair of holes in the strap. It should be
tight. A loose sling is worthless.

Put the sling on your arm before getting into the prone position, and use
the butt of your rifle to ease down onto your belly. Don't lie perfectly in line
with the target, but face about 20 degrees to the right. (All of these
directions are for a right-handed shooter. A southpaw would reverse them,
of course.)

With your belly flat on the ground, your legs spread in a comfortable
position, elbows dug in, left arm *under* the rifle and sling tight, your sights
should be approximately on the target. If they're not, change position until
they hang there naturally. Don't attempt to correct for an improper position
by forcing the muzzle to either side; you'll induce trembling and ruin
accuracy.

Now, I realize there are hunters who are going to say at this point, "Nuts!
Nobody has time to do all that. The game would leave the country before
you were ready to shoot." I know as well as anybody that you don't have

NRA Hunter Safety Instructor Art Owen demonstrates proper use of the sling. First, you lengthen the short, lower strap. Then, slide the keepers (leather bands) up the long loop and give the loop half a turn to the left, as shown.

Then you put your left arm through the loop and pull the keepers down tight.

time for such preparation when you're shooting at running game in heavy cover. Then you shoot your rifle much as you would a shotgun, or you don't shoot at all. In such hunting, however, the target is always close, so you don't need extreme accuracy.

Hold the rifle's fore end this way, with your left hand above the sling's loop. If necessary, adjust the loop until it is tight. Maintain uniform tension from shot to shot.

The sitting position is steadier than standing; the prone position is steadier yet. To get down to prone position, place the rifle butt on the ground and ease yourself down.

Simpler than the military sling is the plain carrying strap Art Owen demonstrates here. First step in using it as a "hasty sling" is to twist sling half a turn to the left. This half turn makes the strap lie flat against your arm and hand.

Then put your arm through the sling and around it as shown. This will allow you to place your left hand in the proper spot on rifle's fore end. Military sling can also be used as hasty sling.

The place where you use the prone position with the sling loop pulled tight is, fortunately, the very spot where you need all the help you can get. It is in long-range shooting, on either varmints or game, in the West and the North. In this open country you may have to take your shot at 300 yards because there is no way to get closer. There is one thing in your favor,

The hasty sling as seen from the opposite side. Notice how strap lies flat against arm and hand. Strap should be tight, which makes it right for carrying the rifle. Hasty sling can be used in all four standard shooting positions: standing, sitting, kneeling, and prone.

however. At such ranges the game ordinarily is not alarmed. You can take time enough to get into the best possible position.

Of course, there are many times when you can't shoot prone. Maybe there is grass or brush in the way, or rocks or logs. Then you may be able to use a sitting position—which is steadier than kneeling or offhand—and again, your sling will help. Kneeling, which puts your rifle about seven inches farther off the ground than sitting, is better than offhand. With your left elbow on your left knee and the sling tight, it's really pretty steady.

Even offhand, I use my sling unless the game is running at short range. In this case, however, I don't put my arm through the loop. Instead I use what is called the "hasty" sling. Holding the rifle in my right hand, I twist the sling a half turn to the left and put my arm over it. Then I put my hand over it again, also from the left, to grip the forearm. When I raise the rifle to my shoulder, the sling is pulled tight across my chest and around my arm, which is directly under the gun.

The hasty sling is equally helpful either sitting or kneeling, and I have even used it prone when I felt that I was really pushed for time. It has another advantage: It works with a simple carrying strap, in case your rifle is not equipped with a military-type sling. Just as is the case with the sling, however, the length of the strap must be properly adjusted. It should be tight when you're in shooting position, and if it has an adjustment to change the length it must be designed so that it won't slip under tension.

Looking back over the past ten years—which is about as long as I can remember on this subject—I can't recall a single head of game that I killed without using the sling. Quite a few of them were on the move, too. I know, of course, that there are skeptics. Each fall, the rod-and-gun club to which I belong opens its range to the public on one or two Sundays preceding deer season. Through the media of press and radio we invite the boys to come out and sight-in their assorted rifles. The members man the butts, score the shots, and assist all who will accept help on the firing line.

You ought to hear the stories! Characters with rifles that would do well to hit a barn door at 50 feet tell about shooting their deer running at 500 yards—offhand, too. When we get down to the serious business of firing and sight adjusting, however, most of them can't even hit the paper, much less the black.

I suggested to one such rifleman, who happened to have a carrying strap on his rifle, that he lie down and use the sling, at least to check his sights. He gave me a contemptuous look. "I stand up and shoot like a man!" he said. He sure did, too, but we had a little trouble helping him because he couldn't seem to get a shot on the target.

Personally, I want all the help I can get, and a sling provides a mighty lot of help for a mighty little bother.

Chapter 17

Beware the One-Wire Fence

In the Great American West you will often see cattle in a pasture with only a single wire around the edge. It will be some 30 inches above the ground. If you look closer you will observe that there are insulators between this wire and the posts that support it. Beware! You are confronted by an electric fence, and it is crossing them that proves the courage of Western men.

An electric fence won't kill you. Obviously, no farmer could afford to use a fence that might kill the unsuspecting calves that touch it. But, believe me, coming into intimate contact with one is an experience you won't forget. And the electrified expression on the face of an unwary hunting or fishing companion when he grabs the hot wire is highly entertaining. In fact, strange though it may seem, even my own mistakes begin to seem funny as soon as I recover from the shock.

One winter Clare Wissel and I shot crows along the creek in back of Jack Frost's farm. We had our blinds in the trees along the stream and they were separated from Jack's alfalfa field by a four-strand, barbed-wire fence—with the top wire on insulators.

Each time we hunted there we gathered up the crows we killed. There were two reasons: first, crows won't come to decoys or a call if many of their dead brothers are lying on the ground, and second, after shooting twice a

Dogs and people soon learn great respect for a hot wire.

week all winter we would have had so many crows in Jack's alfalfa that he would have baled more crows than hay the following summer.

Of course, it was necessary to cross the fence to pick up the crows that fell in the field. The first four or five times we hunted, we cautiously tested the top wire with a straw. We'd find one about 15 inches long, hold either end, and touch the dangerous wire with the other. Then, feeling nothing, we'd gradually slide the straw across the wire until we were actually touching it. If there had been current in the wire, we would have felt a tingle through the straw before the hand holding it was close enough to get a hard jolt.

Although Jack had a few horses grazing the alfalfa stubble, we never saw them near the fence and we finally decided the current had been turned off for the winter. That was a mistake! One day I went to the fence, boldly grabbed the top wire, and swung a leg over. Oooooh!

My feet were on the wet earth on both sides of the fence when the electricity hit me. I ground my teeth down to the gums, my hair stood on end, my eyes crossed, and I thought, "I'm ruined!"

Remember putting your finger in a light socket when you were a child?

That was nothing compared to this! The shock only lasted a second, but it felt like an hour. Then I flew off the fence and stumbled out among the dead crows.

Clare and I have often wondered whether Jack really needed to turn the fence on to keep his horses in the stubble, We doubt that he did. It's an unkind thought, but we suspect he may have been gleefully watching through a knothole in the barn when I had my shocking experience.

The heart of the electric fence is an innocent-looking metal box called a "fencer," and while some of them operate on 6- or 12-volt batteries, the majority use regular 120-volt, alternating current. A transformer in fencers of this type changes the 120-volt AC to direct current of 1600 to 1800 volts, but of very low amperage. One terminal of the fencer is grounded to a rod driven into the earth; the other is connected to the hot wire. The dead-end, charged wire can be as much as twenty miles long. When an animal—or an unsuspecting hunter—standing on the ground touches the wire and completes the circuit, he has learned his lesson for that day.

Most fencers have a pulsing current, which protects the livestock from a sustained glow. A calf can put its wet nose against the wire, get a jolt, and then the current goes off so the animal can pull away. Maybe this is a good thing for hunters, too, but if you happen to touch the wire ever so cautiously when the current is off, then grab it boldly just in time to get the next spurt of current you won't think so.

For the farmer, an electric fence is economical. One wire does the work of three or four and the posts can be farther apart. In fact, you don't even need posts. I saw one electric fence that consisted simply of half-inch steel rods driven into the ground, girl-shaped bottles upended over the tops of the rods, and the wire attached to them. Sometimes a farmer runs a hot wire along an old, tumble-down fence that his stock were going through. After one quick lesson, they never touch it again.

Once in a great while you see an animal that is an exception to the rule. Jim Nettleton had one, a bull calf. He would bawl, shut his eyes, throw up his tail, and charge full bore under a hot wire to eat the greener grass on the other side. I'll bet he grew up to be a bull of character—if he did grow up!

With almost every living creature, however, once is enough. Cattle, horses, pigs, chickens, dogs, people, even mice, soon learn. Once my father stored a bin of seed wheat in the corner of his farm repair shop and when the mice moved in for the winter they were quick to find it. You'd open the shop door and as many as two dozen mice would shoot out of the wheat bin and scamper to cover in all directions.

This couldn't be. Seed wheat was valuable. So one day Dad ran an electric fence around the bin where the wheat was stored. And he wasn't joking. He used 120 AC right off the line and it was on all the time. To prevent inadvertent contact by the hired man, us boys, or other loafers, he put up a sign: Beware—Mouse Fence." A nice touch, I thought.

The first morning after installing his wheat bin fence, there were thirty-two dead mice on the floor. The second morning, there were twelve. The third morning, there were four. But the next morning, there were none!

Had he killed them all? I should say not! The survivors were wise. They still ate his seed wheat, but they stayed clear of the fence. They climbed the wall of the shop, ran along the sill, crept up a rafter until they were above the bin, and then dropped down into it. And when they left they made a flying leap from the edge of the bin to the floor.

In the land of the electric fence you soon learn to be very careful. You look carefully for insulators on any fence you approach and if you see them you either scoot under or step over with all the respect you'd give an angry rattlesnake. Even so, you make an occasional mistake.

Willard Cravens and I were hunting quail one day when we came to a three-strand, barbed-wire fence with the middle wire on insulators—an effective arrangement, as I soon discovered. I had cautiously pushed the top wire down just far enough to swing a leg over and was completing the turn when a covey of birds flushed 30 feet to one side. I forgot where I was. In my hurry to get on over I pushed the top wire down too far and it touched the hot one. Wow!

Electric fences are put to all sorts of strange uses. A farmer living on the bank of the Portneuf River, near Pocatello, Idaho, raised sugar beets. Beaver started climbing up from the river at night, digging his beets, and lugging them away. Beaver were protected and he didn't want to kill them anyway, but they *were* getting a lot of beets. So he strung a hot wire about 6 inches above the ground along the river side of the field.

As it got dark the first evening, he sat quietly nearby to listen. Before long, he told me, he heard a splash that sounded as though someone had thrown a stove into the river. Seconds later, there was another splash, then a wild commotion as the two beaver practically threw the water out of the stream getting away. Not another beet was taken—and no wonder! A wet beaver must get a dreadful wallop.

The instructions that come with some electric fencers tell you never to use them for poultry. Maybe the manufacturers think chickens are too stupid to learn; maybe they're afraid the current might kill the cackling idiots. In at least one case, I can guarantee they were wrong on both counts.

My brother had about a hundred chickens running loose and a big garden, and anybody who knows anything at all about chickens knows where every one of them wanted to be—in the garden. So Burtt strung a wire from his electric fencer down two or three rows and stood back to watch the results. They were great.

An old hen would come pecking along, pulling up the newly sprouted sweet corn or picking the blossoms off the peas, and she would raise her head and touch one of the hot wires, which were about a foot above the ground. Instantly, she'd take off like a pheasant, squawking as though her tail were on fire. And, believe me, in less than a week you couldn't have driven a chicken into that garden with a pack of hounds!

Of all the animals that occasionally come into contact with an electric fence, however, none registers so much shock, pain, and surprise as does a dog. A farmer friend had a pointer bitch and when she was in the condition that attracts every male dog for miles around he kept her in his dog pen. It was 6 feet high and dogproof, but all the dogs in the neighborhood were outside and the frenzy was unbearable. Some dogs spent the night fighting. Others assailed the fence with admirable enthusiasm but an obvious lack of judgment. Several dogs just sat and howled as though their hearts were broken.

After a couple of sleepless nights, my friend ran a hot wire from his electric fencer around the dog pen, attaching it to insulators about a foot off the ground. Shortly thereafter, he saw a visitor lift his leg. This was followed instantly by a startled and anguished howl. Then the unfortunate brute left in a cloud of dust and didn't slow down until he had crossed the first ridge, half a mile away. He may not have slowed down even then; my friend couldn't see. Within a matter of hours, the only dog on the farm was the forlorn and lonely bitch in her pen. I suppose the poor thing wondered what she might have done to lose her charm.

Dogs, like people, vary in intelligence. Some dogs get stung a time or two and never again touch *any* wire. They belly under fences, hot or not, as though touching the bottom strand were certain death. Other dogs innocently blunder into one electric fence after another. A few of them go merrily on their way after the experience, but the usual reaction is to lose all interest in life, love, hunting, and everything else. One canine friend of mine would make a few quick leaps after touching a hot wire, then sit down and stay there and watch his master hunt. It took a long time for the effect to wear off.

The very worst dog-and-fence experience of all, however, was this: Jim Eidemiller was bringing along a little pointer bitch that had lots of promise but she was slow to point, as good dogs sometimes are. He kept working her and letting her flush birds and have fun. At last, she pointed. Jim was 40 yards away. He started toward her.

She was in that ecstatic state pointing dogs enter when the scent of game is hot in their nostrils. Her eyes were glazed, her mouth was opening and closing, and her tail was coming up.

Unfortunately, she had almost—but not quite—passed under an electric fence. As her tail rose, the tip pressed firmly against the hot wire. A pulse of current came through. She yelped, broke point, and ran back to cower behind her master.

Who knows what a dog may think? Did she believe Jim had punished her for pointing? Whatever she might have thought, she made a firm connection between pointing and getting hurt. Despite many hours of patient effort on Jim's part, it was more than a year before she pointed again.

Chapter 18

The Wild, Free Days

When the last of the yellow leaves are twisting down and the haze of Indian summer has given way to the sharp, clear, rain-washed air of fall, the anticipation that precedes each day afield is somehow tempered for me by a feeling of nostalgia. The weathered corn, an apple left unnoticed on the tree, the crunch of frosted stubble underfoot, wood smoke in the evening— these things all remind me of the wild, free days of boyhood, because the best of all those days were the Saturdays of fall.

In the sense that the life of the Mountain Men was wild and free, my days were, of course, really very tame. I was a country boy wandering through a farming community with my gun. But from the time I was in the seventh grade, once the crops were up, Saturdays were mine. I could go where I wanted to and do as I pleased. And for me, then as now, this could mean but one thing—hunting.

I had a buddy, Alvin Morrison, who lived half a mile up the road and loved to hunt as much as I did. He, too, was free on Saturdays. We usually teamed up, starting from either his place or mine, and we often walked all day. I can remember yet how tired I used to be when we dragged in after dark—and how hungry. Somehow I can't recall that we ever took a lunch; being boys, we'd have been hungry anyway. I do remember eating old, withered plums—how sweet they were!—and frosted apples and occasionally a carrot from some neglected garden. A handful of wheat or corn, missed in the harvest and shelled out as we walked along, was standard on our bill of fare.

One gray Saturday in November was typical. Oddly, I don't remember the year, though I do remember vividly many details of the day—the shells I was shooting, for example. They were the old U.S. Cartridge Company's black Climax—¾ ounce of shot in 20-gauge—and modern-day magnum fans should have seen the way they'd tumble a big cock pheasant or a mallard drake! And I'm sure it was November because Thanksgiving came only a few days afterward.

The clouds were hanging low and there was a raw bite to the air as I did my morning chores. I had just finished them when Alvin came walking up the drive with his gun and dog. We discussed which way to go. In those days, long before anybody dreamed of a population explosion, trespass hadn't become a problem. We could hunt all day in any direction, crossing property lines as we came to them; stopping to ask permission was neither necessary nor expected. There was but one exception—a neighbor, Ellis Kaufman, who lived between our two farms, always posted his 80 acres.

His back 40 was hilly and not in crops, and it was a wonderful place for pheasants. From time to time Alvin and I asked if we could hunt there, but we were invariably refused permission. At the same time, Kaufman's friends from town were always welcome. This somehow didn't seem quite cricket, and we reciprocated by keeping him in good running trim. We could slip in, shoot a bird or two, and by the time he had run the quarter mile from his house to put us out we'd be over the hill and gone. Now that he has passed to his reward, I hope he enjoyed these little sprints as much as we did.

At any rate, on this particular day we decided to hunt along the Snake River, which was about a mile south of our starting point. We walked across the road and started through Myron Way's 20 acres, which was half in corn and half in wheat. The stubble looked dull and lifeless in the poor light, and the tattered leaves of the corn rustled softly in the chilly breeze. Coaly, Alvin's black shepherd, and Barney, my brown one, started systematically about their business.

Those unfortunates who in their boyhood never hunted with a shepherd dog may smile at my confession. Let me point out that all dogs like to hunt and that shepherds, being very bright and tractable, as a rule, can easily be taught to hunt in the fashion of a spaniel. Both Barney and Coaly were eager, quick to scent a pheasant and make him fly, and almost infallible on cripples. Both retrieved without urging, though only Coaly would do it from water.

At the end of the corn, in the weedy strip along the fence, the dogs flushed two pheasants, a cock and a hen. One flew right, the other left. We got them both.

We climbed the fence, walked across Elwood's alfalfa field, through a barley stubble, and along the edge of his pasture to the next half-section road. Beyond it, Tony Landa had a big cornfield that we started through, walking down the rows about 20 yards apart. After only a little way the dogs began to make game. Pheasants! Soon Coaly and Barney were loping down two rows, noses to the ground, and we were running hard to keep up. The birds, at least a dozen of them, flushed well out of range at the end of the field. They sailed off to the southwest, into the heavy cover along Stone's drain ditch.

We paused to catch our breath and Alvin said, "Let's surround 'em! I'll cut across Mike Frosig's hay until I'm past 'em, then hunt back this way. You wait till I get to the ditch, then start down it from here."

It was a good plan, and I agreed. Alvin started at a dogtrot, Coaly at heel. I noticed that the wind had picked up a little and was even rawer than when I had been doing chores. The clouds, now showing edges of black, were scudding toward the east. The smoke from Helyer's chimney, a quarter mile to the south, was lined out flat, 30 feet above the ground. Beyond it, a great raft of ducks beat their way into the wind, flying downstream along the river. They finally pitched in near the head of Louie Smith's island.

Alvin and I were 30 yards apart when the first nervous rooster threshed out of a tangle of alkali weeds along the ditch. He flew toward the river, which was 200 yards away beyond a patch of brush, and Alvin tumbled him in a puff of feathers. At the shot the air seemed full of pheasants. The dogs started barking in excitement. I was excited too. Most of the birds were flying my way, some of them directly overhead. I hit a hen too close and missed a cock at 30 yards. Alvin shot again. It was all over before we could reload.

Barney found my hard-shot hen. Alvin and Coaly were beating through a clump of cattails, the down they shook loose trailing off in the wind like smoke. "I've got a cripple in here," my friend called.

Barney and I hurried to help find it, but the rooster flopped out of the cattails into the swift-flowing water of the drainage ditch and Coaly nailed him before we got there. We crossed the ditch—our feet would be wet from that moment on, of course—and found Alvin's other bird. This made five, three for him and two for me, a good start. We climbed a mound of earth that had been dredged from the ditch when it was dug and sat down.

We could see the top of the far bank of the river, the blue hills ten miles beyond, the clumps of trees that marked the farmhouses across the valley. We counted a dozen flocks of ducks following the river, and I told Alvin about the big raft I'd seen pitch in at the head of Louis's island. "I wish we had a boat," he said. "This would be a good day."

We hiked through the brush to the river, flushing a covey of quail en route. Neither of us shot. We didn't have very many shells—we never did—and we hoped to kill a lot of ducks as we hunted along the bank. And we still had three pheasants to go. The limit was four apiece.

The long gravel bar at the head of Louie's island, which we could see when we walked out on the riverbank, was black with mallards. There must have been a thousand loafing on it, with more pitching in and still more drifting in on the water. The first big Northern flight, pushed by the storm that was now imminent, was getting in. "If it would only snow," I said, "the fields would be full of 'em."

"Yeah, but it's going to rain. In fact, it's starting now."

He was right. A cold drizzle, driven by the ever-freshening wind, had reached us. We turned our backs to it and started upstream along the bank. A cock pheasant flushed out of range and flew across the river. The dogs found the quail again and made them fly, and they buzzed back into the brush. A lone duck, probably a goldeneye—in those days there were only mallards, teal, and "river ducks"—pattered and flew away from shore. A cottontail or two bobbed off, speeded by our stern warnings to the dogs.

Upstream from Louie's, where the river curved, we sat down among the greasewood on the point. Ducks cutting the bend might fly over. They did, but nearly all of them were far too high. We resolved to build a skiff before another hunting season because we obviously had to have a boat. We talked about the things boys talk about and shivered in the wind with our light jackets soaking through.

At last five mallards came over closer than any of the others. They were too far for my 20-gauge, but Alvin had a 12. He shot twice and a greenhead tumbled down.

We went on then, past Helyer's, along back of Biship's, and past Snell's to the road at the corner of Fred Gebert's place. I killed a pheasant and two mallards en route; Alvin got another mallard and a green-winged teal. Our game bags were now heavy, it was raining harder by the minute and getting late, and we were a long way from home. I've never been hungrier.

We walked along the road awhile, past Ed Mapes', then left it to cut across John Weidman's wheatfield. It was the time of day when pheasants should come out into the stubble. Near the far side Alvin killed his fourth—a hard, crossing shot at long range. Only a little farther, as we walked through the corner of the orchard, we found several big, crisp, cold Jonathan apples. We ate them as we trudged along.

We didn't see another bird before we came to Morrison's. As Alvin turned in the drive and I started wearily on, with Barney walking as wearily at heel, I was tempted to hike right down the road. It was the shortest way, and the easiest, and the light was almost gone. Still, there was a field of stubble on the south side of Kaufman's hill—not on his land—and I could swing around through it. That wouldn't be much farther and I might get my fourth pheasant.

Halfway across the stubble a bird got up. It was now so dark I could only hear it. Then, suddenly, a rooster rose above the black horizon, against the leaden sky, still somewhat lighter in the west. I threw the gun at him and pulled the trigger. I heard him hit the ground.

Barney found him and brought him to me. I broke my gun and pocketed the unfired shell and smelled the sweet smoke that curled up from the breech. I was suddenly content—and oh, so tired.

My parents and little brother were just sitting down to eat as I opened the kitchen door. My father said, "Where have you been? It's late." My mother said, "Get out of those wet clothes!" My brother said, "Did you get anything?"

I was too weary to answer.

Chapter 19

Make Sure You Missed

Were there no optimists, there would be no hunters. Yet in one area of our sport we are all too prone to let pessimism rule—and at the very time when it may be both most costly and least excusable. This is the agonizing interval after we pull the trigger when high hope quickly plunges to deep despair. A miss? Maybe not!

You should never assume you missed simply because the game at which you shot does not fall instantly. Even though it fails to reveal the slightest indication of being hit, it may be dead within seconds or, at most, a matter of minutes. This is equally true of upland birds, waterfowl, and big game.

One fall afternoon I was walking through open woods along the edge of a narrow, brush-choked swale. The dogs were in it. The cover was 10 feet tall and the grouse knew what it was for; three in a row thundered away low and out of sight.

Then one made a mistake. It came out waist high on my side, passed me, and flew straight away down an open aisle among the trees. No man ever had an easier shot at a ruffed grouse, yet I fired both barrels and didn't turn a feather!

The timber ended about 200 yards away, and right at the edge of the trees, directly on the line the grouse had taken, I knew there was a big clump of haws. That's where it had to be; it wouldn't fly into the open.

Many an experienced gunner has shot at a bird, decided
he missed, and then had his dog pick it up later and bring
it in. This mountain quail flew around a bend in the
creek and out of sight before it fell, but Rip found it.

With the dogs at heel, I stopped 40 feet from the hawthorn thicket to
figure out the proper strategy. I happened to glance up. There, on a slender
branch growing from a scraggly pine, sat my grouse. Now what? I can't
shoot sitting birds with a shotgun. I might shoot the branch off with one
barrel to make it fly, then kill it with the other. Still, I might miss, too. A
bird flying down and away, as this one surely would, is a hard shot. I looked
around for something to throw. There wasn't a stone or knot in sight.

All of this took time and I was still trying to decide what to do when the
bird suddenly let loose all holds and dropped. Believe me, if I was amazed,
the dogs were utterly dumfounded when it thudded to the ground in front
of them.

When I plucked it I discovered several shot against the skin at the front
of its breast. A ruffed grouse is not considered a hard bird to kill. Hard to
hit, yes, but not hard to kill. Yet this one had not shown the slightest

indication of being hit. One shot would have broken a wing and dropped it instantly, yet four or five ranging through it lengthwise were not immediately fatal.

How often do hard-hit birds fly away without faltering? More often, I am convinced, than most hunters realize. In fact, my wife and I had a similar experience with a blue grouse the very next day.

We were walking along a hillside a few yards above a brushy stream bottom in which both dogs were busily working, when the big bird pounded up in front of us. We both shot just as it disappeared behind a tree. But then it curved into view and we watched it light high in a towering yellow pine a quarter of a mile ahead. It, too, fell dead shortly after we arrived.

All of us who have hunted the birds of the open have watched the one at which we shot fly strongly for several hundred yards, then tower and fall. They are always dead when we find them and all I have examined had a single shot through the heart.

Once while hunting sage hens my companion, half a mile away, shot a bird that flew toward me, then towered directly overhead. It was hanging there like a tethered balloon and probably would have dropped. But its wings were still beating strongly and, fearful lest it might angle away, I shot it. I estimated the range at 30 yards, straight up, and that bird fell almost at my feet.

I have never seen a quail or grouse tower, perhaps because of the cover, but my dogs have picked up many that flew out of sight, apparently unhit, then fell dead. Nor have I seen waterfowl of any kind tower, though I have watched both ducks and geese fly strongly for half a mile and then drop. They were always dead when I found them and I suspect from one freakish experience that they may have been dead in the air before they fell.

Back in the days when I believed in heavy loads of big shot, I fired at a single mallard, passing at 45 yards. It didn't flinch. I watched it anyway, and at least a quarter of a mile away it flew straight into a single, tall, dead snag. It was easy to find, since there wasn't another tree, living or dead, in sight. When I cleaned it I discovered that a No. 4 shot had gone through its heart.

A heart shot, whether one pellet in a bird or a rifle bullet in big game, is always fatal—but seldom does it kill instantly. In fact, I suspect a great deal of game is killed but never found because inexperienced hunters expect a heart-shot animal to drop in its tracks. Then, when it shows no sign of being hit, they assume they have missed and fail to follow it.

I had a perfect opportunity to observe the effect of a heart shot on a bull elk early one morning. I was sitting quietly in open lodgepole pine timber along the route a herd of elk took from the grassy south slope where they fed at night to the spruce thicket where they spent their days when I saw a single bull approaching. His route would bring him past me at 75 yards. I didn't move a muscle. The breeze was in my favor and he didn't suspect my presence.

He was walking slowly, taking an occasional bite of the grouse whortleberry that carpeted the lodgepole forest, but maintaining a steady pace. When he was directly in front of me and full broadside, he lowered his head for another mouthful of this dwarf huckleberry. I pulled up my knees, rested my elbows on them, and wrapped the sling around my arm, virtually in one motion. At his next step I pushed off the safety, then shot, holding for his heart.

He didn't drop. He didn't leap ahead. He didn't start to run. He merely kept on walking! I was so confident my hold had been good I didn't shoot again; there was no place he could disappear for 200 yards, anyway. I'd have plenty of time for another shot if it was necessary.

It wasn't. He walked calmly on for about 50 yards, then stumbled over a log and fell. He was dead. When I dressed him I discovered that the 130-grain .270 bullet had blasted a hole through his heart, as I had aimed.

Heart-shot game reacts in various ways, however. I virtually shot the heart out of a little whitetail once, but it wheeled and ran like a gazelle for 200 yards. My hunting partner on another trip shot at a three-point (Western count) mule deer that bounded 10 yards over a rise and disappeared. "I missed him!" he exclaimed in a voice both incredulous and anguished.

"Maybe not," I told him, and when we walked over the ridge we found his buck lying just out of sight. He was dead, shot fairly through the heart.

Still two more reactions, this time on elk. It was one of those cold, rainy, dull, fall mornings when every branch you touch releases a shower and your legs and feet are soon as wet as if you had waded a river. I had been hunting since daylight without seeing even a track when, about 10 o'clock, I decided to sit down on a grassy hillside and smoke a pipe.

At the bottom of the slope, 200 yards below, a stringer of small spruce trees, about 20 feet tall and thick as bristles on a brush, ran up the bottom. I had stuffed my pipe, but had not yet lit it, when I saw two cow elk walking along my edge of the trees. A fat cow was exactly what I wanted; there is no finer meat, and these were as slick as grain-fed thoroughbreds.

I pocketed my pipe and shot at the leader, aiming for her heart. Instantly, both plunged into the trees and out of sight. But seconds later they both came out the far side and turned to the right, again giving me a broadside shot. They were not running full out, but were pacing in that smooth, ground-eating gait elk have. Again, I shot at the leader, holding for her heart. She dropped in her tracks.

While I was dressing her, the rain changed to snow. I finished, got her up off the ground, and was washing the blood from my hands with snow when I happened to look back through an opening among the trees. I saw something that seemed out of place—a brown rock with no snow on it. Everything else in sight was covered. A dreadful thought soaked through; it had to be another elk.

I thought, Oh, no! If there was anything I didn't want to do it was to kill two elk. In the first place, I don't believe in killing game for my hunting partner or in letting him kill game for me. In the second place, the fellow I was hunting with wanted a big bull for a trophy. Now, I would have to ask him to tag one of my cows.

What happened was this: There had been three cows, not two, and one was among the trees out of sight, when I shot. The first cow had plunged about 15 feet into the trees and dropped. When cows No. two and three ran out I assumed I had missed and killed the second elk. Both were shot through the heart; one went 5 yards and the other fell in her tracks.

So you never can tell. The only hit that invariably drops an animal as though struck by lightning is one that destroys the central nervous system—brain or spinal cord. I prefer a neck shot on hoofed game when the animal is close and motionless, but this calls for precise shooting, while any hit in the boiler works will eventually be fatal, even though the bullet may not touch the animal's heart.

Preventing the loss of wounded, though apparently missed, big game is comparatively easy. Go immediately to the spot where it was, whether standing or running, when you shot. Find its tracks, Look very, very carefully for any indication of a hit—such as a chip of bone. A bullet often clips off a little tuft of hair where it enters an animal. I once tracked down and recovered a bull elk I honestly thought I had missed simply because I saw a single drop of fresh blood on a blade of grass.

In any case, whether you find a clue or not, follow any big game for at least a quarter of a mile. Don't hurry. Pause frequently to look for sign, and to study the terrain ahead. I found the bull just mentioned by standing still and looking in the direction his tracks were headed. Though still alive, he was lying down, well screened by heavy cover. Barely moving, I shifted to one side until I found an opening through which I could finish him off with a neck shot.

One of the most common misconceptions among neophyte hunters is that the shock of the bullet will knock down their game. I don't believe that any bullet ever knocks down any big-game animal. It's like saying a fish "threw" a plug. No fish yet has thrown a plug. He may jump and dislodge it. Then the spring of your rod brings the lure sailing through the air toward you. But your rod did it, not the fish.

In the same way, an animal may be standing in such a position that your bullet gives the appearance of knocking him down. He may have most of his weight on one leg, and if you happen to break that leg he's going to flop in that direction. But in the sense that a bowling ball knocks down a pin, a bullet simply cannot knock down big game. Consequently, to harbor the impression that anything you hit will be knocked down is to run a mighty good chance of losing a wounded or perhaps fatally hit animal.

Avoiding the loss of winged game is more difficult, though there are several rules that help:

Pick *one* bird on a covey rise or in a flock of ducks and shoot at it. If you miss, shoot at the same bird again.

Try for another only after you see this bird falling. Never have your heart set on a double and swing to a second bird before the first is coming down.

Whether you shoot at a single, or one bird from a flock or covey, and apparently miss, watch it as far as you can see it. You may be pleasantly surprised.

Though ruffed grouse inhabit such heavy cover you can seldom watch them more than a few yards, try to establish the line of flight. They usually hold a reasonably straight course and they seldom fly far. Even if you made a clean miss, the chance of putting up the same bird again is usually better than trying to find another.

If at all possible, use a dog. Once it learns what hunting is all about, any old mutt is better than no dog at all.

Chapter 20

Hunting Clothes

Before my father made his astounding middle-age intellectual growth—
which, strangely, coincided with the first year or two I earned my own
living—he occasionally volunteered a suggestion about one of my activities.
Hunting, for example. I loved to hunt and he approved. But when I was
seventeen he certainly had some strange ideas.

At that time the well-dressed sportsman wore 16-inch laced leather boots
and things that were, as I remember, called riding breeches. The bottom 6
inches of each leg laced or buttoned tightly around the calf; the pants fitted
snugly at the knees, then flared away from the outside of each thigh so that
the wearer, especially from the rear, had somewhat the appearance of a
tenpin on two pegs.

Like most of the other boys in our community, I thought these outfits
were great. When bad weather gave us an excuse we wore them to school;
the local postmaster wore them all the time. The pictures in *Field &Stream*
showed hardy sportsmen in high laced boots and peg-bottom pants doing
everything from catching trout to shooting grizzlies.

My father, being hopelessly antiquated, didn't even own a pair, and
when from time to time he told me that I'd find walking much easier in 6-
inch shoes and regular trousers it was obvious that this was simply another
of his old-fashioned ideas. His suggestion made no more impression on me
than one of mine made later on *my* teen-age sons.

The boots weighed nearly three pounds apiece. Their high tops constricted circulation, confined sweat, and bound the muscles of my calves. The pants, tight from boot top to well above the knee, were the perfect companion for the boots. It would be hard to imagine a more severe handicap to walking than this combination, yet I struggled along in it for years, lifting an excess pound each time I raised a foot, straining against the tight pants each time I bent a knee.

Of course, I eventually either got wise or else the fad died its well-deserved natural death—probably the latter. The price you pay for being young would be far too high to pay for anything but being young. I confess my foolishness only to prove that while I may never know what the best hunting clothes are, I am closely acquainted with the worst.

I have never subscribed to the adage that clothes make the man; I suspect Caesar in a pair of slacks would have been quite as much a tiger as Caesar in a toga. But I know from experience that clothes can make—or break—the hunt.

I remember a time in Chamberlain Basin when I'd killed my elk and come in to Slim Horn's base camp to wait for a plane out. The weather was stormy and there was no chance of flying, so Slim asked me to be a guide for a day. One of his guests had had nothing but bad luck. I knew the country well and was glad to oblige.

We got an early start and rode out six or seven miles, then tied the horses beside the trail and started hunting. As is often the case, the elk were feeding on the open hillsides at night and spending their days in thickets of lodgepole pine and jungles of spruce. After the first hour of daylight the only chance for a shot was to go into these dense covers after them.

Riding out, my companion wore a bulky down coat with a duck outer shell. I assumed he'd leave it tied behind the cantle of his saddle. Instead, when we started away from the horses he still had this coat on. I suggested leaving it, but he objected, so we went ahead.

That was, without a doubt, the noisiest coat to which I'd ever listened. I could hear a twig scrape against it from 50 feet away, and I've no doubt an elk could hear it four times as far. Furthermore, it was so big and flared out so far that getting through dense cover without brushing against something was simply impossible.

We jumped several elk that day, but we didn't even get a glimpse of them. The noisy coat gave warning of our approach long before they were visible. If my companion did all his hunting in it, the reason for his bad luck was obvious.

Of course, there are kinds of hunting in which noisy clothes make no difference—sheep, goat, antelope, anything in open country where you don't have to make a close approach through brush. But even here quiet clothing is no handicap and could be, at least occasionally, a real help.

And what kind of clothes are quiet? Wool, primarily, or any soft-woven fabric with a nap. I like wool pants and a wool shirt, with a wool jacket over it in cold weather. Any hard, tightly woven fabric, such as duck or denim, is noisy. Rainwear is equally bad. When I'm hunting big game in the rain or falling snow I prefer to wear wool and get wet rather than to endure the hopeless handicap of a slicker in heavy cover.

Shoes, too, can be either a help or a hindrance. Among my other youthful sins I tried boots with leather soles and hobnails. They were heavy, noisy, and cold, and it was impossible to scrape all the mud or snow off them before going into the tent. I now prefer light leather shoes with 8-inch uppers and crepe rubber soles in dry weather, light all-rubber shoes when it's wet.

I've yet to find a pair of insulated pacs that weren't too heavy and stiff for easy walking. An active man doesn't need them when the temperature is above zero, anyway. Pacs with rubber bottoms and leather uppers are fine for day-at-a-time upland hunting, but on any big-game trip where you have wet snow or steady rain, or where the going is tough in marsh or muskeg, they partically guarantee constantly wet feet.

Although I prefer wool outer garments, I've bought my last suit of woolen underwear. Under wool pants, shirt, and jacket, waffle-knit cotton is all an active man needs until the temperature drops below zero. When it's really cold, quilted insulated inner wear is better than wool, and in the usual fall weather light, long cotton is all you need. Shirts and drawers have many advantages over union suits.

Duck hunting, which vies with ice fishing and winter steelhead fishing as the coldest of sports, presents a different set of problems. Here you must sit still. The air is usually damp, and you're often exposed to wind. At the same temperature, I seem to require about four times the insulation in a duck blind that I do in the woods.

I can remember the day when duck hunting meant suffering. There was no way around it. You either wore so many clothes you couldn't move, or else you were cold. Sometimes you wore them and were cold anyway.

Those days are gone forever. I haven't had cold feet since I bought my first pair of insulated hip boots. And I've neither been cold nor rendered helpless by layers of wool since the advent of quilted dacron-insulated underwear. I wear it over lightweight long cotton shirt and drawers to keep it clean, and under tightly woven pants and coat that turn wind and a reasonable amount of rain. I usually wear a wool shirt.

This insulated underwear is simply great. I wouldn't be without it, but it does have one disadvantage: It's an *inner* garment. While you're driving or when you go into a restaurant for a meal you can't shed it without peeling off your outer clothes first, then putting them back on. When you're ready to brave the elements once more you have to reverse the process. And don't let anybody kid you. Any garment that will keep you warm at zero will make you sweat at 70, no matter what it's made of.

Along about the mid-sixties, insulated coveralls hit the market. Since then they've taken my part of the country by storm. Their great advantage is that they are worn over light inner clothing and so can easily be taken off when you go indoors and put on again just as easily when you go out again. Duck hunters and winter steelhead fishermen find them ideal. Farmers wear them driving tractors in cold weather. In fact, all outdoor men whose work or sport requires sitting still under miserable conditions are taking to them like flies to honey. With insulated boots and a suit of these coveralls, duck hunting simply isn't what it used to be.

The best clothes for upland hunting vary with the country and the weather. In the East there are blackberries, and in the South cat briers. In the Southwest almost everything has thorns. You need pants that will keep all these devilish things from raking your hide. The best I ever found were made of light but very tough and tightly woven material, double on the front of the legs. Cuffs are out of place on any hunting trousers.

In the arid West, where we hunt for six weeks in shirt-sleeve weather and there are no briars, I prefer cotton work pants for upland hunting. They're cool, light, and easy to walk in. Furthermore, they're tough, inexpensive, and easy to launder. Along toward midseason—the date depends on the weather—I start wearing light, long, two-piece cotton underwear and a wool shirt with them. Still later when the weather turns cold, wool pants and a wool jacket are in order. This clothing is suitable, of course, only because we don't have to fight our way through heavy cover.

Every so-called hunting coat I ever had was abominable. They were all stiff, heavy, bulky, ill-fitting, uncomfortable, and a real handicap to good shooting. I hunt in shirt sleeves, or else I wear a ski jacket or a light wool cruiser jacket, depending on the weather. And I carry my game and ammunition in one of the sleeveless bird-hunting vests that are available in several styles. They're the only thing for hot weather, which is common in the South, Southwest, and those Western states where the upland seasons open in September.

Actually, the type of hunting vest with straps over the shoulders, which I use, allows for just about any kind of clothing to be worn under it. In cold weather it fits over a jacket.

The best upland hunting shoes are the lightest that give your feet adequate protection. This varies with the terrain, though I prefer 8-inch uppers everywhere. In the rocky chukar country of the West I want stiff counters and toe caps. They prevent bruises and also keep the shoes from running over during the endless miles of walking around steep hillsides. Crepe soles are my choice for upland hunting, as for big game. They're light and quiet and hold well on all kinds of footing.

Oil should be used sparingly, if at all, on leather shoes. Leather's finest quality, aside from its resistance to wear, lies in the fact that it is *not* airtight; rub on enough grease and it loses this valuable feature. You might as well wear rubber. And in wet weather a tub full of boot grease is the poorest kind of substitute for a pair of rubber pacs.

All hunting shoes must fit—fit your feet, that is, not your head. Try them on over the socks you'll wear hunting and make sure there's room for your feet to spread out flat. They'll do it anyway after you've walked ten miles, and if your toes are bound tightly you'll have blisters. A little room to spare is far better than not quite enough.

Socks for hunting, whether they're made of wool, cotton, or nylon, should be thick enough to cushion the feet. I buy fleecy nylon socks because they wear so long, but some hunters don't like them. Wool is always good.

One of the toughest problems in preparing for a hunting trip, particularly in new country, is deciding which clothes to take. My approach is the same as my feelings every time I snap a picture—I hope for the best but expect the worst. No matter where you go, the weather can turn unseasonably hot or cold, or wet, and if you are prepared only for "normal" temperatures you'll be miserable in either case.

A suit of insulated underwear is good insurance against extremely cold weather; cotton pants, shirt, and summer underwear are welcome in unseasonable heat. They're handy to wear around camp, too, while your other clothes are drying. Rain gear is always worthwhile, even though you may not hunt in it. Few experiences are more miserable than an all-day ride in a canoe or on a horse in a driving rain without a slicker. A pair of moccasins to wear in camp, in addition to shoes for both wet and dry weather, are worth their weight; so are an extra pair of gloves and several extra pairs of socks.

Obviously, you can't take everything you can think of unless you go by truck, and even then most of it would only be in the way. But if you are prepared for weather unseasonably warm and unseasonably cold, and for rain—never forget rain—you'll get along all right. With a little planning, you can do this on any trip and still travel reasonably light.

Chapter 21

Hunting in the Snow

The first snow of winter is a magic thing. No other snow is like it. No other manifestation of Nature's alchemy is so obvious, so sudden, or so complete.

I suspect there is no one so leaden that he fails to thrill to the first snow. Certainly, if such a man exists I have yet to meet him. Hunters, because of the very thing in their nature that makes them hunters, are especially susceptible to this magic. We feel almost as though it was worked solely for our pleasure.

Several first snows are vivid in my memory, but one when I was about sixteen is particularly bright for two reasons: It came on Saturday, so I was spared the agony of school when I knew I should be hunting; and the hunting was especially memorable.

By late November, in the farming neighborhood where I grew up, the world was a dull and faded brown. The stubble was weathered. In the plowed fields the rich earth lay dark and colorless. The trees had dropped their brilliant foliage of October, and their naked branches were stark against a leaden sky.

In such a setting, on a Friday evening, my brother Burtt and I worked at our chores, loitering as we always did, and beating darkness by the narrowest of margins. We listened to the mallard gabbling overhead on their way to the stubble fields to feed. This evening their talk seemed

After the first snow, you walk into a new world.

especially urgent. The smoke from the kitchen range hung low, and the breath of east wind that drifted it down across the farmyard to us seemed to bring a hint of something mysterious and wild.

Country people, because they live so close to Nature, and are so dependent on her whims, become nearly as sensitive to her moods as the wild animals. Burtt and I could almost feel a storm.

And so we woke early. The world was strangely quiet. A rooster crowed, his voice half muted. It was still dark, but our father was up, and the lamplight from the kitchen window was reflected by a wall of white. The ground was white. Snow!

It was not long after daylight when we left the house—too early, really, for a snowy morning. But we were anxious and wonderfully excited. The low hills behind the farm were hidden by the falling snow. The familiar orchard, just across the road, was half shrouded and mysterious—a wild forest. The well-known fields into which we turned were remote and half obscured, and it seemed as though we were exploring a strange land.

Ducks were feeding in the corn, which had been husked but was still standing in the rows. We stalked them and killed two fat mallards when they jumped. Then, since others were flying, we concealed ourselves among the stalks, our dog crouching obediently beside us, and killed several more during the next hour.

There is no duck shooting more wonderful than when mallards fly to corn or small-grain stubble in the snow. We loved it—and love it yet—but nearly two months remained during which we could hunt ducks. Quail and pheasant seasons were drawing to a close. So we walked away and left the ducks still coming through the soft and very quiet snow.

We hunted through the corn and along a weedy fence row bordering the alfalfa patch beyond it and through a brushy corner where a covey of bobwhites used. But game was strangely hard to find.

In our inexperience we didn't realize that we were still too early. The upland birds, sensing the approaching storm, had stuffed their crops late the day before. Now they were still snug in their covers. Not until they began to stir around in search of food would they put off scent so Barney, save for sheer luck, could find them.

It must have been 10 o'clock when he first made game. A cock pheasant burst out of a weedy fence corner.

Burtt killed it. Two hundred yards farther we found a covey of quail and got two on the flush, then marked them down and got two more. A pair of pheasant hens were almost where the quail had settled, and we bagged one of them—there was no hen law in those days.

The sky was brighter now and the snow was not falling so heavily. We could see a mile or more. The birds had started to feed; they were everywhere. And the pheasants, which had learned to run like deer after being hunted for five weeks, stuck like bobwhites in the new snow.

We ran out of ammunition—a wonderful experience. We hadn't expected so much shooting. I don't remember how many ducks and quail we had, but we were still three short of the eight pheasants we were permitted. The canvas sacks in which we carried our game were fat and heavy. We were soaking wet and desperately hungry. The few withered prunes we had found still clinging to the trees in Eidemiller's orchard were only enough to whet our appetites.

We hiked back to the house, displayed our game proudly to our mother, soaked up the welcome heat of the kitchen range, and ate everything in sight. Then we stuffed more shells into our pockets and started out again.

The sun was shining when we left the house. The world was new again. The air was crystal-clear. Each bush and tree was bowed under a sparkling load. Yesterday's drab fields were brilliant white and every weed held a proud display of diamonds.

We walked toward the hills where the pheasants were accustomed to find refuge in the brush during midday. The wet snow creaked pleasantly underfoot. Barney, weary from running through it all morning, was content to follow quietly at heel.

As we plodded slowly along—to tell the truth, Burtt and I were a little weary too—we saw a pheasant track. We followed it. At the end of 200 yards it disappeared in a low, thick bush about 6 feet across. We walked around the bush. It didn't come out.

This was great! I was so excited that I can't remember what Barney did. But Burtt and I stood on opposite sides of the bush and kicked it. A gorgeous rooster, his colors doubly vivid in the brilliant light, took to the air. Burtt let him down.

We walked on until we found another pheasant track leading to another bush, and the result was just the same. So was the third—and the hunt was over.

I still like to hunt in falling snow and on snow that has just fallen, particularly when it is winter's first. No doubt my feeling stems partly from the memory of many such pleasant and successful days. I'm sure it comes partly from my enjoyment in being out in the fresh, new world of snow. But there is a practical reason, too: The first day of snow is an excellent time— perhaps the best time—to hunt many kinds of game, both large and small.

Scent, always mysterious to man, whose nose is useful only to support his glasses, is doubly so in snow. I am inclined to think that falling snow carries the terrifying man odor to the ground and so is to our advantage in any kind of big-game hunting. If this is true, it would explain why a good dog sometimes appears helpless in the snow. Yet on other days, when conditions appear identical to me, the same dog will go from point to point as though the birds were whistling to him.

I don't like to hunt in rain. I think the birds and animals hate it as much as I do and don't move around in it any more than necessary. With few exceptions, I have found rainy days to be poor ones for hunting anything from deer to ducks.

Snow is different. Deer and elk, primarily nocturnal in their feeding, frequently browse all through the first day of snow. Ducks feed in the stubble when it snows, trading back and forth between the fields and water, and making for good shooting all day long. Upland birds feed longer, and those that are notorious runners, such as pheasants, chukars, and California valley quail, often stick tight when the ground is covered by two or three inches of snow.

The fastest quail shoot I ever had was on a snowy morning—the first snowy morning—late one fall. A heavy snow fell early, but by the time Clare Wissel and I parked beside the tangle-brush bottom where we planned to hunt valley quail, only an occasional lazy flake was sifting down and the sky was beginning to get bright.

Valley quail are great runners. A covey seems to flow over the ground, every plumed head erect and every foot flying. They look like an army of bugs, but no bugs can run like they do. These little quail can run off and leave the longest-legged man in town behind.

This morning was to be different. A covey of twenty-five or thirty birds flushed when we slammed the car door and went down well scattered in a patch of knee-high greasewood 100 yards away. We went over there with Rip. He pointed. Clare kicked out a single and shot it, and before Rip got to it to retrieve he pointed again.

Clare went on to find his bird. I walked in to flush this one. It proved to be two. We got both. Rip brought one but pointed again before he found the second. He really didn't have a chance to hunt; he could take only a few steps before he had to point again.

Somehow, before we were through with the first covey we were into the second. Before we had put up all of its singles we were into the third. And before we had fairly started hunting we were back in the car with our limit of ten birds apiece, eating our lunch and marveling at what had happened to us.

No bobwhites ever stuck tighter than did these light-footed valley quail. The reason, of course, was snow. They didn't want to get their little feet cold—I guess. To complete the story I must admit what we discovered when we came back several days later. The old snow was crisscrossed with quail tracks and they ran like rabbits!

Actually, it doesn't really matter so much what we hunt in snow as the fact that we are hunting. I remember hunting cottontails in a weedy, briery field, surrounded by New York State's lovely woods, as clearly as I do hunting elk in the wild mountains near the Idaho-Montana line, also in snow, a decade later.

Snow makes good hunting. Snow also makes it good to be hunting. The atavistic core of modern hunters thrills to the first snow as did our forebears ten thousand years ago. Then it warned them to seek food, just as it does the wild animals today. And for all our civilization, we still feel something of this primitive urgency.

If the winter's first snow heralds the Christmas season—and if we are free to hunt—then we are doubly blessed. This is the best time of all to walk quietly afield in the fresh, new world of snow.

Part VI

WHEN THE HUNTER CAMPS

Chapter 22

Selecting the Right Tent

When the beloved tentmaker of Naishápúr died more than eight hundred years ago, he left behind some quatrains that made him immortal. So long as men dream, they will muse over *The Rubáiyát of Omar Khayyám;* so long as they live close to the stars in the clean, far places of the world, their shelter will be a covering of cloth, modified perhaps, but clearly descended from the tents that Omar and his fellows stitched during centuries long gone.

It's pretty hard to come up with something really new in tents. For hundreds of years, wanderers on the desert, in the mountains, and on the

This variety of tents showed up on a spring fishing trip.
From left: modified umbrella, tepee (pyramid), mountain
tent, another pyramid, and finally, as a cook
tent, a 10x12 wall tent with a 10x14 fly as
a front "porch."

plains have lived in tents. Most of them were dissatisfied with their "rag houses," as you'll hear tents called to this day in the West, and tried to make improvements. Gradually, improvements were made, but many of them served only to adapt one particular tent to the conditions peculiar to the area in which it was used.

The tepee of the American Plains Indians is a good example. Being conical and supported by poles on the inside, it withstood the violent winds of the region as though made of rock. Its covering of hides turned wind even when the temperature was 50 below; a fire in the center kept it warm, and an ingenious draft arrangement allowed the smoke to escape from the peak.

But a tepee wouldn't do today. Where would you get the nine or more long, straight poles it requires, and how would you carry them? Besides, pitching a tepee takes time and work. The squaws then were more industrious than they are now.

One winter, on the day after New Year's, my wife and I started on a hunting trip in the desert country of southeastern Oregon. I took my wall tent and the little sheet-iron "sheepherder" stove we use in t, because I expected cold weather. Instead of low temperatures we got wind—violent, continuous wind that blew without letup for three days and nights. It blew so hard that flying dust blocked out the nearby hills like snow. Tumbleweeds, driven by the wind, rolled up the ridge near camp, then sailed a quarter mile through the air.

It was impossible to pitch the tent. In that country, where there are no trees, there is no shelter from the wind. I parked the car broadside to it and blocked the space beneath the body with our food boxes and a canvas. We cooked on the little sheepherder stove in the lee of the car. We ate most of our meals in it and, of course, we slept there.

Toward evening of the fourth day, the wind stopped. It was a relief, though we had become so accustomed to its constant noise and pressure and the blowing dust that everything somehow seemed unreal without it. When we got to camp, I quickly put up the tent and moved in the stove, table, and food boxes, and we enjoyed our first dustless meal.

Half an hour after we finished I was outside chopping wood and Ellen was cleaning up the dishes when the wind struck again. It came with a roar and a cloud of dust and tumbleweeds flying back from wherever they'd gone before. It hit the tent like a wall of water. The canvas bellied halfway to the floor. The ridgepole sagged. The ropes were tight as fiddlestrings.

Ellen was carrying stuff outside when I got there. She knew something had to go. I jerked the chimney off the stove and let it hang through the flapping roof. I grabbed the still-hot stove, using a couple of folded towels, and ran out with it. Then I got the chimney.

The tent went seconds later. There was the harsh sound of ripping canvas, then a wild, crazy flapping, with ropes and stakes and ridge and uprights flying. The wind, once it got inside through the ripped-out wall, raised the tent and tore it into little pieces. The whole thing took only half a minute. We arranged our camp in the shelter of the car again.

A wall tent is great for cold weather in timbered country. You can have a stove inside and cook and eat in comfort. Wet hunting clothes suspended from the ridge dry quickly. But a wall tent wasn't meant for wind. The wide, flat surfaces of walls and roof catch the wind and put tremendous strains on ridgepole, uprights, and ropes. If the canvas and ropes are new and the ridgepole is strong, a wall tent will stand up in wind so hard it scares you. Let that wind blow long enough, however, and eventually something will go.

The comparatively new bungalow tents, which are simply wall tents with

If the weather were always this pleasant on a hunting trip,
you could get along without a tent. But a wall tent
with a stove (note stovepipe) is a good combination
for insurance.

higher walls, are worse. They're great where you have the shelter of trees,
but they won't do in open country. The popular umbrella tents are likewise
vulnerable to wind. I remember yet being asleep in one when it fell in over
me. I woke up thinking I was trapped.

Better than any of these is the wedge tent—a wall tent without walls—of
which there are many variations. Modified wedge tents, variously called
mountain tents, explorer tents, and alpine tents, have been used under the
most extreme conditions on many expeditions. Usually only big enough for
two men to sleep in, with a ridge from 3 to 5 feet high, they can utilize light
material and still withstand a gale, but they are unnecessarily cramped
when the method of transportation permits taking something heavier and
more roomy. I have seen only a few big wedge tents and have never owned
one.

For more than sixty years, the standard tent in the wide-open country of
the West has been what the cowboys and sheepherders call a tepee, but is
more correctly called a pyramid tent, a name that describes it perfectly. It is
the easiest of all tents to pitch—spread it out flat, drive a stake at each

Ted and his wife have used stoves like this "sheepherder" model for many years. When the outside air is zero, a stove like this will make a 10x12 wall tent too warm for comfort in a matter of minutes.

corner, and raise the peak, either with shears outside or with one pole in the center. I have seen a pyramid tent blow down only once. A friend pitched his on loose sand, and a violent wind pulled the stakes out.

One of the finest tents in wind and one that was really new in concept—if such a thing is possible—is the Pop-Tent. It is shaped like an igloo, supported by fiberglass ribs attached to the outside. Named for the way it pops into shape when you set it up and spring the ribs into place, it, too, is very quick and easy to erect. It is not well suited to the use of a stove, however.

There are, of course, many things to think about besides wind when you choose a tent. Most camping is done among trees, and the wind can never reach the velocity there that it does on the prairie or seashore or in the barren Arctic. Weight is always a consideration, and great progress has been made here during recent years. Lighter, tougher, stronger fabrics and aluminum frames have shaved off many pounds.

Most tents are used for summer camping. The umbrella tent or one of its many modern modifications with more room is a good choice. So is one of the new variations of the old standby wall tent. Both are available with inside framing that is easy to put up and eliminates the need for outside poles and guys.

One of the first things to consider is size. How much room do you need? Two adults in separate sleeping bags, which require more space than one double, can sleep comfortably in a tent 8 feet square. You'll have room for clothes and duffel and a 3-foot space between the beds in which to stand while dressing. You can fold the beds back to cook and eat inside if necessary.

This tent provides 32 square feet of floor space per person—an arbitrary figure because you could get by with less and you could use more. On that basis, four people would require 128 square feet. In actual practice, four have more room in a 10x12 tent than two have in an 8x8. The space required for each cot or sleeping bag remains the same, but beds and duffel can be stacked, leaving more free space in which to move around, cook, and eat. On a hunting trip I once slept with five other men in a 10x12 wall tent. We got by, but you should have heard the grumbling when the man in back had to go outside.

Except for families with several young children, I doubt that it's ever a good idea to plan for more than four people to sleep in one tent. Two small ones are easier to handle than one big tent, and in the matter of privacy their advantage is obvious.

Any summer tent, but particularly one to be used by a family, should have a sewn-in floor and screens on doors and windows. Mosquitoes and black flies are an annoyance to a man intent on his fishing; they drive women and children crazy. Fine-mesh nylon screening is best, and the door screen should close with zippers.

If a tent will be exposed to the sun, white fabric is much cooler than any darker color. It's also brigher because the white duck admits sunlight in the daytime and reflects the lantern light at night. Despite this, if you have neighbors, you'll want a tent with opaque walls so your shadow won't show through at night.

The time was when tents were either white, khaki, or dark olive green. Those days are gone forever. You can buy a tent in your choice of many bright, cheerful colors now. One good feature some companies offer is blue, green, or khaki walls with a roof of yellow or white. This lets through more light and is not nearly so depressing as a dark, drab tent when you're confined to it by rainy weather.

For hunting-camp tents, material tightly woven of long-staple cotton, made water-resistant and rotproof by a process that leaves the texture dry, is best. Thickness of fabric is described by the weight per square yard. If the material is topnotch, 7- or 8-ounce weight is strong enough for any normal use. Ten-ounce duck is as heavy as anyone should require.

One point to remember, however, is this: Although a light tent is easier to handle and packs into a smaller bundle, it also requires more care. A thin fabric won't withstand the chafing and abrasion a heavier one will.

When cotton fibers get wet they swell, making the fabric very tight. A tent of 10-ounce, untreated canvas will turn rain or melting snow. At the same time, inside moisture from cooking or breathing escapes. A cotton tent is a dry tent.

Nylon fibers don't swell. Despite its great strength, nylon fabric is inferior for tents. If it has a waterproof coating, it drips with inside moisture or collects frost; if not, you have to stretch a fly above it to keep out rain. The fabric of the best tent I ever had was a mixture of nylon and cotton and combined the good qualities of both, but I don't know where to get another like it.

Tent ropes should be nylon. It eliminates the shrinking and stretching of hemp or cotton, so annoying during and after every rain. And when you break camp after your fall hunt, picking the knots out of frozen hemp rope is no treat.

The majority of modern tents have fairly flat roofs in order to give good headroom clear to the walls without excessive height. This is fine in summer. In late fall and winter a wall tent is better because it's easier to beat the snow off the steep roof.

Most of the tent stakes you buy, whether plastic or metal, are suitable only for soft earth. Bridge spikes about 10 inches long are far better in rocky soil. They're heavy, but they last for years, and if they do bend you can hammer them straight. To pull them, grab the head with a pair of pliers, and twist back and forth a time or two. Then they lift out easily. (I buy mine at the local hardware store.)

Finally, don't worry if your new tent doesn't look as trim and neat the first time you pitch it as it did in the pictures. Nobody ever raised vegetables as handsome as those in the seed catalogue, either. A few slack spots do no harm, and you'll always have them unless you find perfectly level ground. I've been looking for just a *little* patch of that—near good hunting, of course, for more than forty years.

Chapter 23

Knives, Axes, and Sharpening Them

I once watched a friend attempting to haggle the innards out of some trout with a knife so dull it wouldn't cut butter if you heated it red hot. Always helpful, I said, "Why don't you sharpen your knife?"

"Hell," he replied, "I can't sharpen anything. If I tried, I'd only make it duller."

I've heard many similar statements and I never cease to be surprised by them, though I suppose I shouldn't be. I grew up on a farm and went to a country school and every boy in it had a pocketknife that was his pride and joy. They weren't switchblades, either. We hadn't even heard of such things. Our knives were strictly utilitarian, similar to the knives our fathers carried.

Most of them had one big blade, one small blade, and a leather punch. We farmed with horses then, and the punch blade was essential in repairing harness. We used our knives every day, for everything from making willow whistles when the sap ran in the spring to dressing game we shot in the fall.

It was a matter of great pride with all of us to keep our knives sharp. We spent hours whetting them, and most of us finished the job by stropping the blade along the side of a boot. The boy who finally got his knife so sharp he could shave the hair off the back of his hand had achieved the ultimate. He had real status.

I still have a reminder of this—a long, thin scar along the side of one finger. A neighbor boy and I were throwing our knives at a mark on a tree and I foolishly reached to pull mine out just as he released his. The razor-sharp blade made a deep cut two inches long.

I started early learning how to sharpen not only knives but also axes, scythes, shovels, and all the other edged tools we used. This would not be the case with a boy who grew up in a city. He would have little opportunity to use a knife, much less learn to sharpen it. So I really shouldn't be surprised when somebody says he can't sharpen a knife. Yet all sportsmen need sharp knives every day; axes or hatchets, occasionally. A sharp knife makes everything from skinning a moose to filleting a walleye easier; the only thing you can cut with a dull knife is your finger.

Most new knives aren't sharp. They usually have a gradual taper from the back of the blade toward the edge, then an abrupt bevel. The manufacturers put this kind of edge on them because they know a lot of buyers are going to use their knives to peel the insulation off wire, clean spark plugs, open cans, and do similar rough work. The factory edge will take this kind of punishment. But it will never satisfy the man who has learned to use and enjoy a sharp knife.

The best stone for sharpening a new knife is a fairly big one, perhaps 2 inches wide by 8 inches long, with coarse grit on one side and fine on the other. You can use a smaller stone, but the sharpening process will take longer because you must make more strokes. This is the stone you use to take off a lot of metal in a hurry. You'll need it only for a new knife or an extremely dull one. Some experts put oil on it, but I prefer to use mine dry because it cuts faster.

Lay the stone on a bench, coarse side up. A piece of rubber, such as a strip cut from an old inner tube, under the stone will do two things: It will keep the stone from sliding on the bench under the pressure of your knife strokes, and it will keep the stone clean. A dry stone must be clean, If the pores fill up with dirt and grease, scrub it with a brush and detergent, then rinse it well.

Now, the most important thing in sharpening is to maintain a uniform angle between blade and stone for the full length of every stroke. I start at the far end of the stone and bring the blade toward me, edge ahead, as though I were slicing a thin layer off the hone. The knife handle is against the side of the stone at the start of the stroke; the tip of the blade is on the stone when the stroke ends. I then turn the knife over and reverse the process, with the tip of the blade on the stone at the start of the stroke, the base on the stone at its end.

Throughout the entire sharpening process, I try to maintain a constant angle of 20 degrees between blade and stone. This is about right for most knives, and for most purposes such as dressing game, slicing bacon, or whittling soft wood. You can use a somewhat narrower angle with a blade of exceptional steel and wind up with a thinner, more razorlike edge—but the thinner the edge, the more careful you must be to avoid nicking or turning it.

And remember, the edge we're shaping now is for slicing and cutting, not chopping bones or whacking off dry spruce branches. One of the

Closeup shows knife at proper sharpening angle. As you
draw blade across the stone, imagine you're trying to
shave a thin layer from stone's surface.

advantages of a two-bladed pocketknife is that you can leave the abrupt factory bevel on one for rough work and sharpen the other. And if you expect to chop through the pelvis of a deer with your hunting knife, you'd better leave the original edge on it, too, sharpening when necessary to retain it.

During the first phase of sharpening you can safely maintain a fairly heavy pressure on the blade, thereby taking off metal rapidly. But from time to time wipe off the bits of steel and abrasive dust with a dry cloth and hold the blade up with the edge toward you. With good light, you can see a dull edge or any dull spots on an otherwise sharp one. When the edge gets hard to see, turn your stone over and make a few strokes on the smooth side. When you can't see the edge anywhere, you are through with this stone.

Your knife is now sharp. Many sportsmen never go any further because this edge actually serves quite well for many purposes. But a microscope would show that it is actually quite irregular, with little fingers of steel sticking up somewhat like the teeth of a saw. In use these teeth soon become broken off or turned down and the knife needs sharpening again.

For the keenest and longest-lasting edge, you need another stone, an extremely smooth one such as an Arkansas oilstone. This is a natural rock of fine, uniform texture which for many years has had a reputation for putting the best edge on a blade. Put a few drops of light oil on it and, again, sharpen with uniform strokes, the edge of the blade ahead, maintaining the same angle. Only now don't press hard. Your purpose isn't to remove a lot of metal, but to smooth the edge. Half a dozen strokes each way may be enough.

One of the most important rules of sharpening is this: Don't overdo it. Once your knife is sharp, you need only to smooth the edge so it will cut better and stay sharp longer.

There are several ways to test a blade for sharpness. I hold it in my left hand and touch it gently with the side of my trigger finger. I can feel any roughness or dullness, and a really sharp edge will cut into the skin with virtually no pressure at all. But maybe this is a little tricky; I get by because I've been doing it ever since grammar school days.

You can pull the edge over the end of your thumbnail, exerting no pressure but the weight of the knife. If the blade is sharp, it will bite into the nail. You can feel any rough or dull spots. Or you can hold a piece of paper by one side and slice into the other. A keen edge will cut it without tearing or wrinkling. And, of course, you can always shave a few hairs off the back of your hand.

So now your knife is really sharp. How do you keep it that way? You've already done the hard work; maintenance is easy if you don't wait until it is too dull. You can carry a small Arkansas oilstone in your kit and give the blade a few gentle strokes from time to time. Or you can use a steel, the instrument with which butchers have kept their knives keen for ages.

The purpose of a steel is not to remove metal from the blade but to smooth the edge by realigning the microscopic teeth along it. If a knife is really dull, with an edge you can see, use a stone first. But to keep an already sharp knife keen, the steel is excellent. Maintain the same angle you did on the hones and, again, draw the edge toward you with gentle pressure. Don't try to hurry, especially at first.

After you have used any knife a while and sharpened it several times, you may find that a modification of the 20-degree blade-to-stone angle is desirable. A tough, hard blade will hold a thinner edge, while a softer one may require a more abrupt edge. Or, with a relatively soft but tough steel, such as the good new stainless, you may find it desirable to make the final sharpening strokes on the fine stone at a greater angle. This gives a minute dubbing off, similar to the original factory edge, but much thinner. It cuts well, but doesn't turn so easily.

There is one knife that requires a blade shape and sharpening procedure different from the ones I have described. This is the filleting knife. A fish knife should be sharp, of course, but when it comes to peeling the fillets off the skin, a straight taper isn't so good. The edge of a good filleting knife is somewhat rounded on both sides so it will ride over the skin without cutting into it. Of course, a narrow, thin blade is desirable, too, but the importance of having the sides rounded toward the edge is sometimes overlooked.

Like knives, most axes come from the factory with a thick, strong blade for rough work. Such blades are fine for splitting, but not very good for chopping.

You can safely use a power stone to thin an ax blade if you dip it in water frequently to keep it from getting too hot and drawing the temper, or you can use a file to work an extremely dull, nicked ax blade into shape, though veteran woodsmen would never permit a file to touch their axes, only a stone. But then, they never chopped against the ground, so they never had a really dull ax.

An ax blade should be somewhat rounded in cross section for most work. A straight-taper blade bites into the wood easily, but sticks worse. And an ax blade ground somewhat thinner a couple of inches back from the edge frees itself most easily of all.

If you must file an ax, work with the edge toward you and make your strokes toward where the handle fits through the head. A thick edge and abrupt taper, like the factory bevel on a knife blade, are good for rough work but don't cut so well. File with constant, moderate pressure, and lift the file as you return it for each new stroke. Dragging it back doesn't remove any more metal; it only dulls the file.

If you use your ax properly, always having a log or block under the wood you're chopping, you should never need a file after the first sharpening. The fine side of your coarser knife hone or a round ax stone (made with rounded edges, too, so it won't wear holes in pack or pocket) will keep an ax blade smooth and keen if it is used often enough to avoid extreme dullness. With an ax, as with a knife, frequent sharpening saves work in the long run—and you always have a good tool with which to work.

Sharp tools are a delight to use. Dull ones are a constant annoyance.

Sharp tools do good work; dull ones can only haggle. Furthermore, keeping them sharp actually requires little time and effort. And in case you have never sharpened knives or axes properly before, you will soon discover that

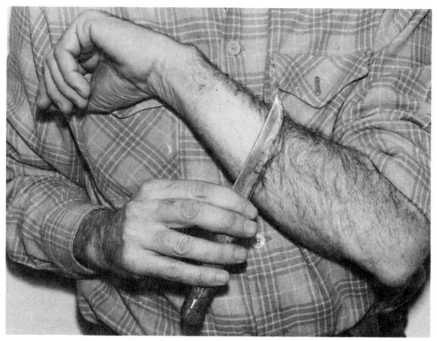

Ted's old knife, made in a mine blacksmith's shop, passes
one of the classic tests for sharpness.

sharpening, like anything else requiring some thought and skill, provides considerable satisfaction in itself.

Like a fine fly rod or an exceptional gun, a good knife eventually comes to occupy a warm spot in a hunter's heart. He treasures it far beyond its monetary value. I have such a knife and I acquired it long before the days of the fine, modern stainless steel and custom-crafted blades.

In the summer of 1933 my brother Burtt and I made a backpacking trip up the Boise River beyond the end of the road. When we came to the old Boise King Mine, we spent the night with Art Stevens and his son Billy.

We got to talking about knives during the evening, and Art said, "I had a world-beater once. You could dress a deer and then shave with it, and never touch it to a stone, either."

Of course, I asked him where he got it, and he told me the following story:

"When I opened up the mine in 1914, I had a blacksmith who was a genius. There was nothing he couldn't do with steel—and in those days, when you might have to send to Salt Lake City to replace a broken shaft, such a man was invaluable.

"Anyway, he was so good that one day I asked him if he'd make me a knife. He said he would, so I sent to Chicago and got a bar of razor steel. When it came I gave it to him and told him to make a knife for himself and one for me.

"After a week or two I was down at the shop one morning and asked him if my knife was ready. He said, 'Yep,' and walked out to the back. When he came out, he had a 60-penny spike in one hand and the knife in the other, and he was rolling shavings off the spike like it was a willow! I said, 'My God, man, that's a nail!'

"He said, 'That's all right. I've got a whole keg of 'em back there.'

"Well, I carried that knife for ten years. Then I either lost it or somebody stole it—I was never sure which. I've had a dozen knives since, but none of them could hold a candle to the old one."

In 1936, I started to work as a reporter for a Boise newspaper. On my beat, I used to pass a little hole-in-the-wall shop where an old guy sharpened knives and scissors and filed saws. One day I noticed a picture of the Boise King Mine in the window, so I went in and got to visiting. I said I knew Art Stevens and the old man said he used to work for Art and we let it go at that. But afterward I would stop in occasionally and chew the rag, and one day we got to talking about knives.

"When Art opened up the Boise King in 1914," he said, "I was his blacksmith. One time he sent to Chicago and got a bar of razor steel and I made two knives out of it, one for him and one for me. After a while he came down to the shop and asked if his knife was ready. I went out back to get it.

"I happened to notice a keg of 60-penny spikes sitting there so I picked up one and when I walked out I was rolling shavings off it with Art's knife." The old man chuckled. "Art never got over that. I reckon he's got it yet."

"No," I replied, "he told me about it. He lost it in twenty-four. Have you still got the one you made for yourself?"

"Yep. Don't use it much any more."

I could feel my blood pressure mounting, but I tried to conceal my excitement and said, "You wouldn't want to sell it, would you?"

He thought that over. Finally he said, "Well, I'm getting so damn old I'll probably never go hunting again anyway. I suppose I might as well sell it."

I asked him what he'd take and he named a figure that happened to be just half my weekly paycheck. Naturally, I bought it.

The ax stone is round and has rounded edges. A good
version to take on hunting trips, it has coarse grit on
one side, fine grit on the other.

As I was giving this chapter the final editing, sixty-three years after my
knife was made in a mine blacksmith shop, I walked out to the kitchen and
got it out of the knife drawer—my wife uses it all the time because it's
always sharp—and gave it the shaving test. Sure enouth, it cut hair off my
arm like a razor, and I can't remember when I last sharpened it!

You want to buy that knife? Hah!

Part VII

LORE OF THE MASTER WOODSMAN

Chapter 24

Tracking Your Game

I doubt that I've gone hunting once in the past ten years without thinking of the fellow who said, "I can sneak up on them all right. The only trouble is, I don't know where to sneak." Obviously, his brain will never be a burden, or he wouldn't have made such a remark, but when you consider it seriously—and he was dead serious—you must admit that he did have something. If we only knew where to sneak, there'd be nothing to bagging any kind of game from mouse to moose.

It is in deciding where to sneak that the arts of tracking and stalking enter the picture. Stalking, which really could be called sneaking, is primarily a skill of the open country. There you often see game at a distance—

Tracks will tell you what game was there and about how
long ago, which way it was headed, and
what it was doing.

sometimes several miles away—and stalk it until you get within range. Tracking is useful anywhere, though the culmination of a successful tracking job is frequently a stalk.

When I come across a set of tracks, I often think, The animal that made these is at the other end. Fresh or old, clear or faint, they connect me with him. They'll lead me to him if I follow them intelligently and read them correctly.

To an experienced woodsman, an animal's tracks tell the story of what it was doing as plainly as if it had left a written account. Suppose, for example, you cut the trail of a band of elk in fresh snow, early in the morning. At first you have trouble telling the direction in which they were heading. The tracks wander back and forth, cross each other, and often turn at right angles.

After you have followed them for a few hundred yards, however, you decide that the band was working around the southern slope of a long hogback. You know it was snowing lightly when you got up to stoke the fire at midnight and there is no snow in the tracks; so they were made sometime within the past six hours. When elk wander like that, they are feeding. They'll feed until shortly after daylight, then bed down in a spruce pocket for the day. With a little luck, you'll be into them by 10 o'clock.

Had your elk tracks been more closely bunched and holding steadily to one direction, they would have indicated that the band was traveling. Following them would probably be futile. They might have gone ten miles before they stopped.

Though this particular example applies primarily to animals such as elk and mule deer that are often hunted while migrating from summer to winter range, it is true to a degree of any game. Wandering tracks indicate a feeding animal that probably won't go far; beeline tracks promise a long trail and a cold bed.

Knowledge of your quarry, which admittedly must come largely from experience, is the most important thing in tracking. As you acquire it you develop the ability to tell what the animal was doing, where it is likely to go, and the kind of spot in which it is apt to stop.

There are many obvious signs that anyone should recognize, however, such as bunched, widely spread, and deep tracks. They indicate a startled, bounding animal. Whether to follow them depends on the species and the relative abundance or scarcity of game. A scared whitetail won't go nearly so far as a frightened elk, but he'll be mighty hard to approach the second time.

Every former country boy or Scout can tell the direction in which an animal was going at a glance. Others can easily remember that the tracks of most hoofed game are shaped somewhat like hearts or arrowheads, all pointing toward the animal at the end of the trail.

Tracks made by a deer that was just poking along show this characteristic shape most obviously. The hoofs of a bounding deer will be widely spread and the dewclaws (rudimentary toes at the back of the hoof) will show in soft earth or snow.

The tracks of domestic sheep or pigs—the only animals likely to be confused with deer—are not so pointed. Sheep hoofs are wide-spaced, blunt-toed, and parallel. Hog tracks are more rounded than heart-shaped.

The tracks of a bighorn ram are very much like those of a big mule-deer buck—bigger than a whitetail's—and the tracks of ewes and lambs are similar to those of does and fawns. Mountain-goat tracks are noticeably squarish, and those made by a big billy are larger than the tracks of ram or buck—nearly as big as those of a cow elk. Antelope have no dewclaws; otherwise their tracks resemble those of deer.

Elk tracks are similar in shape to deer hoofprints, though somewhat more rounded and more than twice as big. Moose tracks are twice as big again as elk tracks, with long, parallel hoofs and with the dewclaws always showing in soft earth or snow.

Cat tracks, whether made by bobcat or cougar, are round—simply enlargements of the ones that tabby leaves in the snow. The typical bobcat track is about the size of a silver dollar, an adult cougar's bigger than that of the biggest dog. Both prints show only the pad and four toes, just like tabby's. Lynx tracks are bigger than a bobcat's and sometimes show the fur fringe. No member of the cat family leaves prints of its toenails, whereas all members of the dog family do. This, coupled with the longer, narrower shape of the latter, should prevent you from confusing the two.

Bear tracks normally reveal the print of all five claws. The general shape of the front feet is rounded. The impression left by the back feet is not unlike that of a barefoot boy's, though if a bear is "on his toes" the print of his back foot is short and wide. With all soft-footed animals—bear, cat, fox, or coyote—the pad is always at the rear of the track and the toes point in the direction in which the animal was going, whether you can see the imprint of the nails or not.

While following a trail don't try to watch the tracks right at your feet. They're easier to see at some distance—possibly 4 or 5 yards. Alternate your glances at the footprints with careful looks ahead. After all, the purpose of following a trail is usually to get a shot at the animal that made it. If your eyes are glued to the ground, you're likely to blunder into your quarry and spoil your chances.

Try to get some idea of the general direction in which the animal was going as soon as you can after starting to follow it. Then if you lose the trail—as we all do occasionally—remember that any game will normally pick the easiest, most logical route unless wounded or frightened. Go ahead a few yards in the direction you'd take yourself, and you'll probably pick up

Track of deer (lower left) and elk (upper right) with
wooden match to indicate size. Photo was taken
about 9 A.M.; both tracks were made in dust the night
before. Deer track is somewhat older.

the trail again. This trick often saves a lot of time when you come to a patch
of rock, and even if it fails you can always go back to the last visible track.

A bear is an exception. You can't guess where he may go, and I question
whether following a bear track without the aid of dogs is ever a good idea,
though I have done it successfully. A bear's brain works differently from
that of any other creature, and what looks logical to him might not to you.
For example, he may get a whiff of carrion half a mile away and make a
sudden right-angle turn to investigate it.

I've heard many hunters say that they could tell a buck track from one
made by a doe. Maybe they can, but I wouldn't bet a dime on doing it
consistently. There are two things on which I normally base an opinion,
however: First, an exceptionally large track was probably made by a buck,
because the biggest deer are bucks—though a big doe leaves a larger track
than many a buck worth shooting. Second, if you observe a lot of aimless
dancing around and pawing, the animal probably was a buck. The male of
the species begins to get foolish in late autumn.

I know of just one sure way to tell a buck's trail, and you seldom get a

This deer track in moist, sandy soil is probably only about
two hours old.

chance to use it. If you find a bed that a deer left without being frightened, you probably will see that it urinated before doing so. The urine of a buck (or a bull elk) will be approximately in the middle of the bed; that of a doe (or a cow elk) just outside the edge.

The most important point to establish when you strike a track is its age. Was it made an hour ago? Two hours? Or two days? Obviously, it would be foolish to follow a trail that is too old. If snow is falling, of course, there is no problem, but we seldom encounter a condition so perfect. Maybe it snowed yesterday and cleared off during the night. If so, it probably frosted. There will be frost in the tracks made last evening, but none in those made early this morning.

The snow often melts a little during the day. The same day's tracks will be clean and sharp, with slick bottoms; those made from the time the snow froze in the evening until it started to thaw next morning will be poorly defined, because of the crumbly nature of the frozen snow.

On dry, dusty soil it sometimes is impossible to tell whether a track is a day or a week old. If you get out early after a frost or a dew, however, you can easily tell tracks that were made after it fell. A recent track in moist earth is sharp and clean; the older it is, the more the dirt will have crumbled down around the edges. Most of the grass pressed down by a passing animal will spring back up within two hours. Weeds with stiff stems that break will stay down.

Droppings are probably the best clue to the time lapse between the

Deer track and droppings, probably three or four days old. This photo was taken near the sharply defined track in the previous photo. But in this photo, grains of sand have gradually tumbled into the track, making it indistinct. The droppings are dry.

animal's passing and your arrival. In a wet spot, water oozing into a track means that he was there very recently. Tracks full of muddy water indicate that he went by several hours before; tracks full of water that has cleared are old.

In the absence of snow, there will be many times when you'll see tracks here and there, but attempting to follow them would be a waste of time. It is always worthwhile to observe them, however, and to read their story as fully as possible. They will tell you how much game there is in the area you're hunting, and whether it is sticking around or passing through. Even though you don't follow them, tracks will tell you where you might see game feeding in late evening or early morning and approximately where it is bedding down for the day.

As you begin to approach the end of the trail—which you may determine from your knowledge of the kind of spot that particular species chooses to bed down in for the day, the distance you've followed it from the area in which it was feeding, or simply a hunch—it is time to sneak. You should now forget the tracks and stalk the cover. Approach very slowly and very quietly and *always* into the wind, even though you may have to leave the trail and make a circle to do so.

There will be many times when you guess wrong. There will be others when you snap a twig or make some other blunder and hear your quarry go out the far side without giving you a chance for a shot. Sometimes the wind will change and betray you. Occasionally, however, everything will be correct, the wind will behave, you'll make a flawless stalk. Then suddenly, as you pussyfoot along, straining your eyes ahead and to both sides, you'll make out the form of your quarry, resting undisturbed and watching his backtrail.

This is the proof of your woodsmanship. And in itself alone it is one of the greatest thrills of hunting.

Chapter 25

Foiling Game's Keen Nose

Scent, as any man who has spent much time behind either hounds or pointing dogs knows only too well, does many strange things. Here it lies; there it evaporates or drifts away. At one time it is strong; at another it apparently doesn't exist. Whatever it may be doing at the moment, however, it is always of the utmost importance to the big-game hunter. All kinds of game are frightened by the scent of man. A sound or a movement may alarm a buck, but he will often hesitate to make sure. Let him smell man, though, and he is gone. Even such keen-sighted game as bighorn sheep put more confidence in their noses than in their eyes.

Under favorable conditions, game can smell a man at an incredible distance. Fortunately for man, with his inferior senses and clumsy walk, conditions are not always favorable for the game. Sometimes the odds are in his favor. I discovered something on an elk and deer hunt years ago that has been extremely helpful a number of times since.

It had been a hard go. We had put in long hours and covered many miles, but now it finally was over. Our deer and elk were skinned, quartered, enclosed in meat bags for protection against flies, and safely hung above the reach of bears. Our packer would be along in a few days to bring them in. There was nothing to worry about.

Nevertheless I decided one morning to revisit the scenes of the various

Test the breeze with dust, smoke, dry snow, or punk from
a rotten log. Then hunt into it. Game can't smell you
when you hunt upwind toward it.

kills and check. A black bear is clever when it comes to getting at a choice
piece of meat, and there were lots of bears that fall. I was on my way,
walking right along through open lodgepole timber, when I saw a bull elk
about 100 yards ahead, facing away from me, feeding. I sat down on a log
and looked at him through the scope. He was a good one, with six points on
each side, and my first thoughts were something to this effect: Wouldn't you

know! I walk a thousand miles before I get a shot. Now that I'm through, I blunder right into one!

As I sat there watching I attempted to figure out an explanation. I had been walking straight downwind for half a mile—I was sure of that because the rain had been hitting me on the back of the neck while my face remained dry. Though I had made no particular attempt to walk silently, the rain had quieted the pine needles, grass, and grouseberry bushes with which the forest was carpeted. It was the matter of scent that had me puzzled. Why hadn't the bull smelled me?

I sat there half an hour, watching him and wondering about it, being careful not to move when his meanderings headed him in my direction. He wandered around cropping grass, sometimes a little above my level on the slope, sometimes below it, occasionally somewhat closer than when I first saw him, and finally fed away downhill into a spruce thicket.

The wind was constant all this time, flowing gently toward him. Never did he suspect my presence. If he had smelled me, he would have bolted.

Man's olfactory sense is so inferior to that of all wild animals that we can learn nothing from our own experience. I've smelled skunks and bull elk before I saw them, but they are about my limit, and I doubt that my nose is much different from anybody else's. We can learn, however, by watching animals that do have good noses, and since most hunters have a more or less constant association with dogs of various kinds, they provide the best opportunity.

Although I failed to hit on an explanation for the bull's not smelling me at the time, I didn't forget about it. A couple of years later, after a fruitless day spent hunting pheasants and quail in good country with a dog of proven ability, the answer suddenly came to me. Here was a perfect analogy.

Pointing dogs depend on body scent to locate birds. Game animals likewise depend on the body scent of man to warn them of his presence. In both cases it had been raining. Could the rain have carried the birds' odor to the ground so that the dog was unable to detect it? Could it, likewise, have washed my scent out of the air so that the bull elk was unable to smell me?

I think it did. I believe that is the only possible explanation. I have hunted many different varieties of upland birds in the rain and I have never done well. Obviously, pheasants don't fly up above the clouds and sail around in the bright sunlight every rainy day. They're right there on the ground somewhere, but they're hard to find because they sit tight, and whatever scent they do give off is washed to earth by the rain.

Once I got to thinking about the matter in this light, I remembered that I had approached game quite closely many times in the rain, frequently when I was just walking along, unmindful of wind direction. Then I began to recall instances when it had been snowing—I once wandered right into the middle of a band of elk during a snowstorm—and came to the realization that snow does the same thing. Raindrops and snowflakes carry your scent to the earth.

So game is less likely to smell you when it is raining or snowing. This helpful bit of knowledge is partly offset by the fact that a storm frequently makes it harder to find game. None of the wild creatures like rain. They're apt to hunt up the densest jungle they can find and stand under a tree in the middle of it until the storm is over.

There is one exception. Immediately preceding a storm, especially a snowstorm, and during its first few hours, all kinds of big game with which I have had any experience feed steadily. Nature apparently warns them to fill their bellies before things get bad. There is no time I would rather hunt than during the first half day of a snow or an autumn rain that later turns to snow. Everything is in the hunter's favor—the woods are quiet, the game is active, and scent is no problem.

On a warm day, in particular—and to a considerable extent in cold weather if the sky is clear—scent seems to rise. Game is much less likely to smell you when you approach from above. Consequently you have a better chance to get within range of a buck by walking along near a ridge than you would have in the valley below.

As a general rule, during calm weather in hilly country the air flows down the draws early and late and up them during the rest of the day. It normally changes direction shortly after sunrise and again about half an hour after sunset. Therefore, if you would hunt up a canyon in hope of spotting feeding deer, the best time to start is just as soon as you can see your sights. You can cover a lot of ground moving slowly and quietly, too—between first light in the morning and the time when the sun reaches the bottom and starts the daily upward movement of air.

I remember one time that this phenomenon worked to my advantage. I had started hunting up a canyon, walking along the bottom, just as soon as it was light enough to shoot. I had left camp quite a while before, of course. I continued up the narrow valley, following the game trail near the stream, until the sun finally came over the high ridge to the east. The air was perfectly motionless for a few minutes, then shifted. Knowing that it would be futile to continue with the breeze, I climbed about 300 yards up one side and started to circle back.

Deer at this elevation, whether still feeding or already bedded down for the day, would not have smelled me as I went by below because the air was then flowing down. Nor would they have a chance to smell me now, because the air movement was up—up the valley and up the sun-warmed slope. I had gone only a little way when I was fortunate enough to see a nice buck about 30 yards away before he saw me.

A year later I started up the same draw at the same time—the minute it was light enough to see the crosshairs in the scope—and had gone only about a quarter mile when I saw a fat buck, with four points on each side, at a range of 75 yards. He was feeding across the brook and twenty yards above it, and he never knew what hit him.

A wind that blows steadily from one direction doesn't present much of a problem in flat or gently rolling country unless it is violent. A hard wind seems to make all game found in timber nervous, although I never could see that it bothered sheep, goats, or antelope. At any rate, you can hunt into or across wind with reasonable certainty that your quarry won't scent you before you can see it.

In broken, mountainous terrain, however, such a wind whips around the peaks and ridges and seems to blow from all directions at the same time. You walk half a mile facing it, then cross a saddle or circle the point of a ridge, and suddenly find it going with you. Alter your course accordingly, and you soon feel it on your back again.

Probably the best solution in this case is to follow a ridge, occasionally walking back and forth across the top to look into the valley, on either side, and hope that the wind will carry your scent above the head of anything you see in the "wrong" direction. Fortunately, this often happens. Once you locate game, you can plan your stalk to approach it from the best direction possible or wait for the wind to die.

Frequently in the fall there is no steady wind except, perhaps, on the highest ridges. Little breezes eddy and puff back and forth, blowing willy-nilly first in one direction, then another. Many times I have gotten almost within range of game only to have the wind shift and spoil my chances.

Obviously, you can't change direction with every little whiff. You'd never get away from camp. Here again, it helps to stay above the area where you expect to find game, but other than that I have no solution except to keep hunting. It always pays to keep hunting.

Determining the direction of a brisk wind is never difficult. It is the gentle breeze, the barely perceptible movement of air, that can betray you. There are several tricks for detecting it. Moisten a finger in your mouth, then hold it up. The side that cools first is toward the wind. Or hold a handful of dust (or, if the ground is wet, punk from a rotten log) shoulder high and allow it to trickle down. Moss hanging from branches will show the direction of a breeze so gentle that you can scarcely feel it.

You can't always hunt into the wind, nor is it possible to stay continually above your game. In fact, the ideal situation that we visualize before a trip seldom occurs. In hunting, as in anything else, we do the best we can under the circumstances. This may mean walking straight downwind for a mile in order to approach a promising spot from the proper direction.

One thing for sure—no matter how much effort is involved in approaching game from the downwind side, it always is worthwhile. If there is any cover at all, an animal that smells you first will never be seen. In open country you may see him, but he'll probably be running and out of range.

I have sometimes wondered if a man doesn't smell worse to a skunk than the skunk smells to the man. Whether he does or not, his odor is terrifying to all game animals, and the successful hunter is the one who can, in one way or another, keep them from detecting it.

Chapter 26

How to Sit Still

One autumn morning my wife and I were walking quietly through an open stand of lodgepole pine when we saw the backs of two elk, 75 yards ahead and somewhat to our right. They were moving slowly, apparently feeding down a shallow swale that concealed their heads and most of their bodies, and they were obviously unaware of us.

The wind was favorable and the elk were coming closer at every step, so we simply stood still. At 40 yards they climbed out of the swale, a cow and calf, and started walking almost straight toward us. We were completely in the open. We didn't move a muscle. On and on they came, finally walking past us at a distance—which I later measured—of 30 feet. They gave no indication whatever that they saw us.

There is no hoofed animal in North America more wary, wild, and alert than an old cow elk in an area that is hunted regularly. The incident illustrates perfectly one of the cardinal hunting axioms: Game does not see the man who is motionless.

The art of immobility must be mastered if you hope to be consistently successful in hunting waterfowl. It is invaluable in big-game hunting because, nearly always, it provides the best chance for a sure shot at a standing target. Even in the uplands it occasionally pays off. How many

Ted was sitting here, in the open, when five deer appeared on the
ridge half a mile below. They came toward
him slowly, nibbling a bush here and there until they
were in range. Then he killed one. Because he had
held perfectly still, they never saw him till he raised
his rifle to shoot.

times has some distant hunter flushed a pheasant that flew toward you until
it was almost in range, then veered off? This has happened to all of us.
Nearly always it turned because it saw us, and it saw us because we moved.
Even in such an unlikely situation as chukar hunting I have bagged quite a
few birds simply by standing perfectly still at the right time. One time Buzz
Fiorini and I were walking down a rocky canyon when a hawk flushed three
chukars close to the rimrock, several hundred feet above. They flew a little
way, then coasted straight toward us on set wings, apparently headed for a
clutter of rocks and brush on the opposite slope.

We stood motionless until they were almost directly overhead, then threw up our guns. It was a typical duck shot, high and fast, but we killed two of them and might have gotten the third as well if we had been quick enough. Judging from other experiences, I'm certain that the chukars would have veered off if we had revealed our presence by moving.

Holding still, which should be the easiest of all hunting skills, is actually one of the most difficult. It requires no effort. It is restful. It gives you a chance to think. Yet it is desperately hard to sit still, really still, even for a few minutes. I would rather walk steadily all day than sit perfectly motionless for an hour.

There is a world of difference between sitting on a stump and sitting *still* on a stump. You can sit and visit with your companion, or eat your lunch, or simply rest, and an hour will fly by before you know it. But when you sit down with the deliberate intention of remaining absolutely motionless, the seconds become minutes, the minutes hours, and the hours days.

First you develop an itch somewhere, and the longer you resist scratching, the more persistently it bedevils you. Then you want to cough or blow your nose or turn your rifle over because the bolt handle is digging into your leg. If the weather is cold your feet begin to get chilly, and if it is warm the insects make a deliberate attempt to drive you insane. You discover that you are sitting on a knot that is getting bigger and harder by the moment and will undoubtedly make a permanent dent in your hipbone if you don't move.

This is only the start. The more you dwell on the tortures, the more they prosper. At the end of ten minutes they will be all but unendurable, and then you'll discover that you have the squirms and wiggles worse than a fourth-grader sitting at his desk beside an open window on a warm spring day. You'll want to move first one leg, then the other; one arm, then its mate. You'll positively yearn to shift.

Fortunately, you have now hit rock bottom. If you can only remain motionless a few minutes longer, the job will get easier. It takes about ten minutes for the birds to forget about you and start flitting around again; for the squirrels, chipmunks, and other little woods creatures to resume their normal activities. With the never-ending show of the woods in progress—a show, incidentally, that no restless person has ever seen—you will have interesting things to watch and the time will fly.

One fall, while I was sitting motionless near a spring at the head of a meadow where we had seen fresh elk tracks, three Franklin's grouse walked out of the alders on a log. They hopped off and started pecking here and there in the grass, not 20 feet away. A few minutes later a pine squirrel started shrieking bloody murder. The grouse, instantly alert, hopped back onto the log where they had first appeared and began looking around in all directions.

It was lucky they did, because a weasel soon popped out of the grass and dashed at them. But he was not quick enough, and they flew into a tree. He glared at them, then went bounding away, and in a little while they were back on the ground feeding. All was quiet for a few minutes—then the squirrel started chattering again. Once more the grouse hopped up on the log and again the weasel rushed them, this time nearly catching one. He didn't quite make it, though, and came bounding toward me, disappearing under a log that was scarcely 6 feet from my outstretched legs.

The grouse stayed in the tree. The squirrel continued his scolding. In maybe half a minute the weasel appeared from behind the log carrying a deer mouse. He laid it on the end of the log, then went searching busily through the grass and around the other logs nearby. In the course of his exploration he hopped around behind me, out of my line of vision and so close—scarcely a yard away—that I couldn't resist turning my head slightly to watch him.

Instantly he saw me, hissed, rushed back to his mouse, seized it, and bounded away. That was the last I saw of him, though the three fool hens continued feeding nearby and the squirrel stayed with his fir-cone husking until I finally decided that no elk would appear in the meadow that morning and went on.

The first requisite for sitting still while big-game hunting—whether on a deer stand waiting for a buck that might be driven to you or watching a crossing alone—is to get into a perfectly comfortable position. Find a spot facing the right direction—downwind from where you expect the game to appear, of course—and cut any nearby branches that might obstruct your vision. Dust off a comfortable seat, preferably in front of a tree or log against which you can lean, and test it for fit. If you want to smoke during these preliminaries, go ahead. After that, no. This is not because game can smell tobacco any farther upwind than they can a man, or that they fear it any worse than the man odor; it's simply because you can't smoke without moving your hands, and the striking of a match can betray you as readily as if you got up and stomped around.

Finally, when you are *sure* that everything is just right, sit down. Lay your rifle across your lap with the muzzle to the left (for a right-handed shooter) or over a convenient log with the muzzle ahead so that you can get it into shooting position with minimum movement. Now suffer. After ten or fifteen minutes you should begin to see interesting things—I've had both fox and coyote come trotting right up—and after half an hour you might see game.

If you undertake the ordeal of sitting still, be patient. Remember that undisturbed wild things are never in a hurry. They mosey along, picking a leaf here and a twig there, and it might take a deer an hour to come half a mile. And the noise of your movements before you decided to sit down probably frightened everything within half that distance.

Compared to remaining motionless while watching for big game, sitting still in a duck blind should be easy. The ordeal lasts only a few minutes at the longest—from the time the ducks appear until they finally decide to come in to the decoys or to go on. Judging from the men with whom I've hunted ducks, however, it isn't easy. Few of them can do it.

The hazard here is not discomfort or itchy-scratchiness or biting bugs. It's curiosity. Where are they? What are they doing? Are they coming? Are they in range yet? These are the questions that race through the eager duck hunter's mind, and his success or failure will depend in many cases on his reaction to them.

The movement of a hand is enough to flare off a flock of mallards or blacks. A face upturned, even for a second, has saved thousands of ducks from meeting a load of chilled 6's.

If your blind is placed correctly in relation to your decoys, you know where your shooting will be. When you first see ducks coming, put your right hand on the grip of your gun so that you can bring it up into shooting position, hold your call in your left—if you use a call—lean forward against the front of your blind so that you can peek through it, *keep your face down,* and don't move.

Several years ago I put out my duck decoys on a bar beside the upstream end of a brushy island, only to discover, when I finished, that some other hunters had already made a setup for geese on the bar at the lower end. I apologized for intruding and said I'd move. When they told me to stay, I volunteered not to shoot at geese, or at ducks when there were any of the bigger birds in sight.

Just as anybody might have known under the circumstances, a flock of lesser Canadas came in about 10 o'clock, made two or three circles, and then lit on *my* bar among the duck decoys. I didn't know what to do. I'd promised not to shoot at geese, but there they were, walking around among my duck decoys, not 30 feet away. Finally I decided simply to wait and see what happened.

I didn't bat an eye for seven or eight years—anyway fifteen minutes—and then I saw one of the other hunters slipping along the riverbank. He had dropped downstream in a boat, crossed over, and was now coming back to be in a position under the geese in case they few in his direction. Then I heard one of the hunters coming up through the brush behind me, and I later learned that the third had gone to the upstream tip of the island while the fourth remained near the lower end.

Their plan was for the man coming up behind me to flush the geese, maybe getting a shot or two in the process, and for one of the others to clean up on them, no matter which way they went. Unfortunately the geese also heard the man behind me, and they probably saw the one on the bank as well. Their heads began to come up, and an instant later they took off downstream over the channel.

That experience was a perfect example of what holding still can do. My blind was open—simply a hole in the brush—and one movement either before or after the geese lit would have sent them on their way. I have had equally interesting experiences with other kinds of waterfowl and upland birds, and with game both large and small. Holding perfectly still will do as much for any other outdoor lover, from bird watcher to bear hunter, who is stubborn enough to give it a thorough trial.

Chapter 27

How Not to Get Lost

A herd of elk fed every night on the open south slope about a mile west of camp, but they didn't come out of the timber until dark and they went back into it before daylight. One morning when I stepped outside the tent before dawn I discovered three inches of fresh snow. Perfect! Now I would learn where they spent their days.

My wife and I were hunting approximately in the middle of Idaho, about thirty miles from the nearest road, in an area of rolling hills, lodgepole pine timber dotted with spruce thickets, mountain meadows, and a few grassy, south-facing slopes. It was great elk country. The wapiti, however, rivals the Eastern whitetail for craftiness, and even where there are many you earn every chance you get.

Now the snow had evened the odds. I left camp just as it was getting light, and half an hour later I found where the herd had entered the timber.

I followed the trail, plain as a highway, for about two hours, mostly through an open stand of lodgepole. The elk had passed a couple of spruce thickets, which we call elk jungles, and eventually came to one that was simply huge. The tracks led straight into it. The breeze was in my face, so I followed, moving along just as cautiously and quietly as I knew how.

The jungle grew thicker and thicker. Soon I was on hands and knees, both to avoid the drooping spruce branches and to see under them. After

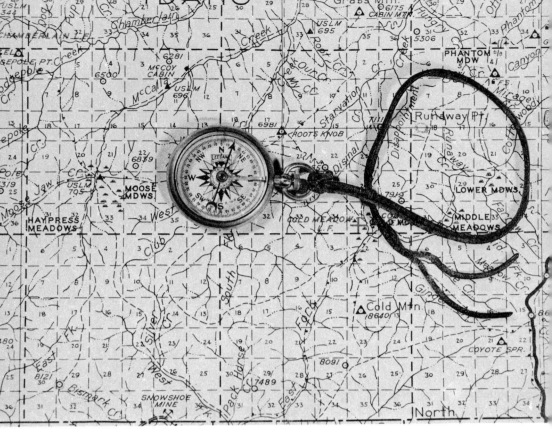

The first thing to do before starting to hunt in new territory is to orient your map—establish correct north and south—with the aid of your compass. Shown here is part of a U.S. Forest Service map, scale half an inch to the mile. The magnetic declination in this area is 19 degrees east of true north. Before you make another move, try to memorize the more important features of the area. When you start to hunt, check your compass occasionally as you hunt *away* from camp. Your compass won't do you any good if you wait till you're lost to look at it.

crawling endlessly I saw elk legs ahead, lots of elk legs! But they were all I could see. They weren't far, less than 50 yards. I lay on my belly in the snow and tried to see an entire elk. It was impossible. Whether I could have crawled closer I don't know because it suddenly occurred to me that there was no way we could get pack horses into this jungle to take an elk out. It would be silly to kill one here.

I fought my way back out of the jungle and discovered time had been racing. It was noon and I was hungry. I boiled snow water for a can of tea and ate my sandwich. By the time I had eaten and smoked a pipe it was snowing. I was delighted. Elk often leave their daytime hideouts to feed when it is snowing.

I hunted several hours without seeing game or a fresh track, however, and finally decided it was time to head for camp. I set out, walking briskly.

Suddenly, I was brought up with a shock. There was a pole leaning against a tree and I recognized it. It was where I had killed an elk the year before. I had used the pole to hang the quarters between two lodgepole pines. And for twenty minutes I had been walking straight away from camp, not toward it!

I was in an area of low hills and ridges where several small streams headed, and but for the lucky accident of noticing the pole I might have walked much farther before realizing my mistake. Yet I was so completely turned around I couldn't believe it. Even though I knew, I still couldn't believe.

I sat down on a log and put my compass on it beside me. Sure enough, I had been walking north when I should have been headed south. I ate my candy bar and apple, lit my pipe, and drew a map in the snow. It must have been twenty minutes before I was able to reorient myself so north seemed north, not south. Then I started for camp, checking my compass occasionally because I had to circle blowdowns and elk jungles and it was too late in the day to risk getting turned around again. I came out on the east-west trail about 200 yards from the tent just as darkness was falling.

I have never been so badly lost that I had to sleep out, but I have been completely turned around dozens, possibly hundreds, of times. I have friends who claim a sense of direction like a homing pigeon's. Not I. On an overcast day in an area without visible landmarks, I would be helpless without my compass.

I hunted grouse one fall in Michigan with Peter Barrett, Leon Martuch, and several of Leon's friends—not all at once, of course. Two is the ideal number, and three is the limit as far as I'm concerned. It's too hard to keep track of more hunters in heavy cover. And if I don't know where my companions are I don't shoot.

Immediately north of Leon's house were several hundred acres of dense pines dotted with small, relatively clear areas where big oak trees grew. The grouse were eating acorns. We could step out the front door and be hunting, with an excellent chance of putting up birds, in five minutes. There was only one problem: I absolutely couldn't hold a straight course through the pines. That's essential when your companion is 35 yards to your right, you can't see him, and you want to maintain this distance.

Pete had bought a pin-on compass when we got our Michigan licenses, but I had the pocket compass I carry big-game hunting and thought it would serve. Not so. I had to stop walking to use it while Pete kept moving ahead. I'd hurry to catch up, then try to match his pace. But after two or three stops, I never knew whether I was ahead of Pete or behind him.

After we had been there a couple of days, Leon went to town for groceries and I had him bring me a pin-on compass. I put it on my jacket and the problem was solved. I could glance at it frequently without pausing and hold the course Pete and I had decided on before entering the woods.

All hunters and anglers can benefit from map and compass, even in familiar territory, and in big, wild, remote country they are essential. On the day I got turned around hunting elk, I knew I was north of the east-west trail that passed our camp. Consequently, walking south would take me to the trail somewhere. But I had also studied the map carefully. I knew where the streams headed and in which direction they flowed. So even if I had continued walking the wrong way until I came to Deer Creek, a small stream flowing east here, I still would have known where I was in relation to the trail and camp.

For National Forests, you can get maps from the headquarters of each, and often from district ranger offices. Most of the Western range is administered by the Bureau of Land Management, and you can get a map of the area in which you're interested from the district office. Forest Service and BLM maps are usually adequate; I use them all the time, though some are not minutely accurate and they don't show elevations, save for the highest peaks. There are many other sources of maps, and even a highway map is better than none. The best are those prepared by the Geological Survey, which show elevation as well as many other details, such as ponds, buildings, and swamps, that are not on the others.

Most cities have stores that sell Geological Survey maps of nearby areas, as well as other maps. (Look in the Yellow Pages.) If you can't find what you want locally, write to U.S. Geological Survey, 18 and F Sts., N.W., Washington, DC 20242 or, for states west of the Mississippi, including Louisiana and Mississippi, to U.S. Geological Survey, Federal Bldg., Denver, CO 80225 and ask for the free index sheet of the state in which you're interested. From it you can order a detailed map of the quadrangle in which you plan to hunt.

The best compass for use with a map is one with rotating dial and sighting device so you can set a course in any desired direction.

With any compass and any map, however, do this: In an easily identified location, such as the spot where a road crosses a stream, lay the map on a flat surface and use the compass to orient it. This means rotating the *map* until its north coincides with the north shown by the compass. Look at the map from its south end so north is straight away from you, west to your left, and east right.

Our elk camp was near the spot where the trail crossed Pup Creek, both shown on the Forest Service map, so it was easy to pinpoint my location, square up the map, and study the surrounding area. It showed me, for example, that Deer Creek flowed east for about a mile from its source in a big meadow, then turned and flowed a bit east of south. Dog Creek, which headed nearby, flowed southwesterly.

Your Geological Survey map will have a little sketch at the bottom showing the declination. This is the difference between true north and magnetic north. Where I hunt, the declination is approximately 20 degrees east. This means I must turn the compass until the needle settles down 20 degrees east of N to have true directions.

A few final words on compasses: First, never argue with your compass; if you think *it's* wrong, *you* are. In some compasses the north half of the needle is blue, the south end, silver. If you have one like this, scratch on the back of the case, "B-N." I can tell you from experience that when you are *really* turned around you can't remember. Another point: Keep your compass out of all magnetic fields. I once laid a good compass on the shelf directly above a magnetic tool bar. When I next looked at it the needle pointed south. And finally, don't use your compass near iron or steel. The pin-on compass I used in Michigan was okay if I held my shotgun at arm's length straight down. To get a true reading from my pocket compass, I must lean my rifle against a tree and walk away 6 or 8 feet.

This dope on maps and compasses is rudimentary, but there are other points I want to touch. First, the best compass in the world is not worth one cent unless you use it going *away* from camp. If you wait until you're lost, your compass can't help you. But if you know that you started hunting to the southwest and held generally to that direction, as proved by checking your compass occasionally, then when the time comes to return you know camp is northeast.

Then, always try to establish a base line of some sort. It might be a road, trail, or stream. Get its directions firmly in mind, and memorize the position of your camp in relation to it. If you hunt to the north, you know you'll return by walking south. Even though you may not hit your base line right at camp, you'll be able to find it.

As you hunt away from camp, pause frequently to look back. This, I think, is the secret of good woodsmen who never carry a compass and scarcely know what a map is. The woods, deserts, or mountains look different from the other direction. Yet if you hunt to the east, you must be able to recognize rocky hills, odd trees, or any other landmarks as you return to camp—walking west.

For about ten years, Phil Fairbanks, his wife, my wife, and I hunted sage hens and antelope from the same camping spot on a high plateau in southwestern Idaho. Four big mountains are always visible in the distance. Two are in Idaho, one in Oregon, and one in Nevada. One morning after breakfast, as we were about to start hunting, I noticed Phil pull a compass out of his watch pocket, square around to face north, and study it. I said, "Phil, why do you bother with a compass here? You can see four good landmarks. And we know the road past camp runs northeast and southwest."

"Well," he answered, "when I was a boy in Utah I was hunting sage hens in country about like this. There was a good dirt road. I parked beside it and took off. I walked all morning and part of the afternoon. Then a storm moved in. I turned around and started back to the road, but it wasn't there! I realized I was lost. I couldn't see 100 yards.

"I built a sagebrush fire and huddled near it all night. The sky cleared in the morning. I could see my landmarks and made it back to my car okay. But ever since then I've carried a compass—and I always know which direction I'm going when I leave camp."

Chapter 28

Lost!

In the previous chapter I discussed the precautions hunters should take to prevent getting lost, particularly in big, wild, remote, or difficult country. Anglers sometimes get lost, too, of course, but the weather is warmer during fishing season and spending a night or two out is not so serious.

There are various degrees of being lost.

The first is simply getting turned around in country devoid of landmarks or when the weather is foggy or snowing. I once led a companion in a complete circle on a big mountain meadow during a snowstorm. This wasn't serious. I knew we were north of the east-west trail that passed our camp, and I had merely to use my compass to maintain a southerly course.

Then, I've been completely turned around, walking east when I should have been headed west toward camp, for example. I know from these experiences the panic that must seize an inexperienced outdoorsman when the cold realization that he is really lost first grips him. Sometimes it has taken me twenty or thirty minutes, with the aid of my compass and a crude map scratched in earth or snow, to reorient myself.

Third, there is the situation of merely hunting too far from camp and suddenly realizing that darkness will fall long before you can get there. You're not really lost; you know the general direction to camp. But the sky is overcast; there will be no stars or moon to help you, and the terrain is

If you should get lost or break a leg, these things—spread
out on the little day pack in which you should carry
them—could save your life. They are: dehydrated food,
flat can (with wire bail) for making soup or tea, tea bags
inside can along with salt and the day's sandwich,
sheet of plastic, nylon cord, hatchet, waterproof
matchsafe, and fire-starting tablets.

difficult. It is better to prepare for the night and stay right there than to
attempt traveling in the dark.

Harper Saunders, my brother Burtt, and I once did an extremely foolish
thing. We were hunting mountain goats in typical, precipitous goat country
and Burtt killed one on a ledge far above. It teetered on the brink, from
which it would have tumbled almost to our feet, then simply settled down
right where it had been standing.

We left our rifles where they were, beside a tiny alpine lake, and went
after it. Darkness was falling when we got back. We discussed building a
fire and staying there. That is what we should have done. Instead, we
started the eight or ten long, rough, dangerous miles to our camp.

There was no trail anywhere. We decided to get down off the mountain as quickly as we could, then follow a mountain stream to camp.

It was a clear night but there was no moon and we soon discovered that starlight alone was not enough to make walking safe. The mountain had a series of grassy slopes, but between these benches and slopes were many vertical cliffs, most of them 50 to 100 feet high. We each began carrying a handful of pebbles and tossing one ahead every few yards. If we heard the pebble strike the earth, we went on; if we couldn't hear it we angled right or left.

We finally reached the stream and turned down it. Here we didn't even have starlight to help us and while there was no longer any danger of a deadly fall, we bumped into blowdowns and boulders, fell into beaver ponds, and struggled through endless alder thickets until about 1 A.M. Food and bed were never more welcome, believe me.

The fourth, and final, degree of "lostness" is being *really* lost. Perhaps you followed a big buck all day, wandering in every direction, either lacking a compass or neglecting to use it in the excitement of the chase. Finally, you notice that darkness is approaching. You suddenly realize that you don't have the faintest idea which way to turn toward camp.

This has never happened to me because in difficult country—rolling hills with little streams flowing in various directions, thick timber, and no visible landmarks—I use my compass frequently. In fact, I use it anyway to be sure whether I'm north or south of the base line mentioned in the previous chapter and east or west from camp. If a storm moves in, cutting visibility to 100 feet, I know which way to go.

But I've talked to many hunters who have been completely lost. Invariably, they said the first reaction was dreadful panic—described by Webster as "a sudden overpowering fright; *esp:* a sudden unreasoning terror often accompanied by mass flight."

One bull of a man, about twenty-five, told me of running and walking for five days, much of the time stumbling down the bed of a mountain stream because somebody had told him all water led to civilization, until he finally blundered upon the camp of another hunting party. He fell in the water the first day and got his matches wet, and the ground was covered with snow. But for his amazing physique, he surely would have died.

Yet before panic seized him, he knew he was hunting on a long slope with a well-beaten trail on top of the ridge. When he gave way to panic, he headed downhill!

The first thing is to whip this deadly enemy. Sit down and smoke a pipe or eat a candy bar, meanwhile drumming into your consciousness something like this: "I may be lost, but I'm in no danger; I may be lost, but I'm in no danger."

Survey your surroundings. You need two things—dry wood for a fire, and water. You can easily go for several days without food, but water is essential. A shelter of some kind—a lean-to of spruce or hemlock boughs or even a flat-faced rock or big log to reflect the heat from your fire—is desirable, but you can get along without it if you have water and fuel.

Before darkness settles in, try to find a spot near a brook or spring with an abundance of standing dead saplings, or big dead trees with part of their branches up off the ground. (Once the fall rains come, any wood lying flat on the ground will be wet and hard to ignite and will make a poor, smoky fire.)

In coniferous woods you can nearly always find pitch. You can ignite it dripping wet, and it occurs near the butts of lightning-struck trees or blowdowns or in pine knots you can kick out of punky logs. The dead twigs near the lower trunk of big spruce trees are always brittle, dry, and good kindling, even after a week of rain.

In deciduous forests, birch bark will ignite when wet, but I would never peel a birch save in the most dire need. A fallen tree, leaning to the south and hung up on another, will nearly always have dry wood on the underside. Most off-ground dead saplings and branches of 2-inch diameter or more have dry wood in the center and, if finely splintered, will start easily and ignite the larger kindling. I only wish I could remember the variety I have used to start fires in the rain in New England, the West, and the South. As you gather kindling in the rain or snow, put it under something to keep dry.

No hunter these days should find himself in such desperate straits. In new or difficult country I carry a few fire starters that burn with a hot flame about ten minutes and will ignite even damp kindling. Lacking them, a stub of candle is worth two dozen matches. I also carry a 7x9-foot sheet of .004-inch plastic and nylon cords with which to erect it as a lean-to. It can be put up in a couple of minutes, eliminates the need for the time-consuming bark shelters and spruce-bough lean-tos described by Nessmuk and Horace Kephart, reflects heat, and protects you from wind, rain, or snow. Plastic and cords weigh 22 ounces.

I carry a waterproof matchsafe that holds eighteen kitchen matches—and I don't use them for smoking! Two precautions: Don't pack the matches in tightly in order to take a couple more. You may have to get one out with numb or wet fingers. Second, scratch an arrow on the barrel indicating which way to turn to open. Otherwise, when you're cold and desperate you won't remember.

My tea can, with light wire bail, measures 1¾x3⅞x6 inches, weighs next to nothing, and holds a pint. I make tea or soup in it, let it cool, and drink out of it. My lunch for the day—a sandwich, candy bar, tea bags, and a little salt shaker—go into it, and a plastic bag keeps it from getting everything else in my pack black.

The most valuable thing I carry is my hatchet, which weighs 28 ounces. I use it to quarter and skin big game and to cut fuel for lunchtime fires. In a really bad situation, it and matches alone could save my life. I also carry two days' rations of dehydrated food. This, carefully spaced out, and perhaps augmented with a grouse or squirrel, would hold me for a week. The emergency food weighs 21 ounces.

With all of this, my red day pack weighs 4½ pounds, including the weight of the pack, and has room for my jacket in case the day turns warm. Since I don't carry a belt knife, I usually hang the hatchet on my belt. (I do carry a pocketknife, of course.) Hunting game larger than deer, I add a lightweight block and tackle and 25 feet of ¼-inch nylon rope to the pack. I can then tie a pole between two trees and hang the quarters out of reach of bears.

Too much to carry? You don't feel it on your back. Yet you are completely independent. Should you break a leg or become hopelessly lost, you have no cause for panic. You can make tea from spring water or melted snow. You have food. You have everything you need to stay warm and dry.

Now, before you stretch your sheet-plastic lean-to, scrape away the duff and build your fire on the spot where you will sleep. Let it burn there, 5 feet long and 2 feet wide, for an hour. Then scrape it about 6 feet away, heap it up, and add a couple of good chunks. If you can find dry leaves or soft fir twigs, spread them over the heated earth.

Finally, put up your lean-to, the back edge flat on the ground, preferably weighted down with earth or snow, but tied securely at the corners. Tie the front corners to give a slope of about 45 degrees, centered over your bed, and well back from the fire.

You should sleep comfortably until about 2 A.M. When you wake, get up, rebuild your fire, and smoke a pipe. You will probably sleep comfortably then until daylight. I have done this very thing hundreds of times when I was *not* lost. (Thirty years ago we used oiled silk, which was more expensive and probably not so good as sheet plastic.)

In the morning, you will have a fresh outlook on life. Make a can of tea, eat, and smoke your pipe. You will have proved that you can survive alone, that there are no mysterious dangers in the woods, and that you are self-sufficient in an emergency. Wait until you feel sure your companions are up, then gather an armful of green boughs. Get your fire going well, and fire three shots into the air—the universal distress signal. Then throw the boughs on the fire so they will put up a great smoke.

Wait an hour and repeat the process. You may be only a mile from camp, but you may be six or eight. It will take your friends a while to get there.

On the other hand, if you now feel sure where you are and you want to walk into camp on your own, do this: If you have anything to write on, leave a note saying you have marked your trail. Then, as you walk away from your camp, taking everything you own, break twigs every twenty or thirty feet so you can come back. If your calculations turn out to be wrong and you don't find the trail, you will be better off to remain exactly where you first stopped than to keep on wandering. In fact, of all the things that contribute to lost-hunter fatalities, aimless wandering is Number 1. Better to stay put, fire three shots occasionally, and send up smoke.

Advising hunters to carry emergency equipment may seem like advising drivers to put on the brakes before they approach an accident—good, but impossible. Not so!

A few pounds on your back could save your life. Those who die take off with light hearts and loaded guns, wearing summer jackets in November, with only a paper packet of matches and a hunting knife. They are inviting disaster. The friendly woods at 8 A.M. can be cruel and demanding by 4 P.M. Yet they are never too much for the man who knows them well and is prepared for the worst as well as the best.

Part VIII

A DOG MAKES A DIFFERENCE

Chapter 29

How Not to Train Hunting Dogs

If you ever see anything in writing on how to train hunting dogs by a guy named Trueblood, his first name won't be Ted. After some forty years of association with various four-footed companions—during which time the dogs taught me more than I taught them—I have come to the reluctant conclusion that I was not cut out to be a dog trainer.

Consider a Chesapeake named Bill. When Bill made up his mind to something, it was permanent. Nothing I might do could change it. His attitude toward chickens was a good example. Bill decided early in life that chickens were put on this earth for only one purpose—for him to catch.

Joe was getting old when this photo was taken and was
content to rest awhile. But Rip was just approaching
his prime and was raring to go.

This is a reasonable assumption on the part of most puppies. What could
be more fun than to make an old hen run, flapping and squawking, and to
see the feathers fly? I don't begrudge them that. But the difference between
Bill and the others was that Bill never changed his mind. Most pups learn,
after a couple of lessons, to leave chickens alone. Not Bill. When he saw a
chicken, that chicken was as good as plucked and in the pan.

I really wouldn't have minded the chickens so much if he had been more
open-minded on the subject of retrieving. He had his own ideas about that,
too. I've seen him swim a quarter of a mile through ice-cold water in chase
of a crippled bluebill, and finally bring it back. But if he didn't want to
retrieve, he wouldn't pick up a green-winged teal paddling air one foot
from the bank. What I wanted him to do was of no concern.

There is an old saying to the effect that you don't need to know more
than a dog to train him; you just need more time. This did not apply to Bill.

In those days I had more time than he did, but I never convinced him that any of my ideas were worth considering.

My experience with Bill should have taught me that whatever talent I might possess lay in other fields. It didn't. More years and more dogs—none, fortunately, such original thinkers as Bill—were required to force that conclusion. Now that I have resigned myself to the fact, however, it is really rather nice. I don't worry if my dogs aren't perfect; neither am I. We go out together and have fun, and that's the purpose of hunting. I only hope the dogs enjoy it as much as I do, because I'm quite sure nobody gets greater pleasure from his canine campanions than I.

This, I think, stems primarily from the fact that whereas I may not be any great shakes as a trainer, I do understand dogs fairly well. I have a dog's outlook, so to speak. Each dog is an individual, as truly as is each person, and I suspect sportsmen would enjoy their dogs more if they paused occasionally to consider this. A dog isn't a machine to find birds or retrieve ducks or follow a trail.

He can do these things better than any machine, of course—even better than Ed Zern's Mechani-Mutt, an imaginary mechanical bird dog—but he is also an individual with dignity and feelings and at least some ability to figure things out for himself and decide on a course of action that appears wisest under the circumstances.

A good example of this occurred one fall before the bird season, while I was bass fishing. Rip, a white-and-black pointer, shared the boat with me. He was pretty bored with the whole thing; so when I saw a big covey of chukars along the shore I decided to let him have a little fun, too. I ran the boat in 100 yards away from the birds and started walking toward them. Rip began hunting at once and I angled up the steep sidehill a little because it's best to approach chukars from above. Otherwise they're almost always sure to run.

The maneuver didn't work this time—the covey flushed wild before Rip even scented them. They flew about 200 yards and lit in some thick sagebrush. We went after them, and this time they ran. The mountain above, easily a 45-degree grade, was mostly lava rockslides with patches of grass and sagebrush among them. Long before we got close I could see the chukars hopping from rock to rock up a slide as they rapidly made their way away from us.

Rip saw them too—a dog that hunts chukars soon learns to depend almost as much on his eyes as on his nose—and I let him go. Meanwhile I changed my course to climb at a steeper angle in hopes of being within range when they began to fly. I had no gun, of course, but I still wanted to be within range when they flew.

Rip soon caught up with the stragglers and began putting them into the air one at a time. The leaders, however, were still running up the mountain, getting farther from me by the instant and almost outrunning Rip. He did his best, but a chukar can actually outrun a slow dog uphill and almost hold its own against a fast one.

Rip got 400 yards above me, then pointed! Most of the cackling idiots had flown, but one elected to sit tight, and Rip had pointed it. This was exactly what I didn't want. Already several hundred yards above the lake, I had no desire to climb higher. But Rip was as solid as a rock, so I had no choice. I started up to him.

I was nearly there when I pushed a chukar out of hiding. It ran uphill through the grass, six feet behind the motionless Rip. I saw him when he heard the running bird. He turned and looked back over his shoulder, then swung his head around toward the one he was pointing. Then he looked back again as the rustling in the grass continued. He did this three or four times, obviously trying to decide what to do.

I saw him make up his mind. He left his point, dashed back and flushed the runner, then returned to his original stand and pointed again!

Now, there, I submit, was an example of a dog's thinking—and if you insist that dogs can't think, you must at least agree that he made a decision and acted on it. And in view of his experience, he made the right one.

Most of the birds Rip hunted were notorious runners, especially pheasants and chukars, and the two western quail with which we spend the most time. After a pointing dog has learned the habits of these birds he eventually adopts a philosophy that, if he could only talk, he'd state about as follows: "I'll set 'em if they'll set, and I'll make 'em fly if they won't."

This is a good philosophy. It is what I want a dog to do. A slow, poky, timid dog could never get chukars off the ground. Nor point them either, for that matter; they'd never quit moving away from him. I've long suspected how my dogs felt on the subject, but never before had I seen such a clear demonstration of it.

Bird-dog men may shudder at the thought of encouraging a pointing dog in this kind of goings-on. And I do think it does tend to make a dog short of patience with his game—if they shuffle their feet, he's likely to rush in and make them fly. I've seen quite a few pointers, however, that would make the pheasants rattle out of a cornfield, where they never hold, then point them as solid as Gibraltar in the sugar-beet fields in the evenings, where they nearly always do hold.

In fact, one of the most unusual points I ever saw was made by a dog that had pushed literally thousands of pheasants, chukars, and running quail into the air. Joe, Rip's daddy, was eleven or twelve years old at the time. My brother Burtt and I had hunted a canyon for mountain quail, and as we came back down it toward the car I let Joe run ahead.

We were out of the canyon, nearly to the car, when we came around a clump of brush and saw Joe pointing. He was on ground like a concrete floor. When we had gone a few yards farther we saw a cock pheasant, also completely in the open on earth as bare as if it had been swept, crouching motionless. The two were 20 feet apart, with not one blade of grass between them.

We had not seen Joe for fifteen minutes; so it seems reasonable to assume that he must have held the cock at least a third that long. They were both like statues, and not until we had taken several steps toward the bird did it break its trance and fly.

Burtt killed the cock, and Joe brought it. As we walked on to the car we tried to reconstruct what must have happened. Very likely it was a sight point. Joe, loping along the trail, must have rounded the brush and caught the pheasant in the open. They both froze and stayed frozen until we got there.

I have observed that the more bungling and inept a hunter is, the more likely he is to find fault with a dog, as though perfect dog work could make up for his own shortcomings. Of course, I except out-and-out beginners, who are likely to be awed by the miracle of a dog's scenting and pointing game.

Maybe I err too far in the other direction. When any dog bumps a covey of quail I am inclined to excuse him by thinking of the many times he has pointed perfectly and I have missed. It probably is not good to think of your own shortcomings when you are dealing with dogs, children, or women. Still, it has its compensations. You're always so pleased when they do the right thing!

This is true even if the right thing results purely from luck. Once, hunting Huns in the foothills, Joe swung 300 yards into a little grass basin and came up in a solid point. I walked over, expecting Huns, and a cock pheasant cackled up. I killed it. At the shot twenty-five or thirty more pheasants got up. They were all over the place, and every one was a hen! No dog can tell a cock bird from a hen, nor would he give a whoop if he could. Joe's point was pure luck but it was the kind of thing you remember.

Dog have good days and bad, the same as people. These are times when scent conditions are impossible and no dog can smell a bird. On such days any dog will run over more birds than he'll point, and it won't be his fault. There are conditions under which a dog can't hear properly—and I mean this seriously. We've all seen the hardheaded dog that would get to chasing birds and not hear call or whistle, but I don't mean that.

I was hunting grouse one day with Ray P. Holland and a wonderful setter named Peter. Ray was on a ridge and Peter and I were in the bottom, which was 150 yards wide and bounded on the far side by a rather high, steep hill. I could see Ray when he called Peter, but the dog probably couldn't see him because of waist-high cover. At the sound of his master's voice Peter turned and ran straight away. Ray called again and Peter ran faster, still directly away.

"What," Ray called down to me, "is the matter with that fool dog?"

I said, "Wait until he gets to the hill. Then call again."

Peter ran 50 yards to the opposite hillside—it was open and we could see him clearly there—and stopped. Ray called a third time. Peter ran straight to him.

The explanation? Strangely, in the tangled bottom I could not hear Ray's voice direct, but I could plainly hear its echo from the hill. If, like Peter, I had been unable to see Ray, I would have gone in the same direction Peter did.

I often think of that echo when a dog does something stupid, or fails to mind the way I think it should. But for the fact that I was near Peter, Ray Holland would not know to this day why a near-perfect dog suddenly decided to run away when called.

Of course, I'd probably be a better trainer if I didn't think about it. A good trainer shouldn't make alibis for his dogs. But I suspect that, lacking a little sympathy and understanding, he might not enjoy them so much as I do, either.

Chapter 30

Is That So?

In view of the fact that dogs have been man's closest animal companions since long before the first historian began recording the momentous events of his day on the walls of a cave, we harbor a surprising number of pretty shaky ideas about them. Consider one of the most common, the matter of dogs' vision.

A lot of folks will tell you dogs can't see very well. I've read it in books. I've even heard dog men, who should know better, express themselves along that line.

This is a far cry from my experience. I had a pointer named Rip who hunted chukars for eleven seasons. Hundreds of them were killed over him, and if any living dog knew how to hunt chukars Rip was that dog.

Now, chukars are not hidey birds. They prefer arid country with sparse vegetation, and they make no effort to conceal themselves on the rocky hillsides. They wander around through the scanty grass or perch on the boulders and watch you go past below. Consequently you often see chukars long before you are in range. In fact, the distance at which you can see them usually depends solely on the sharpness of your vision.

No man is better at seeing chukars than Rip was. When he was walking at heel along the bottom of a canyon he kept his head cocked up, watching first one slope and then the other. A number of times I actually saw him

These pups didn't know what to think of their first game
bird, a sage hen.

stumble over a stick in the path because he was looking up for chukars. If I
sat down to rest he spent the time watching for them. He saw them, too,
often before I did.

Another favorite pastime of his was to sit up in the car and watch first the
fields and then the desert as we drove out hunting each morning. It was a
rare day when we'd pass a pheasant in an alfalfa stubble or a covey of quail
along the road without Rip's seeing them. Nor was he alone in this. I

hunted in those days with Willard Cravens and discovered that his little Brittany, Queenie, was, if anything, sharper than Rip at spotting birds as we drove by.

One year, I made a January cougar hunt along the Middle Fork of the Salmon River, in Idaho, with Rob Donley. We covered about fifty miles of the deer winter range—because cougar live on deer—walking along the river and up every tributary stream as far as there were any deer tracks. During all this time, except when they were actually trailing a big cat, Rob's two hounds walked at heel.

Like any dogs, they would have enjoyed nothing more than to take off after some of the deer that were almost constantly in sight. Naturally, Rob wouldn't let them go, but that didn't keep them from looking. We usually traveled with Rob in the lead, followed by the two dogs, while I brought up the rear. This gave me a perfect opportunity to watch them. They were always looking. Time after time they saw deer or other game on the slopes above before we did.

I have no doubt that some dogs, like some people, have better vision than others. Very likely their eyes are subject to the same ailments as ours, too. A friend has a farsighted dog that can see a cat at 100 yards, but she can hardly make out a dish of food in front of her nose. On the whole, however, I think dogs' eyesight is far better than is generally believed.

Sometimes we forget that dogs have to look at everything from a lower viewpoint. The man who can't understand why his retriever fails to see a duck on the water should remember that the dog's eyes are only two feet above the surface, even when he's standing on shore. From this low angle the duck could easily be obscured by waves. If the dog is swimming, his handicap is even worse. In cover over which a man can see easily, everything except the immediate surroundings are often completely out of sight to a dog.

One thing we have to remember in discussing dogs in general is that you simply can't discuss dogs in general. They're individuals, the same as people. Dogs differ in stamina, brains, memory, likes and dislikes, temperament, scenting ability, courage, and the many other features, both mental and physical, that set each one apart. Some dogs even have a sense of humor, an attribute that appears to be totally lacking in others.

Rip's father Joe did many funny things, and the only reason we could figure out for them was simply that he thought they were funny. My wife and I used to scuffle occasionally for Joe's benefit and he invariably got into the act by growling and barking and biting me with mock ferocity. Not once did he bite her.

But one evening she and Joe and I were in the kitchen. She had on slacks. When she bent over to get a pan out of a low drawer, Joe walked up behind her and gave her a sharp nip in the most appropriate spot—right where the slacks were the tightest. She squealed and jumped. Joe ran around behind me, and if ever a dog laughed, he laughed then. So did I.

Like all good dogs, as Joe got older he knew from experience where birds were likely to be. He was an excellent judge of cover, but he could also remember where he had found birds before. Too many times to leave any doubt I've let him out of the car and seen him head straight for the particular clump of brush where he'd found quail when we were there before. And sometimes a year would have gone by since that last visit. I can't go along with the common idea that dogs have poor memories. Maybe some of them do, but some don't.

Lest I be accused of prejdice in favor of our canine friends, here's another misconception, this time on the other side, that I can't go along with. It's common practice to run a young dog with an old one on the supposition that the pup will learn from example. I don't think dogs are capable of learning from example. At least I'm sure that none I ever had could do it.

My doghouse is built inside the garage under a workbench, and a dog-size door goes through the garage wall from house to run. In cold weather this opening is completely covered by a dozen 2-inch-wide strips of rubber cut from an old inner tube and attached at one end above the door.

One winter I kept a friend's bitch for three months. In all that time she never learned to go through the rubber door despite the fact that she saw Rip do it several times every day. No matter how bad the weather, she would stay outside and shiver until I rescued her. She slept in the garage, but I had to put her in each evening and take her out again the following morning. You'd think after three months it finally would have dawned on her that if Rip could go in and out through the flap door she could too, but it never did.

My theory is that a pup runs along with an old dog because it's fun. Beyond that, instinct and his master's training decide the rest. I've yet to see a young pointer or setter, not yet pointing, either point birds on his own or honor a point simply because he saw an old dog do it.

Because dogs have so many human attributes—they're subject to fear, jealousy, greed, and anger, and they also possess courage, tolerance, friendliness, and loyalty—it's easy to forget that they are, after all, dogs. Their understanding is limited. Dogs can't make the connection between two related events such as disobedience and punishment unless they occur at virtually the same time. Even the most intelligent are capable of acquiring only a limited vocabulary.

One little-recognized quality that all dogs have, though it is much stronger in some than in others, is a sense of dignity. This is particularly true of working dogs, whether one of the pointing breeds or retrievers. Believe me, kind visiting lady with no dogs at home, my dogs don't like to be gushed over! But worst of all is laughing at a dog, particularly when you catch him in an embarrassing or awkward moment.

I remember Rip in his first season. My wife and I were hunting with him along a little stream—scarcely a trickle, really—when we came to one of the few big, deep pools. It was completely covered with green algae. No water at all was visible. Rip went at it full bore. It looked perfectly solid to him, and he intended to run across. Instead, he plunged in out of sight and had to swim and crawl out. When he emerged festooned with green slime, we laughed. It broke his heart. No person ever looked more obviously embarrassed and crestfallen than Rip did at that moment.

The most widely accepted and completely erroneous bit of misinformation about dogs, however, is the old myth that your dog will quit hunting if you miss too many birds. We've all heard friends say, with but slight variation, "Never had such a slump in my life. I couldn't hit *anything!* Why, along in the afternoon old Spot got so disgusted he quit hunting. He just walked along at heel, and when I finally got back to the car he was really ready to go home."

I've read this in stories. I've seen paintings in which the artist depicted a bored and uninterested dog behind a hunter who couldn't hit a bird. And if I've heard it once I've heard it a thousand times. Years ago when my state first adopted the hen law, I even heard hunters claim with perfectly straight faces that letting so many hens get up and fly away without shooting them was ruining their dogs.

Now, a retriever might get bored and go to sleep in the blind if his master kept shooting and shooting and never hit a duck. I've never seen it, but it might happen. But no pointing dog or spaniel with which I ever hunted gave a whoop whether we killed the birds he found or not. Their job is to find and point, or flush them. It's their life, the highlight of their existence from one year to the next. As to whether we kill these birds, or even shoot, they couldn't care less.

It's true there are dogs that hunt to the gun and actually seem to want their masters to kill game. And there are pointing dogs that enjoy retrieving. But there are many others that simply hunt for the love of hunting and are kept under control in the field only by firm discipline.

The best bird-finder I ever hunted over was a hardheaded, hard-going pointer whose sole desire was to find birds, set them if they'd set, and make them fly if they wouldn't. He was a determined self-hunter whenever he got the chance. If I sat down to smoke my pipe, I had to keep an eye on him every instant or he'd be gone, trying to move every bird in the county and having a marvelous time doing it. Whether I was there to shoot them made absolutely no difference to him.

Of course, the clincher to my argument is the fact that we all work our dogs on birds before the season opens. These birds are never shot. Did you ever hear of a dog that got discouraged and quit hunting because of this preseason training? Neither have I.

So the next time some expert gives you the lowdown on the canine psyche, a grain or two of salt might be in order. Unless it happened to fit in with my own experience, I'd be inclined to take the salt and leave the wisdom. After all, if a premise was faulty to begin with, age doesn't make it any truer.

Part IX

THE UPLAND-BIRD MYSTIQUE

Chapter 31

The Great Dove Gun

September. Labor Day, vacation over, school starting, September morn. I never think of them. I think of mourning doves. In my state the dove season opens on the first day of September.

Most articles on dove hunting get into a lot of biological facts and figures or else waste a lot of space talking about how hard doves are to hit. Maybe the authors would like to tell you how to hit doves, but don't know how to do it themselves. Well, it's really quite simple and I can tell you exactly: Just point your gun so the charge of shot will arrive where the dove is going at the precise instant he gets there. (If you have difficulty following these simple instructions, don't blame me. I've told you all there is to it.)

All you need if you hope to hit an easy-looking shot like
this is a pattern three times as big as the one you've got.

But every once in a while things all come together right
and we get a dove.

Once, possibly because of the little-understood gravitational effect of the moon on a charge of shot or some other obscure reason, I missed some doves myself. It occurred to me that what we need is a bigger pattern. Now, if you enlarge the pattern in the conventional way by reducing the choke, that pattern will also be thinner. A dove is a small target. If the shot are too far apart, the dove will fly among them unscathed.

It was then I got the idea for the three-barrel gun. If I had a gun with three barrels, all flared slightly away from each other so their patterns wouldn't hit the same spot, as with conventional double guns, but would, instead, strike in three separate and distinct, but barely touching circles, you would have a total pattern area three times as big. That is, if all three barrels fired at once.

Excited at the possibility, I arranged three coins in a triangle on a piece of paper and drew a line around them. Sure enough! The shot from three shells would cover three times the area and still be just as thick. Of course, the coins revealed that there would be a blank spot in the middle, but since nobody ever hits a dove in the center of the pattern anyway, I decided this was inconsequential.

I even read the law that limits shotguns to a capacity of three shells. It didn't specify whether they had to be fired one at a time or could all be fired at once. I was in.

My next step was to contact the celebrated technological wizard and inventor Ed Zern, the originator of the mechanical bird dog, and ask him to design a 12-gauge gun such as I have just described, firing three shells at once from three 26-inch improved-cylinder barrels. I could already hear the plaudits of America's millions of frustrated dove hunters as I sat back to await his reply.

Imagine my disappointment when Ed declined to accept the assignment, even though I had generously offered to share the profits with him. His reply was brief, even blunt: "I wouldn't touch your invention with a 10-foot pole," he wrote. "Such a gun would be inhumane."

He then added a second short paragraph: "The recoil resulting from firing three 12-gauge shells simultaneously would probably knock a lot of hunters silly."

Now that we have touched on the serious aspects of dove shooting, let us turn to the lighter side.

It was, indeed, September 1. My brother Burtt and his wife, my wife, and I walked away from the farmhouse at 4:30 P.M. It was hot. We stood for a few moments in the shade of the last tree before starting out across the open fields upon which the sun was beating down with all its fury from a cloudless sky. Three doves whistled over in their rolling, darting flight—headed toward the field where we intended to shoot. Nobody's gun was loaded, of course, but it was a hopeful sign. My pulse quickened.

In our neighborhood, the doves feed in the morning and go get a drink. They then fly to an orchard or a grove of trees, where they sit around cooing and acting innocent all day. Late in the afternoon they return to the feeding fields and fill up again. After that, they get another drink and go to roost for the night.

The field we planned to hunt had raised a crop of wheat—now harvested—and then the stubble had been mowed. This was good. Doves don't like high stubble. They prefer to feed in an open field or one with only low cover so they can keep an eye out for danger.

There was an irrigation ditch along one edge of the field; a weedy fence row bordered the opposite side. Burtt and I sat down along the ditch, 75 yards apart, with our backs to the field. We sent the girls on to the other side where they would find adequate concealment along the fence.

Then we all went through the same interminable wait that we have gone through on the first day of every dove season for as long as I can remember. The cloudless sky was also doveless. The sun beat on my back, and sweat trickled down my face. A few specks in the distance grew steadily larger and larger—and turned out to be blackbirds. I glanced at my watch repeatedly between looks at the sky and watched the hands crawl around toward the end of legal shooting time. I wondered, as I always do, whether the doves would really come.

Just as I was filling my pipe for the third time, I saw them. Doves! Four of them were coming straight toward me, and fast. And how did they get so close before I saw them? I laid my pipe down and dropped my tobacco. I put my hands on my gun, which was lying across my knees, but didn't raise it yet. I didn't want the doves to spot the movement and flare off.

I caught myself muscling up, clutching my gun as though my life depended on it. I was tense as a cat crouched ready to spring on a mouse. My palms were slick with sweat. How can a little, 4-ounce bird have such an effect on a 160-pound man? However it may be, tight muscles are fatal to good wing-shooting. I made a conscious effort to relax.

Now! They were coming into range, I raised my gun, put it to my shoulder, and shoved the safety off. The birds were not yet overhead. It would be my favorite shot—a straight incomer. I swung ahead of one, blotted it out with the muzzle, and pulled the trigger. The solid push of the recoil—the first time I had felt it for eight months—felt good against my shoulder. I had to be right. But the dove flew on.

Undoubtedly, I had shot behind it. I always shoot behind the first dove. Leaning back to take a bird that was now directly overhead, I swung faster. The trap load of 7½'s found its mark and the dove fell dead, 75 feet out in the wheat stubble behind me. A few feathers were drifting slowly down as I walked out to get it.

Back in the ditch, I reloaded my gun, gathered up what I could of the spilled tobacco, and resumed stuffing my pipe, meanwhile watching closely in the direction from which the first doves had come. Would more come in time? Would they come at all? Again, the sky was blank.

I had smoked the pipe half down when I saw a single coming. I laid aside my pipe, hunkered down, and held my gun ready but unraised. The speeding dove was boring straight at me. I didn't move an eyelash, but at the last instant that bird veered off toward brother Burtt. I saw him raise his gun, miss, lean back, and connect on the second shot, just as I had done.

"I'll bet you didn't lead it enough the first time," I called.

He answered, "That's right," as he walked out to pick it up.

We waited. The time came when we had only thirty minutes left. I was uneasy. Then I saw more doves, at least a dozen, coming from the southeast. And off to the south was a little wad of four or five. Three were coming from due east. And there were still-more-distant specks in the sky behind the birds I could unmistakably distinguish.

Maybe what happened during the next brief span of time explains why you don't read detailed descriptions of dove shooting. After waiting for two hours, first confident, then hopeful, then despairing, we were suddenly overwhelmed by doves. They were boring in at us from every angle of the eastern sky. High and low, right and left, doves were barreling past Burtt and me and fluttering down in the wheat stubble behind us to feed.

We did the best we could with what we had. My gun was hot. The edge of tension was off now. I was relaxed and shooting as well as I ever hope to shoot. But I can no more remember every shot than I can remember the day I was born. Things were happening too fast. It became a frenzied routine of shoot, reload, pick another target, swing with it, and shoot again.

Suddenly, when the lowering sun was a great, red, blazing ball, almost touching the western mountains, it dawned on me that I had heard no shooting from the west. Mary and Ellen were down there, along the western edge of the field, and all the doves were coming from the east, northeast, and southeast. Like good, obedient wives should, they had done exactly what Burtt and I had told them: "Go to the fence and stay there."

I was ashamed. Burtt must have had the same thought about the same time. We stood up, waved our caps—ignoring the doves that were whistling around our very heads—and shouted, "Come up here!"

They were ready. They came on the double. You never saw women make better time across a five-acre wheat stubble!

We spread out along the irrigation ditch, four in a row. To those unfortunate (or fortunate) husbands whose wives don't hunt, I must say this: You can't believe how much ammunition two women can burn up in ten short minutes! Burtt and I soon quit shooting with our limits of 10 apiece. Mary and Ellen all but melted the solder from between their gun barrels. The doves were like a swarm of bees now. They hadn't been shot at this year, and they were in the habit of feeding in this field. They were whipping over us in waves. And the women, frustrated, eager, and forgotten—for twenty minutes, anyway—did their best to fight them off.

The hour, the minute, the final deadline of legal sunset came. Burtt and I told our still-eager wives to quit shooting. Then we gathered up all our doves and sat on the ditchbank and looked at the glowing western sky. We had a smoke and laughed at this and all the other opening days of dove season when we had waited and waited and waited and, finally—after we had decided the birds would never come—had suddenly been overwhelmed.

And then we walked slowly back down the winding lane among the fields and watched the swallows soar and dip and smelled the clean odors of alfalfa and ripening corn.

Chapter 32

The Wild, Wild Pheasant

Late of a wintry day in the year 12,000 B.C., two birds huddled uncomfortably in the scant shelter of a bamboo thicket on the side of a mountain in China. The lonesome wind rattled the stalks dismally and the cold rain drove through.

In the valley below, beside a tiny field hacked from the forest, was the hut of a peasant. Dim light from a flickering fire shone around the edges of the goat hide stretched over the door, and smoke rose from the chimney. The hut boasted neither patio nor swimming pool, but it looked like heaven to the two birds. Their own bamboo shelter was very well ventilated, and now as the raw dusk settled over the countryside it was obvious that they would spend a long, cold night.

One of them, a jungle cock, finally shook the rain off his feathers and said to his companion, "Kid, this is for the birds. Look at that farmer down there. He has a snug house and a warm fire. He has plenty to eat and he doesn't have to scratch for it in the dead of winter, either. Tomorrow, I will become his chicken. What I want is security."

The other bird, a pheasant, also shook the water off. "You can chicken out if you like," he said, fixing his companion with a contemptuous glare, "but by the law of the gods only one thing will buy security. That is freedom. If you are willing to trade your freedom for security, go ahead.

Once in a great while a cock pheasant makes a mistake.

You will live in a chicken house with a pen around it to protect you from the foxes, and the farmer will feed you every day. You will never be hungry and you will never be cold. But neither you nor your grandchildren will ever be free again."

The cock thought it over, but it was a miserable night and every time the wind rattled the bamboo and woke him up he imagined how nice it would be to live in a snug chicken house with plenty to eat and no foxes prowling around. So the next morning he rustled up a jungle hen and sold her on the idea and they hiked down to the farm and became chickens. That was the beginning of the poultry business and to this day nothing has more security—or less freedom—than a chicken.

The pheasant weathered it out. He gritted his beak and got even wilder and tougher, if that was possible, and each spring he'd sit on the bamboo fence and show the chickens to his children and grandchildren and great-grandchildren and even great-great-grandchildren (for he was an extremely wise pheasant and lived to a ripe old age). "Look at 'em come running when the farmer rattles the feed bucket," he'd say with a sneer. "They're getting their unemployment compensation. They couldn't make a living now to save their lazy lives. Why they can't even fly!"

Then he'd crow disdainfully and peck a few holes in the farmer's melons just for spite and fly away into the woods with all the young pheasants before the farmer could knock one of them over with his slingshot. He really dinged that lesson into them and they dinged it into their children and they, in turn, dinged in into theirs and as a result the pheasant is now one of the very few creatures that have lived in close proximity to man for thousands of years and still retain all of their original wildness.

In fact, according to my friends, they are getting wilder every season. I doubt that. I suspect my friends are getting older. I think pheasants always have been wild, ever since that memorable evening when the jungle cock decided to become the forebear of our domestic chickens and the wise old rooster coined an expression that has been popular ever since.

They were wild when Pliny wrote: "In Colchis, Asia Minor, there is the pheasant, a bird with two tufts of feathers like ears which it drops and raises every now and then." They were wild when Caesar's Romans took them to England; they were wild when Judge Owen N. Denny brought them to the United States in 1881, and they are wild now. And smart.

A friend and I were coming in from duck hunting one day in January. There had been a snow, but the wind had blown some of the fields clean and now the sun was shining. Pheasants were everywhere, enjoying the sunshine and picking up waste grain and weed seeds from the bare ground. We must have seen a hundred or so in a ride of a few miles, and a great many were cocks. We saw as many as six cocks in one small field.

"Well," said my companion as we drove along, "I see the winter hatch came off all right."

I said, "The what?"

"The winter hatch. There were no cocks when the season ended. You said so yourself. Remember that last day when it was raining and we couldn't find a rooster for love nor money?"

I did remember the day, a fruitless one during which we tramped endless miles, soaked to the skin, and the dogs found nothing but a few stray hens. I also vaguely recalled making a remark, sometime during the dismal afternoon, to the effect that all the roosters must surely have been killed.

My friend continued. "I have the answer. As soon as the season ends, the hens nest again. They bring off a brood that is all roosters and they mature quickly. By January, the country is full of them."

I laughed. I had been had.

Ask any old pheasant hunter what happens to all the cocks a few days after the season opens. He'll say, "They hide out."

Then ask him where. He'll scratch the back of his head and say, "Well, I, um, uh, oh, in bog swamps and brush patches and swales and things. Anyplace where you can't find them."

In that, he'll be exactly right. In fact, it is a pretty safe bet that the average cock pheasant, especially if he has survived one hunting season, is more than a match for the average pheasant hunter. Maybe he isn't actually smarter—after all, men kill more pheasants than pheasants kill men—but he knows the country better and he knows when to flush wild and how to pick cover that he can get out of without being shot at.

Mostly, we shoot pheasants because there are a lot of them—nearly always more than we realize if we get any at all—and out of the total number, some are unlucky. The limiting factor on pheasants is habitat. Repeated studies have shown that in good pheasant country, where they have adequate food, cover, and water, it is virtually impossible to kill enough cocks to endanger the next year's supply. They are too wild and smart.

There are, however, ways in which it is possible to bag an occasional pheasant after the going gets tough. One of the best times to hunt then is early in the morning. Pheasants like to roost in stubble or grass where there is nothing overhead so they can make a quick getaway in case some predator finds them during the night. They walk or fly out of their safe daytime cover late in the evening, usually after it is too dark to shoot, and return in the morning. They don't, however, enjoy the dubious blessing of the alarm clock and they sometimes loiter in the open to feed for half an hour or so.

At this time, as soon as it is light enough to distinguish cocks from hens, I have occasionally enjoyed excellent and easy pheasant shooting. I watch for roosting areas, which are always marked by piles of droppings and are usually near cornfields, brush patches, or swamps, while I am beating my brains out during the middle of the day. Then I return early in the morning. Even lacking this knowledge, it is always well worthwhile to hunt open fields adjacent to good cover as soon as light permits.

Of course, in those states where an arbitrary shooting hour prevents this early hunting, and everywhere once the sun starts to melt the frost off the stubble, you don't find pheasants in open fields. The only chance then is to seek them in the spots of their own choosing. These are invariably places where the cards are stacked against the hunter.

Where corn is grown, it provides good daytime pheasant cover and the accepted way of hunting is by driving. Several hunters station themselves at one end of the field and wait quietly for the pheasants to come to them from the opposite end. This is an effective way to hunt because most of the pheasants run up the rows ahead of the drivers, but I don't like it. I prefer to hunt with one or, at most, two companions and sometimes I hunt alone. One man can't drive a cornfield.

There is, however, a way to get pheasants out of corn, even alone, if you have a dog and know the covers well. A pheasant, along with all other upland birds, usually has his mind made up where he is going before he leaves the ground. If there is a cornfield surrounded by poor cover, but with a brush patch 200 yards away, all the pheasants in the corn will head for that brush when they get up.

One day in November, I killed a couple of cocks early and returned to the car about 9 o'clock. It was parked at the end of a ten-acre cornfield near the middle of an eighty on which a fellow I know raises mostly hay, small grain, sugar beets, and potatoes. I hadn't hunted the corn.

I had put Rip in the car and was sitting on the front bumper enjoying a sandwich and a cup of coffee in the morning sunlight when I heard a cautious movement nearby. A cock pheasant was looking at me from the corn, not 20 feet away! He looked me right in the eye while I, without moving a muscle, tried to decide what to do. My gun, the action open, was lying across the hood behind me. Rip, of course, was in the car. By the time I could get my gun, load it, and let him out, the cock would be far gone. I'd never get a shot at him.

I knew, however, that the closest good cover was near the upper corner of the field, on my side. The cock would probably fly toward it. I set down coffee and sandwich—at this first movement he was gone—got Rip out of the car and sent him into the corn, grabbed my gun, and ran as hard as I could for the corner of the field, loading as I went. I got there in time to draw a few deep breaths before the cock threshed out. He was a little farther into the field than I had expected, but he flew straight toward the cover and gave me an easy crossing shot at 20 yards.

Rip was still far down in the corn. I picked up my rooster and stood quietly at the end. A minute later, four more pheasants flushed from the middle of the field—evidently Rip had pushed them pretty hard—and they, too, flew toward the brush patch out from my corner. One of them was a cock. I let him down, thereby completing my limit of four as easily as I have ever done it after opening day, called Rip when he came to the end of the field, and went back to my interrupted sandwich and coffee.

Of course, I was lucky. I'll go so far as to say that anybody is lucky to kill four cock pheasants before 10 o'clock in the morning after the season is well advanced. But I did know which way the pheasants were most likely to fly when they left the corn, and I was there waiting when Rip pushed them out.

Aside from corn, the best daytime spots for pheasants are those that are hardest to hunt—hardest to get at and hardest to work out with the chance of getting a shot once you do reach them. In one such spot, a clump of willows and wild roses, far from any road and completely surrounded by barren and unpromising ground, my companion and I found a very plethora of pheasants. I doubt that it had been hunted before that season, certainly not for a week or more, and it was fairly stiff with them.

It was about 300 yards long and a fifth as wide, tapering to a point at each end. We separated while we were still some distance away and approached as cautiously as we would stalk a herd of deer. My companion pussyfooted to one end and stood quietly; I took Rip, who has been taught to heel at a whisper, and walked to the other.

Once in it, I let him start to hunt, but held him close, and began to carry on a continuous, if somewhat one-sided, conversation. That's all you need to do to drive pheasants—just talk. Cows and horses crash brush, and pheasants are not afraid of them. But cows and horses don't talk. A pheasant knows, once he hears the human voice, that he may get shot at any moment. He takes steps to prevent it.

In this case, that was exactly what I wanted them to do. I wanted them to run to the far end of the cover where my companion was waiting. Before I had gone 50 feet, Rip's actions told me we had hit the jackpot. I didn't see a bird, however, until I was two-thirds of the way through.

The first indication of what was about to happen was two quick shots from the far end. Then, suddenly, the air was full of pheasants. Cocks and hens flushed ahead of me and flew toward the end. Others, flushing near the end, flew back overhead. I hit one cock and missed another and heard my companion shoot twice more. I missed again, then killed my second cock.

I had momentarily forgotten about Rip. He was in the middle of the brush between me and my companion and the pheasants were pouring out. Two roosters flew overhead while I was reloading. By the time my gun was ready, the sky was vacant. I picked up my birds and went on to the end, but I didn't get another chance.

When I reached my partner, I learned that he had killed four cocks without moving out of his tracks and had let as many more fly away. And, of course, I should have had my four, too. Nobody should miss a pheasant. Even so, six roosters out of one small cover late in the season was better than a jab with a sharp stick.

Perhaps I should add, to complete the story, that we returned to this cover a few days later and hunted it again. There was not a cock in it! We put out three or four hens, then worked all the other promising spots in the vicinity and never did discover where the others had gone.

Whenever possible, it pays for two hunters to separate and approach a cover from opposite ends. One can wait while the other comes through, or else they can meet in the middle. This often works well if each has a dog. In any case, to enter side by side, talking happily and bumbling along, is futile. The pheasants are likely to be gone before you are halfway through.

One time a friend and I hunted a long swale surrounded by cultivated fields. We hadn't seen each other for six months and had a lot to say and we just walked up to one end and started hunting, full of ignorance and enthusiasm and surplus words. About two-thirds of the way through the dog pointed and we flushed a hen. She was the only bird we saw.

On past the end of the cover, the farmer, whom I knew, was digging sugar beets and we walked over to pass the time of day. "Boy!" he said, "I wish I'd had my gun. You hadn't much more than crawled through the fence when the pheasants started running out. Nine of 'em came right past me down the beet rows, all in easy range!"

Pheasants aren't much afraid of men on tractors because they see them working in the fields all the time. It would hardly be economical to buy a $20,000 tractor with which to hunt pheasants, however, and, besides, I'm not so sure but what they're smart enough to tell a city slicker on a tractor from an honest farmer. There is another aid, much less expensive, that's effective.

A fellow with whom I hunt occasionally is a hound for calls. He has all kinds and he can call virtually everything but his own dogs and children. He has deer, antelope, and elk calls; fox, bobcat, and coyote calls; crow, magpie, and squirrel calls; duck and goose calls; quail and chukar calls; and pheasant calls.

I have seen him call a quail up until he could almost touch it and he can call a pheasant out of a cornfield or a bog swamp. I have never seen him call a pheasant as close as that quail came, but he can bring them near enough so it is a cinch to flush and shoot them even without a dog.

So far, although I've watched him call, I haven't tried it myself. It seems sort of sneaky, though why it should be any worse than calling ducks I wouldn't know. Certainly, the pheasant call provides an effective way for a lone hunter to bring them out of cover where he wouldn't have a chance to get a shot otherwise. It also helps by locating them. They will frequently answer, even though you might not want to sit and wait for them to come.

Fortunately, it takes quite a bit of practice to learn to blow a pheasant call properly. I can see that it would be a ludicrous situation if every pheasant hunter had a call and they all started calling at once. I can imagine hundreds of hunters hiding in the brush and hopefully calling each other.

As soon as the pheasants caught on—as they certainly would—they'd get a tremendous kick out of it. No doubt, pheasant calls would then save as many pheasants as duck calls now save ducks!

Chapter 33

Pheasant-Hunting Wisdom

On a bright October day way back in 1926, Mr. Davis came down to our farm to hunt. He brought his family and a lunch, as many of our autumn visitors did in those days, and he went out alone in the morning. At noon Mrs. Davis and my mother combined forces, and we all—the four Davises and the four Truebloods—ate at the big picnic table on the lawn, enjoying alternately the mellow sunlight and the thinning shade as the golden leaves came tumbling down.

After we had finished and the grownups were enjoying their last cups of coffee and we kids were fidgeting, Mr. Davis (he signed his name C.W. and his cronies called him Fat, but not for another ten years was I to venture that familiarity) said to my father, "I have a little 20-gauge double in the car, and if you think it would be all right I'd like for Ted to take it and go out with me this afternoon."

My father thought the proposition over—for an hour, it seemed to me—and finally answered: "Yes, I think it would. He's been hunting with a .22 for several years, and I'm sure he'd be careful. And this summer we've been shooting quite a bit at tin cans tossed up in the air. I believe he could hit a pheasant with a shotgun."

Mr. Davis got the gun out and explained the safety to me and gave me a pocketful of shells. Then we walked out past the corral and started through

When you're hunting pheasants, there's no substitute for
a dog that knows how to handle them.

the corn. My feet didn't touch the ground for 200 yards, and if that gun had
been made of glass I couldn't have carried it more carefully.

We were walking across the rows and I had barely come back to earth
when I looked down the row I was stepping over and saw a cock pheasant.
Apparently our approach had rattled him, because he was only 50 feet
away, pressed tight against the earth, trying to hide behind a weed that was
entirely inadequate. I looked at him and he looked at me. Then he flew.

Having spent all my thirteen years on a farm in good pheasant country,
the sight of a cock pheasaant, either on the ground or in the air, was
certainly no novelty. But let me tell you, I'd never seen a pheasant before!
Nothing sharpens the senses like a loaded gun. The noise he made
threshing up through the corn was petrifying. It was a wonder I ever got the
20-gauge to my shoulder.

Foolishly the bird, instead of flying straight down the row toward Mr.
Davis, where I wouldn't have dared to shoot, chose to come out of the corn
in front of me. This made a crossing shot, quartering away, and I can see

Rip, son of Joe, soon learned the ropes on
handling pheasants.

him yet against the smoky-blue October sky. His colors, bronze and green and red and black, all iridescent and glittering, and his magnificent shape are as vivid in my mind's eye now as when I pressed the trigger.

And press the trigger I did. I knew nothing of lead, of course. I hadn't even heard of it. Nobody had told me to swing my gun with my target, and I was blissfully unaware of the disastrous effect of stopping that swing. But I'd been shooting at tossed cans with my .22 and I must have swung fast to catch up with the crossing pheasant. I probably pulled just as the muzzle passed him, and the unintentional swing must have continued long enough.

At the crack of the gun there were only feathers against the sky where he had been. He was tumbling down. I ran and picked him up.

No more birds flew my way that afternoon, and it was just as well. One was enough. A hundred couldn't possibly have been a greater thrill, and more would only have blurred the memory of that first thrilling instant—the first time I'd ever fired a shotgun at any flying game.

Before the Davises left for home, I had bought the 20-gauge. I gave Mr. Davis all my money and agreed to pay the balance as soon as I could earn it. He gave me what shells he had.

Naturally, my record for the rest of the fall suffered sadly by comparison with that first afternoon. I made some ridiculous misses. I must have shot at birds 100 yards away, because I had no idea of a shotgun's limited range. And I killed one—but only one—pheasant on the ground.

I can't remember how many I got that season, but the old diary tells me that I killed forty-five pheasants in 1927, when I was fourteen years old. I'm rather proud of that now, but only because they were all killed legally and all flying. Otherwise, it's nothing to brag about. I hunted nearly every evening after school and many mornings before school, and always on Saturday during the six-week season.

I mention it for another reason—to make the point that pheasants are not easy. Despite years of experience, I'm still learning how to hunt pheasants. I recall a sports magazine that blurbed on its cover, "American Game Birds— All You Need to Know to Get Them," but there still are times when I don't know enough to get pheasants. The pheasant is the most underestimated bird there is.

In the first place, you young pheasant hunters must remember that you are dealing with a crook. A pheasant was hatched sly, sneaky, and cunning and he develops these traits at the expense of more forthright ones as he grows older. There is not a straightforward bone in his body. If you hunt him as you would quail, you will bag no pheasants save the local halfwit or maybe the occasional bird whose luck runs out at the wrong moment.

I am not downgrading pheasants. I admire them and like to hunt them. But it takes devious methods to outwit a devious quarry. Oh, I'll admit that during the first few days of the season, before the pheasants realize the war has started, you can take a gun and simply walk across the fields and kill them. But that's no criterion. If the situation were reversed, the pheasants would kill a lot of people before the people got wise.

After that, you'd better assume your quarry knows more than you do. He has better ears, possibly better eyes, definitely better legs, and he knows the entire area he calls home as well as you know the way to the bathroom. You should assume that he will never hold for a point, that he will always run when he hears you coming, and that he will always flush out of range.

Of course, he won't. Sometimes in the right cover, usually early or late in the day, a good dog can nail pheasants down like bobwhites. And sometimes he won't run or flush wild. But if you assume at the start that he is going to do these things and hunt him accordingly, you'll bag many more pheasants than the hunters who don't.

The first big aid toward hunting any kind of game successfully is knowledge of its habits. Briefly, a pheasant's daily routine in the fall is somewhat as follows:

Early morning finds him moving on foot toward safe daytime cover, feeding as he goes. He'll usually pause for a drink if the weather is dry and he won't walk farther than necessary, but by midmorning it's a sure bet that he'll be safely ensconced in the toughest, thickest, hardest-to-hunt spot available—a cornfield, brush patch, swamp, or swale.

There he'll stay till late in the afternoon. Then he'll move out cautiously, ready to retreat at the first sign of danger, and retrace his route of the morning. His roosting area will always be devoid of cover overhead so that he can fly quickly if a fox or feral cat attempts to catch him. Stubble, moist grassy swales, any fields with low but reasonably thick cover, are to his liking. Look for piles of droppings as you walk through such places, because pheasants return regularly to the same roosting areas, and knowing where they are is helpful.

This daily routine points up the two best times of day to hunt wherever it is legal: very early morning and very late evening—just as early and late, in fact, as you can tell cocks from hens. A farmer friend one fall had a ten-acre cornfield bordered on the east by five acres of new-seeding clover with the stubble from the cover crop of wheat still standing, and on the west by twelve acres of mixed grain stubble.

Several times during the season I parked my car near the corn just as daylight was breaking. As soon as it was light enough I began hunting the two adjoining fields. I always started near the corn and worked away from it, moving slowly and quietly and giving the dog ample time to cover the ground carefully, because a pheasant still on the roost gives off very little scent. I was always successful.

The same two fields were also excellent late in the evening. Pheasants that spent the day in the corn roosted in them, and by always hunting *away* from the corn I had the birds in a position where they were more inclined to hold for the dog than to run. Had I started on the far sides of the stubble fields, especially in the evenings, most of the birds would have run for the safe cover long before I was in range.

Of course, some states don't permit hunting before sunup and after sunset, and sometimes you want to hunt all day. This means going after pheasants when it's tough. The most successful method is driving, and it is the only one that offers much chance to men who have no dogs. Two hunters can do it, but three or four are better.

Station one or two men at one end of the cornfield or other cover and let the others approach them slowly and noisily. And always, of course, in corn the drivers must walk parallel to the rows. Pheasants run down them, and if you attempt to drive the other way most of them will slip out to the side long before you reach the end.

Most brush patches, heavy swales, and swamps are wider one way than the other and come to a point somewhere. They should be driven the long way toward the point, and a hunter stationed there will get shooting as they come out. The drivers should move even more slowly in this kind of cover than in corn, giving the pheasants plenty of time to move ahead. And don't worry about whether they will—it's their nature.

Of course, the hunter or hunters stationed at the end of the cover must be perfectly quiet. They should get into position without making a sound. Once there they should stand still and, above all else, keep their mouths shut.

My brother Burtt coined a phrase that has now taken the place of "driving" in our hunting parlance. We wanted to drive a brush patch that was half a mile long and 200 yards wide. That's a lot of cover for one man, and unless one of us stayed at the point we would get no shooting. "I'll sneak around and talk 'em out," he said.

He did, too. Starting at the far end, he came through, talking and shouting continually. By the time he was three-fourths of the way through, the pheasants were buzzing out like bees from a hive!

For the remainder of that season we "talked 'em out," and it has always worked. We don't talk, however, when we are preparing to hunt a stubble in the morning or evening or while hunting any other kind of cover where there is a chance that the pheasants may stay put.

Chapter 34

A Day
on Fluster Flat

Some thirty years ago H. L. Betten called the California valley quail "the greatest game bird in America." He was taking in a lot of territory and a lot of birds, but Harry Betten was not given to careless statements. His stuff had the temper of experience and the ring of truth.

At that time I had never hunted valley quail. I was skeptical, but I remembered Betten's description because it was not the kind of thing any devout bird hunter could easily forget. Now that I have hunted them, I sometimes think his words were a masterpiece of understatement. But I must admit that sometimes, when the agony of frustration is upon me, I am tempted to call him an old faker who wouldn't have recognized an honest game bird—say, a bobwhite or a ruffed grouse—if he saw one sitting on a fence post.

Both emotions alternately prevailed during a short but memorable day in October. And California valley quail, the little devils, the darlings, were responsible. It was in one of my secret covers, a place we call Fluster Flat. We named it that on our first hunt there because it had so many game birds—mountain and valley quail, chukars, Hungarian partridge, and pheasants—that I became utterly flustered, for the only time in all my

One valley quail is hit, and Ted has a chance for a double.

experience with a smoothbore gun. I was flustered and my dog was flustered. I had to call him in, sit down, and smoke a pipe before I could resume hunting with some degree of sanity.

Anyhow, as we rolled down the hill onto Fluster Flat a few valley quail buzzed up out of the greasewood beside the road and settled down again 20 yards away. We stopped the car, put on our hunting jackets, dumped shells into the pockets, let out Rip, the pointer, to perform his preliminary ambulations, uncased our guns, loaded them, and started walking toward the cover where the quail had lit.

Now, for the benefit of those who have never hunted in the arid West, I must explain that cover here is far different from that of Alabama or New

Hampshire. The vegetation is sparse, though in some spots the brush is so dense that a dog can scarcely get through it, and is higher than a man's head. In most places, however, there is scattered low brush, a great deal of bare ground, and only short, thin grass.

The end of Fluster Flat on which we stopped the car was like that. Greasewood, four-wing saltbush, and rabbit brush grew in widely scattered clumps, none more than a foot through or two feet high. There was some bud sage, which never seems to get more than six inches tall, and very little grass. The ground was dusty, powdery dry. Little puffs of dust squirted out from beneath our feet at each step. This condition, coupled with the pungent odor of many of the plants, soon gets a dog's nose into such a state that he couldn't detect the presence of a billy goat, much less a recently air-washed quail. So I made Rip walk at heel as we started toward the spot where we had marked them down.

We were halfway there when we saw the birds running ahead—far ahead. They didn't trust us. They were 50 yards away, dodging rapidly through the open brush, and there were more of them than we had seen at first, probably twenty-five. We angles out to separate our paths by 30 yards and thereby flank the covey, and continued toward them. Two hundred yards ahead was a patch of thicker brush. Maybe they would hold in it.

They didn't. That is, most of them didn't. It is characteristic of running valley quail that a single or a pair will sometimes see a bit of cover that looks inviting and decide to stop—and when they do they stick tighter than ticks. My companion kicked out a single and killed it. Rip, still walking at heel, pointed a clump of greasewood after I had passed it. I flushed a pair, hit one, and missed the other.

Meanwhile, passing through the brush, the covey picked up more recruits, and we were now following 50. We trailed them across an utterly barren wash, swept clean by a summer cloudburst, and toward the slope beyond. At its foot there was a fringe of brush, and again we hoped they might hold. Again, they didn't. Instead they flushed wild, apparently tired of running, and flew to the top of the ridge, 250 yards away at the end of a 30-degree slope.

Ahead of us, when we reached the top, was a little valley, well grown up to sagebrush on our side and with thick greasewood along the dry wash in the bottom. Here, at last, we thought, they will surely hold.

We started down, expecting momentarily to be surrounded by buzzing, darting, dodging quail. But halfway to the greasewood I looked ahead and saw them going up the mountain on the other side of the draw. The covey had again doubled; now there were 100 quail if there was one.

We were already sweating in the intense heat, and the mountain ahead— a real mountain, a mile to the top—was as barren as the flat. It looked hopeless. We stopped and watched the quail, flowing like an army of bugs, weave their way upward. Each bird seemed to run independently of the others, little feet flying but body as erect and steady as though riding a bicycle, yet all went along in a compact blue-gray carpet.

My partner elected to quit. But my dander was up—I was getting stubborn. Not that I wanted to kill all those quail, or even the 15 that the law permitted. I just wasn't willing to admit that they were smarter and faster and tougher than I. If I could only get around them, make them fly back into the little valley with the good cover, we would have shooting until the world looked level.

Ah, futile thought! Oh, foolishness of the chase! Who ever made any game bird fly where it didn't want to fly? But I started. With Rip still at heel, I ran along the ridge and around the head of the little valley, then started up the mountain 200 yards to the right of the running quail and completely out of their sight.

I ran, walked to catch my breath, then ran again until my cap and shirt were soaked and the sweat trickled down out of my eyebrows into my eyes and the grip and the fore end of my gun were slick with sweat. My lungs were bellows and each leg was lead and weighed a hundred pounds.

At last I knew that I was higher up the mountain than the quail. I had to be. They wouldn't climb so far, and there were a few pockets of brush in which they could have stopped. I swung out to the left on a contour until I knew I was well past them. I didn't see any, nor did Rip detect an odor of their passing. I was above them.

I let Rip go then, for the first time, and we hunted the mountainside down to the dry wash at the bottom. Not a quail! Not a single, solitary, measly quail. They were gone. Where? How? I only wish I knew. I threw myself on the ground, completely beaten. Rip flopped down beside me, panting.

Meanwhile my companion had been walking back and forth over the bottom and shooting occasionally. I joined him after a few minutes, and with Rip's help we found six or seven more quail. These birds were not there as the result of my efforts on the mountain. They were singles and pairs that had stopped off in the cover while the others went on.

During this interval of easy hunting, there occurred one of those odd things that sometimes happen in the uplands and are long remembered. Rip pointed. I walked in, and as I put up two quail a single flushed a few yards to the left. I hit the first bird and missed the second. But the single, 10 yards farther out and unseen till then, flew into the shot pattern. So it worked out that I hit one and missed one—and still made a double with two shots.

After we'd hunted out the bottom, we worked around the end of the ridge and back to the car. We gave Rip a drink out of the water can, had one ourselves, and drove on across the flat toward the spot where we planned to camp. Here was a big lone cottonwood, though the soil was dry and sandy, and when we stopped the car we saw that the sand was dimpled with quail tracks. We wouldn't have far to go to find hunting that afternoon!

We ate our lunch in the welcome shade of the old tree and then rested awhile. But the season was still young and we were impatient to be after the birds that had left their footprints in our campsite.

Close to camp, the brush was comparatively thick, and we hoped to find them in it, because the chance they might hold was better. But we didn't find them. We walked possibly half a mile, then saw quail running ahead. This time we tried rushing them, but they flushed wild, flew around the end of a hill, and, like the big covey of the morning, completely eluded us. Again a few singles stayed in the fringe of sage along a wash, but most of the birds vanished utterly.

By the time we had tramped out a hundred acres of brush looking for them, it was late afternoon. It was hotter and, if possible, drier and dustier than it had been at 10 o'clock. Poor Rip, thirsty and hot, his nose clogged with dust and the aromatic odor of the desert plants, was completely at a loss.

We started down a swale with fairly decent cover and he apparently bumped a small covey that might have held. We followed them—not so much because we hoped to find the singles as because they had flown in the general direction of the car. Rip was not alone in his condition, and I fear that if Mr. Betten had appeared suddenly before me my feelings about his evaluation of the valley quail would have made his ears burn. Road runners! Flying rabbits! Why, an old cock pheasant wasn't in it with these topknotted idiots when it came to running!

We did collect a couple of singles on our way to camp, however, and spread our afternoon's bag on the canvas to cool with those from our first foray. We now had fifteen between us, half our limit. At least ten times that many had run away. Getting our duffel out of the car, we put up the tent, gathered a pile of wood, set up the grill, and placed the grub boxes handy. Then we collapsed. It had been a long day; we had left home at daylight. Rip, asleep, would occasionally whimper and kick. I suppose he was running a covey of quail that always managed to stay just out of reach.

The sun dropped behind the ridge and the air got fresher. My companion said, "It really wasn't so bad. Fifteen quail is better than a jab with a sharp stick. Maybe we ought to get dinner and not try to hunt any more."

I was on the point of replying when we heard the clear, whistled *wh-wh-whew* of a quail. I answered and it whistled back. Another chimed in off to the left, then a third. Rip jumped up and stood looking intently into the brush.

There was now no need for me to answer my companion. We started in the direction of the quail and Rip pointed the covey, a nice one of 40 or 50 birds, before we had walked 100 yards. We both doubled. The singles scattered like a handful of tossed pebbles into the best cover on the flat. This was better!

We collected our four birds, then hesitated. It never pays to rush after the singles until they have had time to move around a little and put off scent, but the day was getting short. Waiting as long as we dared, in view of the time we had left, we went on and got about to where we thought the first of the singles ought to be. When Rip pointed, my companion flushed and killed a bird. On the way to retrieve, Rip slammed into a beautiful, half-turned-back point. I got that one.

Rip brought it in and I helped him find the other, about which he apparently had forgotten; I have never yet been lucky enough to own a dog that was a genius. And then, 10 yards farther on, he pointed a third.

It was the same story until we had killed our 15 birds and were through. I doubt whether it took thirty minutes; it didn't seem one-third that long. It

Ted with a daily limit of valley quail.

was perfect. You wouldn't have thought Rip was the same dog, nor would you have believed we were hunting the same kind of quail. Apparently the humidity rose slightly when the sun set, so that Rip could smell them, and in this better cover the valley quail stuck as tight as bobwhites ever did.

That is not to say it was easy shooting. Valley quail are never easy. They buzz. They come up high enough to clear the brush and then they buzz away over it, low and fast. In flying away from you they're often lower at 30 yards than they were at 10, and that trick never makes for easy shooting. And sometimes, in cover that is only waist-high, you don't see them at all until they are out of range.

I put Rip at heel and we walked back to camp. It was a different day. Rip was a different dog, and I was a different man from what I had been at 4 P.M.

Chapter 35

Magnificent Midget

When the game warden checked us, we had two quail—one apiece out of a wild covey that had flushed barely in reach of the full-choke barrels. It was 4 P.M. of a gray November afternoon.

There are days when quail are hard to find. This had been one of them. Drizzling rain had fallen most of the time since early morning. Though we had tramped through many covers that were usually productive, the dog had failed to strike the scent of birds. Now we were undecided where to turn. We had no thought of giving up, however. You don't quit with daylight and only one bird and the season coming to a close.

We drove a couple of miles farther down the dirt road and turned in at another farm. After speaking to its owner we walked out into his fields—fields that we knew well and that we also knew held quail.

We tramped across a corn patch. It had been picked. The stalks were broken down and weathered, and there was much spilled grain on the ground. Previously, we had found two coveys feeding here along toward evening. This time there were none.

Finally, just before dusk, we started across a weedy swale to another field. The cover here was dense. Thick, waist-high sweet clover made pushing our way difficult. I couldn't see the dog. Suddenly, when I was nearly through, I came upon him. He was pointing.

Ted pauses to put a brace of bobwhite quail into his
hunting vest.

My companion was a little behind. I waited for him to catch up, and we moved in. Two quail buzzed out. One went his way and one went mine, and we got them both. Three more flushed at the shot, and we got one apiece.

Three or four came out while we were reloading, but they were still getting up when we were ready to shoot once more. One, two, or three at a time they came. It was a big covey. We stood in our tracks and filled out our limits, and there were plenty left for seed.

That kind of shooting doesn't happen often. Bob is clever. It is always tempting to say that he is getting wilder. Maybe he is; a lot of folks think so. There were wild coveys in Frank Forester's time, however, just the same as there are now.

The weather has a lot to do with the behavior of all kinds of game, including quail. One autumn we had an early snow. That morning when we started hunting there was three inches of it on the ground and the sky looked as though more might fall at any minute. The quail didn't want to fly. We quit hunting when we had found three coveys because we had killed all the law allowed us.

At the other extreme, I have always found quail to be jumpy, wild, and hard to handle on dry, windy days. Wind, of course, seems to make all upland birds nervous. It also makes scent conditions difficult. A dog that never bumps a covey on a damp, still day is likely to run through one after another when the wind is blowing.

Another factor in the behavior of quail is the cover—not only the cover from which they are flushed but also the kind available for them to fly into. If they are feeding in a field bordered by woods or a swamp, they naturally are going to head for it, particularly if the covey has been shot into before, and you won't see them again that day. Of course, this sort of behavior is more marked where they are hunted hard. On the other hand, quail in areas where all the land is cropped can only fly into another field when they are put up.

Bob is the favorite of many sportsmen because he holds so well for a pointing dog. His Western cousins, the mountain, valley, Gambel's, and scaled (or blue) quail are notorious runners. Admittedly, the birds are different, but I feel that the kind of cover in which they live has a lot to do with it. Often the Western birds can't hold because there is nothing for them to hide in. A few times I have found bobwhites in similar cover, and their behavior was not a great deal different.

There is fairly good bobwhite shooting in a few spots in the West. One that I hunted several seasons had open sagebrush on two sides of the cultivated fields. The birds fed in the wheat stubble and corn. They usually spent their loafing hours in a stringer of willows and wild roses along an irrigation ditch.

When they were flushed from either spot, however, they flew into the sagebrush. I never got a decent shot at them there. They wouldn't hold for a dog. Instead, they ran over the barren, dusty soil until they reached the crest of a hill. Then they flew 150 yards down into an orchard on the other side where it was impossible to hunt them.

What makes quail hunting great? What is there about it that makes men, rich and poor, neglect friends, business, and family to hunt quail? There are many facets to charm the mind and delight the spirit, but the greatest of these is the magnificent midget himself.

Bob is a sweet bird. I love to hear—and watch—him whistling from a fence post during the spring and early summer. Later, nothing gives me a greater thrill than to discover that a covey is using in the berry bushes out back of the house. We usually don't see them until the chicks are two-thirds grown and capable of flying well. Mrs. Bob is a cautious mother. From the day we first discover them, however, it is a constant game to see whether we can observe them at their daily feeding, dusting, or loafing.

During the summer, these "garden quail" become quite tame. If we sit motionless, or even if we go about our work cautiously so as not to startle them, it is not unusual to watch them undisturbed at a distance of 50 or 75 feet.

As summer fades we see them less often. By the time there has been a touch of frost and the hazy days of Indian summer have arrived, our backyard covey is gone. It has moved out into the fields, where the spilled grain and ripening weed seeds afford a diet more tempting than the berry patch that was its summer haven.

When November comes and we can once more go afield with gun and dog, Bob is an entirely different bird. He is wild, wary, clever—well able to shift for himself. Our friendly covey that hung around the house all summer is now no different from any other.

Of course, quail are not alone in this trait. Pheasants and grouse and ducks have it. The deer that watched you curiously along a trout stream in July becomes invisible in October. All game becomes wilder as the year progresses toward the hazardous days of winter. Perhaps Nature in her wisdom is preparing it for survival until spring again brings ample food and safe cover.

Whatever the mysterious force may be that prepares him, Bob is ready when we go afield. He is a brown, feathered, buzzing bullet, ready to flip out of his cover with a rush that freezes minds and paralyzes reflexes as he streaks away to safety.

My early quail hunting was a strange mixture of tingling excitement, bitter disappointment, and, occasionally, high elation. I was puzzled a good share of the time, too. Quail look absurdly easy to hit when you're a boy tagging along behind your father and watching him shoot.

Then came the first gun, the first season, the first covey. I was out by myself after school on the day the season opened. Just back of the field we had in corn that year was a little patch of waist-high brush. I knew a covey was using there, and I made a beeline for it.

Strangely, I found myself becoming more and more nervous as I approached. I began to tighten up until I held my gun like a drowning ant clutching a straw. I was not conscious of walking into the cover where the quail were. I simply seemed to get there, as though transported by some invisible force, and suddenly, with a paralyzing roar, the quail were in the air. Quail did not make a noise like that when it was my father who held the gun.

I squeezed the wood and metal as though the quail were going to take it away from me. My mouth probably fell open. More than likely, I shook. Suddenly, when the quail were 20 yards gone, I realized that if any of them were going to be shot, I was the boy who had to do it. I slammed gun to shoulder, pointed it at the spot where the quail seemed to be the thickest, and pulled one trigger, then the other. Naturally, I didn't turn a feather.

Of course, I knew better than that. I had tagged along behind my father too long not to know that you have to shoot at a quail. But I had just discovered one of the basic facts of wing shooting: All birds fly slower when you don't have a gun.

My hands were trembling as I dropped in fresh hulls. My knees felt a little weak. My heart was pounding. I had also discovered the devastating effect of a covey rise on an overanxious gunner.

I had been too excited to watch the covey down. I didn't have any idea

A bobwhite isn't very big, but neither is a diamond.

where they had gone—and I knew better than that, too. So I struck out in the direction that the covey usually took when it left this cover.

When I had walked perhaps 150 yards, the dog suddenly became very busy. He was making game, and I began to tighten up once more. He flushed a single. This time I would not wait too long. My gun was up and the shot was off before Bob had flown 10 yards. I have no idea where the charge went. The other barrel was forgotten.

How infinitely more difficult it became when I was doing the shooting! I watched my dog hurrying through the cover—pointers and setters were unknown to me in those days—and loaded again.

Shortly, another quail buzzed out. This time I was ready. I brought my gun up deliberately, held carefully, and pulled the trigger. I was sure I was right, but the bird, a straightaway, didn't miss a wingbeat. I now think that I waited until he leveled off and shot over him, but at the time my miss was a complete mystery. I simply couldn't believe my eyes.

Another single flew. This time I knew why I missed him with the right barrel. I was away off to the side when I pulled the trigger. I managed to get the second shot off at him, but he probably was too far. At any rate, I thought my hold was right—and he flew on.

By this time I was getting angry. I could hit quail. I *would* hit them. Unfortunately, as every experienced smoothbore shooter knows, determination can't point a shotgun worth a darn. I missed another quail twice, and while I was reloading a couple more got out.

The dog dashed back and forth over the spot where they had been while I watched tensely, but he could find no more. Evidently they were all gone. I relaxed gradually as I watched him. He finally worked away toward the right in the general direction that a couple of singles had taken.

Convinced by now that I would get no more shooting here, I swung my gun down, balanced it ahead of the trigger guard in my right hand, and turned to follow him. I had not taken three steps when a quail fluttered out of a low bush almost at my feet.

The gun came up somehow and shot. To my complete amazement, Bob dropped. A puff of feathers followed him slowly down. I ran and picked him up. I had killed my first quail.

Thirty seconds before, I had been utterly dejected, depressed, completely without hope. Now, I was in the clouds. The fields suddenly were beautiful in the evening sunlight. The world was a lovely place, and I was the center of it. I followed my dog on, walking buoyantly through the crisp stubble, scenting the sweet wood smoke.

The emotional wringer through which this little grown bird can put a hunter probably is beyond comprehension to all who do not pursue quail. It can't be explained, because there is no sense to it, really. After all, a quail is only a few ounces of flesh and a handful of feathers. What has he that can hurl a man to the depths of despair and then lift him to the peaks of happiness, all within a short November hour?

I can't explain it, but I have experienced the full spectrum of emotions many times. That is what makes quail hunting. It isn't the country and it isn't the autumn weather and it isn't the dog work or the honest outdoor companionship of old friends. It is more than that. It is something that Bob himself possesses. Not any one trait or ability, of course, but the sum of them all. There is none other like him—the magnificent midget.

Chapter 36

A Hint of Fall

When August comes, even though the weather may be hot and muggy, my thoughts turn automatically to hunting. This dates back to boyhood. After threshing, when the haze of summer still lay thick across the valley, we would often have a day or two of rain. Then, on the first bright morning after, when we went out to do the chores it would be snapping clear and we would need our jackets and any country boy could tell a hint of fall was in the air.

The haze was gone. There was a new freshness. It was different from the soft freshness of May. It was sharper and it held the promise not of warm days ahead as May had done, but of frosty nights and crisp, golden days and Indian summer. When I was a boy this first hint of fall always set me wild for hunting. It does yet!

Forty years ago our first hunting each year was for sage hens in August, and before my time they were hunted in July. The excuse was that only in the summer could you tell young birds from old, and the old birds were too tough to eat. This was malarkey of the purest distillation. The real reason was that the birds were more vulnerable then, easier to find and easier to kill, and the brave old-timers shot them by the wagonload.

The season has gradually been moved back a little at a time and now we hunt sage hens after the middle of September, and this is better. The birds

Phil Fairbanks has killed the second sage hen from the
right and is swinging toward another as he
pumps his gun.

are wilder and fly faster and they are scattered on the rocky ridges and out
on the open plains, rather than being concentrated around the meadows. A
man has to hunt to find his game and this is as it should be.

But despite the fact that the dove season comes first these days, when the
early showers clear the haze and break the heat of August and the first hint
of fall is in the air I still think of sage hens and the great days I've had with
them. It is unique hunting, because of both the country and the game.

I have often wondered why some Western state didn't adopt the sage hen
as its state bird because nothing—not even the coyote, antelope, or
jackrabbit—is more typically Western than this great, gray grouse of the
arid sagebrush plains.

The original range of the sage hen—and it is pretty much the same today
except that it includes many large blank areas because of man's activities—
ran from the Dakotas westward to Washington, Oregon, and British
Columbia and Alberta, and south across Colorado and Utah. Lewis and
Clark called the sage hen the cock of the plains. It is the largest of all

American grouse, and the book says old cocks sometimes top six pounds, though the largest I ever weighed came to only four and a half.

Imagine now that you are in our sage-hen-hunting camp with Phil Fairbanks and his wife Bob and my wife Ellen and me. It's the first morning. We're on the high northern desert, more than a mile above the sea, and it stretches away endlessly into Nevada on the south and Oregon on the west, and for as far as you can see in all directions there is not one house or fence or any other sign of man save the road by which we got here. It is a road over which you crawl slowly in four-wheel drive, and making twenty miles from early morning until late afternoon is a big day.

The sun is coming up, a red ball fractured by the sagebrush on the eastern ridge. Its first rays are touching camp, starting to melt the white frost from the cars. There is ice on the washpan. Phil is starting the breakfast fire and a wisp of sweet sagebrush smoke drifts over to where I'm sitting up in bed, putting on cap, shirt, and jacket before venturing full length out of my snug sleeping bag.

September mornings are always frosty in this high, dry country. They send you shivering from bed to fire and make your coffee steam while you hold the cup in both hands to warm your fingers. You sip cautiously and the scalding aromatic liquid tastes better than coffee ever tasted anywhere before.

Bob is up now. Soon she will have hotcakes sizzling on the griddle and the smell of bacon frying will mingle with the aroma of the coffee and the delightful fragrance of the fire.

Ellen joins Bob, helping with the breakfast, and it seems fitting for Phil and me to have a little nip by way of celebration now because this will be a great day after a year of waiting. We hear a coyote sing his lonely morning song somewhere in the distance and realize that his remote country is really more a wilderness than many areas that have been officially set aside as wilderness by law. And then, as though to confirm the thought, specks of brilliant white appear on a low ridge two miles west of camp. The sun has caught the heliographic rumps of a herd of antelope, and the binoculars reveal a dozen of them.

How better could a day begin? We eat quickly, though food never tasted quite so good. We drop our dirty dishes in a pan and pour a little of our precious water over them because it takes less to wash a whole day's dishes at one time and in this country you conserve water. Then, shivering, we shed our jackets. The temperature will be in the 70s by midmorning. We put on our light shell vests and uncase our guns and start away, Phil and Bob in one direction, Ellen and I in another. We will come back at noon for lunch. We'll rest and loaf awhile and maybe hunt again in the late afternoon, though nobody thinks that will be necessary. This will be a great day; we can feel it in our bones.

How do you look for game birds in a country such as this? There are no trees, not even willows along the dry streambeds—and sage hens wouldn't be near them if there were. There are widely scattered clumps of big sagebrush, some of it three feet tall, but the birds seldom use them. The remainder of the cover, stretching endlessly for miles, is sparse, ankle-high sage growing among a hundred million rocks. Here and there a clump of ryegrass breaks the monotony, and little tufts of native bunch grass hide furtively among the black stones.

Well, one clue to finding any game is knowing something of its habits. Sage hens fly to water every day at sunrise, then start feeding slowly back up toward the rocky ridges on which they spend the nights. Thanks to having hunted here before, we knew several water holes. Phil and Bob started in the general direction of one; Ellen and I walked toward another. It was about a mile and a half from camp, and we reached it without seeing any game save the band of antelope, still eyeing us warily from the ridge.

Antelope tracks were thick around the water, but we weren't interested in them. Then in the soft mud bordering the dwindling pool we saw the big chicken-like tracks and droppings of the birds we were looking for. Sage hens had been here for a drink. This morning! Which way did they go?

They might have wandered away in any direction, but it was still early and, wherever they went, we knew they would not be far. For the first time since leaving camp we let Rip leave his hated position at heel to lope happily through the still-fresh brush. And because it never pays to argue with your dog and he obviously wanted to go that way, we followed him up a long slope toward the north.

We heard Phil and Bob shoot. We knew who it was; there were no other hunters for twenty miles. Suddenly Rip was walking on eggs. We hurried, climbing hard up the rocky hillside. Rip moved ahead. We climbed harder, guns at ready. I could feel the sweat beginning to trickle down my forehead and into my eyebrows. It was getting warm.

Rip pointed. He was 50 yards ahead. We gave it all we had for a final 25 tense yards. Then, with a pounding of strong wings, a great, gray bird was in the air. Another, and another, a dozen, twenty. There were sage hens everywhere. How could so many of these big birds have been so perfectly hidden in this sparse cover that really was no cover at all? How well they blend into the black rocks and gray sage and autumn-yellowed grass!

I heard Ellen shoot. I concentrated on a bird angling downhill to my left, swinging with it, and when I pulled the trigger I knew my hold was good. I heard it hit the ground. Ellen shot again and then, quickly, I heard her third and final shot. I picked another sage hen, also flying to the left, and sent it plunging earthward near the first, a lone black feather left hanging briefly against the Kodachrome blue sky. I looked for a third target. They were all gone. I watched eight or ten disappear over the ridge ahead, then turned to ask Ellen how she'd done. "Two," she said.

Rip was already dancing toward us proudly with one of her sage hens, the first one down. We found the others and I drew them quickly, removing the crops, too. After the grass and little annual weeds dry up, sage hens feed almost exclusively on the leaves of sagebrush and unless they are dressed promptly it gives their flesh an unpleasant bitter flavor.

It was time to take five. We sat down on convenient rocks and let our birds cool a bit before putting them into the backs of our shell vests. I lit my pipe. Away off to the south we saw Phil and Bob crossing a low ridge and soon we heard them shoot again and we were both silently grateful that the four of us could have this great, free country and these magnificent birds all to ourselves—doubly grateful that we, so far, have been able to enjoy it this way year after year.

After a while, prompted more by Rip's anxious whining than by any doubts that now remained as to whether we might find more birds before noon, we started on up toward the ridge, following the sage hens I had watched disappear. There was a flat on top and we walked across it. After a quarter of a mile, Rip found the birds again. We killed two more and we were through.

Back at camp we put on a pot of coffee and sat in the shade of the canvas fly because it was quite warm now. And while we waited for Phil and Bob, one of my very favorite animals entertained us by flitting around over a pile of boulders 50 feet away. A little antelope ground squirrel lived there and he was not disturbed by us at all.

These little rodents, chipmunk-like in action, size, and appearance, are actually mistaken for chipmunks by some people, but there is one obvious difference: When the antelope ground squirrel curls his tail up over his back, as he often does, the underside shows brilliant white. This explains how he got that name.

Phil and Bob came in a few minutes after noon and they had six birds, too. We spread them out in the shade to cool and ate our lunch and we were happy. It had already been a great day and it would come to a proper conclusion.

At sunset we built a hot fire and laid potatoes, double-wrapped in foil, around it to bake. We quartered a head of cabbage, sprinkled the quarters with salt and pepper, and rubbed in butter. Then we wrapped them in foil and laid them beside the fire, too.

The women made a salad. I split two sage hens, which we had picked during the afternoon and rubbed them with salt, pepper, vegetable oil, and A-1 Sauce, and when the fire had burned down to coals I broiled the four halves over it, just like steaks.

What a meal that was! There are folks who complain of the flavor of sage hens, or of how tough the old ones are, but they are the folks who cook them in a pressure cooker. You could put the best steak that ever came out

Sage hens in winter. In these bleak surroundings, they
thrive on a diet of sagebrush leaves.

of Kansas City in a pressure cooker and make it absolutely inedible. A sage
hen properly broiled over a bed of coals, in the proper setting, is one of the
great gustatory treats of this world.

After dinner we built the fire up again and sat around it and watched the
stars pop out in the clear sky, and listened to the coyotes singing near and
far, each one trying to outdo the other. May their voices always quaver in
the desert night! And may the sage hen and the open country it requires be
with us always, too.

To a Southerner or a New England Yankee, accustomed to the woods
and fields and little covers that a man can walk through in an hour, this
country might seem bleak and desolate, even forbidding. But to the four of
us, all natives, all with memories of other great days on the desert and other
great evenings around a sagebrush fire, it left not one single thing to be
desired.

No wonder I think of sage hen hunting when the heat of August weakens
and the first hint of fall is in the air!

Chapter 37

The Education
of Ruff

Each autumn for the past twenty years my wife and I have engaged in an educational project of singular interest and unique reward. We have been educating grouse, ruffed grouse. The trouble with ruffed grouse in Idaho, where we live, is that they are too tame. With the exception of only a few areas, they have never been hunted enough to develop those frustrating but delightful traits that have earned their Eastern cousins top spot in the esteem of countless experienced scatter-gunners.

Some thirty years ago in *Field & Stream,* Hamilton M. Laing made this statement: "Any bird must be educated to the gun." He was writing about the grouse of British Columbia, but the same truth applies to the grouse of Idaho. It applies, or at one time did apply, to all grouse everywhere, of course. The jittery and unpredictable ruffed grouse of New England was once a fool hen. Some grouse, unfortunately, can't seem to learn. The trusting little Franklin's grouse and the spruce hen are prime examples. They can be shot to extinction without ever discovering that man is their most deadly enemy. Ruffed grouse are different. They can, and do, learn from experience.

Ruff has another point in his favor: His is the boldest, swiftest flight of all. Dan Holland and I were hunting elk one time in some remote spot when we came upon a grouse that probably had never seen a man before. It

The king himself: Ruff on his drumming log.

strutted and *prrrrt*-ed and finally hopped up on a low branch, where it sat and craned its neck at us foolishly.

Dan tapped the alder in which it was perched with his rifle barrel. Instantly we heard the familiar roaring takeoff. Then, open-mouthed, we watched the tilting, rocking flight as the bird bored away down the tangled bottom to disappear in an incredibly short time. "He may be tame," Dan commented as we walked on, "but once he flies, he flies just like them all."

So Ellen and I in our work of educating grouse didn't have to teach them how to fly—only when. At first this wasn't easy. Grouse strutted around on the ground, making the funny little talk they make when they're bothered about something, and if the dog, Joe, didn't happen to get too close they stayed there. Grouse hopped up into trees and looked at us and at him, and sometimes we could scarcely make them fly at all.

I remember one in particular because he was the only grouse I have ever killed on the set with a shotgun. I've killed a lot of them with a pistol or a bean-flipper for camp meat while big-game hunting in the back country, of course, but not with a shotgun. A bird that is to be the target for a shotgun deserves the chance to fly.

This particular grouse, however, flew up into a pine tree and lit on a limb about 30 feet above the ground. Ellen stood ready while I threw rocks at him to make him fly. There weren't many available, and I exhausted the supply without making him move. Then I threw what limbs and knots I could find. Still he didn't fly.

Finally it occurred to me that if I shot the branch off he'd *have* to fly. It was dead and only about an inch in diameter, and I felt sure the load of shot would break it. I walked around to the opposite side of the tree, told Ellen to take him if he came her way, and shot the limb between the grouse and the trunk, breaking it completely.

He flew out my side, but before I could get on him he dropped to the ground. He was dead and there wasn't a pellet in him! A shotgun is a potent weapon at 30 feet; it had whipped the branch up with deadly force.

The scene of our educational project is a narrow valley, completely surrounded by mountains, with a river curving through the bottom. Here the flats are grown up with willow, alder, red birch, vine maple, hawthorn, serviceberry, wild rose, elderberry, and other shrubs. There are a few small clearings and a scattering of pine and cottonwood. The mountains are steep, with several small streams emerging from narrow canyons to meander across the bottom and join the river. The slopes bear abundant thickets of chokecherry and bitter cherry, both of which are well liked by grouse.

Along the tributary streams grow the same shrubs that grow in the bottom, and where the valleys widen there are clumps of quaking aspen, their white trunks and golden leaves reminding us of birches in New England. Grouse like these spots. We like them too. When Ruff flushes from the shrubby undercover and thunders away among the aspens, he makes very sporty shooting.

Along the brooks, their frequency increasing with the distance from the river, are thick clumps of Douglas fir on the north and east slopes and scattered ponderosa pine on the more arid south and west hillsides. And farther up, usually along the ridges in the hunting season, 2,000 feet above the river, the blue grouse stay. Occasionally a single, or even a covey of blue grouse, wanders down into the ruffed grouse covers in the river bottom or along little streams.

When this occurs, we welcome the opportunity to collect some of the larger birds. The time was when we gave them preference, but now we seldom climb the long slopes to find them. We tell ourselves Ruff gives us more sporty shooting in his heavy covers—which is surely true—but maybe we are getting older, too!

So this is the country in which we hunt, and our game is the same as ruffed grouse everywhere, even though the men who decide such things may have put it in a different subspecies from the ruffed grouse of Vermont. We kill gray-phase and brown-phase birds in the same cover, just as everywhere, and no Michigan "pat" hunter could detect the slightest difference between our grouse and the one he shoots.

Memory tends to retain the unusual. Over the years the tricky and difficult shots, the odd occurrences, and the singular behavior of individual birds remain vivid. Routine, easy shooting is hard to recall. Yet we did get easy shooting.

I remember a day when I surprised a brood of grouse feeding under a big elderberry on a little rise where the river bottom joined the hills. Behind them lay a thicket of alder and aspen bordering one of the brooks where it emerged. This cover was only a few yards away. Ahead of them and down the slope was the jungle of the river bottom. But the slope for 60 yards was bare.

I approached, coming up from the bottom, along the edge of the 30-foot-wide strip of brookside cover. Joe was in it. He came and pointed, probably a sight point, since I saw the birds on the ground 15 yards away just as he stiffened.

The smart thing for these birds to have done, and the thing I think most educated grouse surely would have done, was to plunge into the closest cover. Instead, one after another, at widely spaced intervals, they flew down the barren slope toward the river. I was in the ideal spot, and I killed three of them—my limit—in easy, crossing shots. Not all our early shooting was easy, of course. I also remember missing three grouse in succession as quickly as I hit these.

Half a mile from the river, along one of the brooks, there was a little flat with a profusion of food and cover, and we nearly always found grouse there. This particular time, Ellen killed one shortly after we started through it from the downstream point. Then we didn't fly another, nor did Joe make game, until we were almost at the opposite end. Here the two forks of the creek came together. Each was tightly screened by brush, but between them there was a grassy flat 50 yards long and varying in width from a few yards at the downstream end to 30 at the upper end. The good cover began there again.

In the very point of the V, where the two brooks joined, there was a big chokecherry, dead and half broken down and smothered by a clematis vine. It was a sore spot, a place where we often found grouse, and as we approached this time Joe pointed.

Ellen crossed one fork of the brook and stood at the edge of the clearing, 15 yards from the vine. She'd get an open shot if the grouse went her way. I walked toward it from the side, farther downstream. If the bird flew toward the big cover, through which we had just hunted, I'd have a chance. There was heavy brush, no more than shoulder-high, however, along the brook. The aspens above it were clean-trunked and fairly open.

It is a nice feeling to know you have a grouse surrounded. I have experienced it many times—nearly always with identical results. Our bird burst out with a great threshing and a vine-shaking roar of wings. And he must have skimmed the water like a bufflehead. I got a flash of gray at 30 yards as he hurtled up into a clump of alders and I threw a load of shot at him in vain.

I slipped another shell into the magazine, and Ellen asked, "Did you—" She was interrupted by a second bird leaving in the same way and flying down the same groove, and I missed it in the same spot.

"Did you—" she started to ask again, and the third grouse thundered down the tunnel and once more gave me a flash of gray in the same spot at which to throw the third load in vain.

And so, for a decade and a half of golden autumns, we pursued the ruffed grouse of these covers. And not once did we see an empty shell other than our own. Surely, other hunters must have been there, but we never saw one, nor did we see evidence of his presence.

Gradually we began to notice a change in the birds we hunted. We were thwarted by more impossible shots. We flew more grouse we didn't see. There had always been some, of course, because the Idaho season opens when the leaves are on—and some years they are still on when it closes. But we were flying more grouse we couldn't shoot at, and hitting—also missing—more that we couldn't see when we pulled the trigger. And fewer birds lingered to look us over.

During these twenty years the grouse had their ups and downs. Some seasons they were abundant and others they were extremely scarce. Any kind of game becomes exceedingly wary when it is scarce. Perhaps this is Nature's way of preserving the brood stock. Discounting this phenomenon, however, our grouse steadily grew harder to hunt. There were still foolish ones—the kind we killed—but there were more and more that appeared to be very smart indeed.

I remember one in particular. Approaching a hawthorn in the open, I saw a grouse beneath it, where he had no doubt been picking up the thorn apples. It was a big bush, possibly 10 feet in diameter, but the lowest branches were 2 feet off the ground. Consequently I could see the grouse and he could see me.

Since I had just topped a little rise and was only 20 feet away, and the closest cover was to the left, I started around the bush in that direction. If Ruff flew toward cover, which can usually be expected, I'd get a shot. Instead of flushing, however, he scurried in the opposite direction, keeping the hawthorn between us. Once he was a yard off the ground, of course, it would screen him as effectively as a forest. I doubled back and started running around to the right. That was all he needed. He ran a few steps left and flew the 50 yards to the cover. I couldn't move fast enough to get off a shot.

Ted, Rip, and a brace of ruffed grouse.

During this little drama, which occupied only a few seconds, Rip, Joe's son, was investigating a cherry thicket on the hillside. I called him in and we went straight to the spot where Ruff appeared to have lit. We found him, too, and made him fly, but I didn't see so much as a feather. I might have known I wouldn't. Not *that* grouse.

I sometimes wonder why I enjoy hunting such a bird. And why should I be pleased because they're getting steadily wilder, smarter, and harder to bag? Even tame ruffed grouse are tough enough to hit when they fly through typical ruffed-grouse cover.

Superficially, one reason is that nobody needs an alibi when he misses Ruff. When I miss a pheasant in the open I always feel ashamed of myself. But I don't feel that way often in a grouse cover—only when I miss one of the rare clear shots. The man never lived who could hit them all.

Basically, the appeal of grouse hunting lies in quality. Ruff *is* quality, in his appearance, in his wild alertness, and in the way he flies. And to some of us—"patridge" hunters and fly fishermen among others—the more difficult a sport is, the more attractive it appears.

We had a wonderful lot of grouse one fall. Usually our hunts ended all too quickly—not because we hit them all, but only because we flew so many that we completed our daily quota of misses much too soon.

The nesting season the next fall was a failure, probably because of local weather conditions. Grouse were abundant in other covers 50 miles away, and I suspect a severe thunderstorm at just the wrong time may have depleted "our" broods.

That fall, hunting was hopeless. There was a good carryover of adult birds. We found plenty, but they were always alone, and killing them was next to impossible. If we saw them, it was only when they flushed out of range. If they waited to get up until we were close, we didn't see them. As I recall, we finally killed one or two and went elsewhere. And believe me, no grouse in New England were ever wilder than these.

The fall after that was another good one—lots of young birds and plenty of old ones. We had good shooting. One day I killed my limit too fast when

In this Western grouse country, the blue grouse stay on
the ridges and the ruffed grouse along the
brushy creek bottoms.

I surprised a brood under an elderberry on a hillside with no other cover whatever within 20 yards. Ellen, unfortunately, was on the wrong side of it. But getting a limit too fast is seldom a problem any more. In fact, I sometimes suspect that we may have overdone a good thing. The last bird we flew illustrates exactly what I mean.

Rip pointed him. It wasn't such a bad spot, really. The brush, though thick, was low and there were several wide-open avenues among the trees. Ellen and I both walked in, about 10 yards apart so that if one couldn't shoot the other might.

I tossed a stick into the thicket ahead of Rip and the grouse flew. We knew he flew because we heard him! When he was 70 yards away, he climbed to an elevation of 20 feet and we saw him, too.

We marked him down and went after him. This time he didn't hold for a point. He flushed before Rip found him—but he was in range. We just couldn't see him. Again he stayed low, securely screened by the dogwood along a trickle of water, until he was safely out of range. We watched him down once more.

On the third attempt he didn't even let us get close. He flushed wild, towered to treetop height, and left the cover, curving away across the river out of sight.

The education of Ruff, though long, was an obvious success.

Chapter 38

A Day with Huns

Ben Dobson doesn't like Huns. He likes quail, and I have never shot a quail on his ranch. He's more or less neutral about pheasants, and I have killed a few. But he says Huns scare his horses and so he doesn't like them.

That, I'm for. There is nothing I would rather do than to accommodate a man who wants me to kill Hungarian partridge. One fall, however, it was late in the season before we got around to helping Ben with his problem. Then Al Miller called one evening and said, "We ought to go out and help Ben Dobson suppress his Huns."

The next morning we rolled into Ben's immaculate ranch yard about 8:30. Nobody was home, so we parked near the gate and let Al's Brittany, Bing, out to trot around and talk tough to Ben's collie while we put our guns together and loaded our pockets with shells.

It was a perfect morning. The sun was shining brightly in a cloudless sky, although there was a heavy frost in the shadow of Ben's red barn. All but a few withered leaves had fallen from the gnarled cottonwoods, but the red osier and willows and alders still traced lines of color along the streams. The air was sharp and clean.

Ben's ranch is in a basin, a lovely place of round-edged hills that roll up and away from the buildings, corrals, and hay meadows in the bottom. In spring they're green, of course, but by midsummer they have turned to a

Hungarian partridge fly low and get away fast.

golden hue that has the soft texture of velvet in the distance. In autumn, the gold becomes a blend of tan and gray, laced with the bright foliage along the little creeks and accentuating the still-green alfalfa of the meadows.

In this setting, the gray partridge of Europe, commonly called Hun or Hungarian because the first successful stocking came from Hungary, has prospered. He likes the open, grassy, south slopes where the sun never allows the snow to linger in winter. He likes the brush along the streams when hawks pursue him. He likes the sparse cover of the hillsides because it enables him to elude that more deadly, two-legged predator who disturbs him only in the autumn. And he stays fat on a diet of green grass, insects, grass seeds, tiny bulbs that grow on the grass roots, and an occasional weed seed or berry.

Al and I walked through the corral on the little bench north of the house, carefully closing the gates behind us, and started angling up and around the point of a long ridge. We were chilly. You are always chilly on a brisk morning if you wear only enough to be comfortable while you're hunting.

As we climbed, we discovered that the ground was still frozen on the shady side, but in twenty minutes we were glad we had not worn our jackets. Those gentle, rolling hills of Ben Dobson's become steeper when you start up them. Sweat was already beginning to soak my cap.

We walked around the hill, 50 yards apart, and up to a saddle maybe a mile, as we had come, from the ranch house. This was the spot where, two years before, Dan Holland and Al had practically disowned me because of a fluke shot I made. A covey of Huns had flushed wild. All but one of them flew angling away to my left, but that one came toward me, making a crossing shot at 30 yards. I killed it. As I watched it pitch down toward Al 100 yards below, I saw, out of the corner of my eye, a bird drop from the covey.

Al picked up the close Hun. I called my dog and walked up to the spot where the remainder had disappeared over the saddle and where I thought I might have seen another fall. To my amazement, he found not one but two. They had been far out of range, so far that I hadn't even considered shooting at them, but stray shot had hit them in the head and killed them.

The saddle, sore spot though it had been in seasons past, held no birds today. And Bing had worked well coming up. He must surely have covered at least four miles to our one, and he had yet to show the first sign of making game.

Al and I sat down for a few minutes in the mellow sunlight. Two hundred yards below us a little creek, part in sun and part in shadow, chuckled contentedly down toward the ranch house. Across it, a steeper, higher ridge led up eastward to the blue timber in the distance. Around it, out of sight, we knew there was a little basin that Huns sometimes liked. A gently sloping "flat"—in the West any land not broken by hills and ridges is a flat, even though it may be quite steep—lay below the basin and the ridges that hemmed it in. On our side, it was bordered by the stream below us; on the other, by a dry wash, and beyond that a steep slope leading to a narrow ridge.

Al and I dropped down the hillside to the creek, crossed it, and climbed up and around the opposite ridge into the basin. We hunted it but saw no game. We angled down and started across the flat. Here a covey of Huns flushed 200 yards ahead and flew out of sight over the far ridge. We followed them, separating by 50 yards as we went over the top so that one or the other of us would be more likely to get shooting.

Bing finally found them near the creek beyond. We saw him strike the scent and he came in close, but not too close, and then he had them solid. We started down, swinging with long strides down the steep slope, but the Huns refused to wait. Again they flushed wild. I was closer and tried two hurried shots at long range, but missed.

Again we followed them, this time around the sidehill and down, back toward the ranch buildings. Another quarter mile put us within sight of the cottonwoods that shaded the white ranch house. Then, with Bing searching vainly 100 yards above, we walked right into them. We topped a little ridge that angled down from the big one and the Huns flushed in the pocket below it, almost at our feet.

Al shot twice and I shot twice, and one bird fell. This was disgraceful, but Huns do that to you. They keep flushing wild and you keep getting more edgy and when you finally do get fairly into them your overanxious nerves catch up with you. You miss. We followed the covey on around the mountain but failed to find them. Probably they'd flown across the creek behind the ranch house and over the north corral and onto the hillside where we had started our hunt nearly four hours earlier. But now it was past noon and we were almost back to our point of starting.

We walked down to the gate and unloaded our guns and went through it and across the yard and out a second gate to the car. We laid our guns across the hood and put Bing in to make sure he'd rest instead of making fight talk with Ben's collie, and got our lunches. Then we walked over and sat down with our backs against Ben's big woodpile.

It was good to be there. It was good to be resting with the sunlight soaking into us and the hard-packed earth beneath feeling soft as down. No man who has never gotten honestly tired can appreciate how good it was simply to be there, leaning back against Ben's woodpile and unwrapping our sandwiches and smelling the delightful aroma of hot coffee from our bottles.

Of course, in one sense, our hunt so far had been a failure. We had not found one-tenth the birds we'd hoped to, and when we had finally gotten into them we had shot poorly. One of us, I'm not sure which, had killed one Hun. I'd shot four times; Al twice.

But neither of us felt dejected. After you've hunted as long as we have, you take such things in stride. You do the best you can and forget the alibis. Were hunting a sure thing, any hunter worth his salt would quit. I wondered sitting there what I'd be doing at that precise moment if I were a millionaire, able to go anywhere and afford anything.

I could think of no place I'd rather be. We had the afternoon ahead of us. We ate and drank our coffee and gazed off up the valley and watched the last cottonwood leaves come tumbling down. We rested a little and planned a little. Pretty soon we got our guns and Bing and walked down past Ben's red barn and crossed the big creek behind it and the meadow beyond.

We climbed the first sidehill, across the valley from the area we'd hunted in the morning, and Bing started making game. The Huns didn't hold for him. They flushed wild, before he had come within 30 yards of them, but they tried to swing around the hill ahead of us. They were on Al's side, a long crossing shot, and he killed one. Bing retrieved it proudly.

We watched them down. When Al had reloaded and pocketed his game, we went on toward the spot where they had disappeared behind a flat-topped ridge. They could be some distance beyond and they could be barely over it. We were ready when we reached the top.

Here, in a level spot possibly 100 feet wide and twice as long, a sort of saddle, Lady Luck broke the stern visage she had turned toward us all morning. She smiled from ear to ear and we were ready. The sear grass came alive with Huns. This was not the covey we had been following: It had held only a dozen birds or so. This was a new one, four times as big. The air was full of them, flashing their rusty tails, curving to the right and left, and boring straight away.

The Hun's grays and browns blend well into its
surroundings. The rust-colored feathers on its breast
sometimes form a rough horseshoe, as they
do on bird at left.

Al and I stood 20 yards apart. I heard him shoot twice to the right and I shot twice to the left, and I saw two birds fall at my reports. Bing, who had been below me, saw them fall, too. He brought one to Al quickly and bounded away after the other, which had fallen below the rim of the saddle. Al said, "Bing, you darned fool, come back here. I've got two birds down."

I said, "He's after my other Hun."

"Oh!" Al exclaimed. "Did you get a double, too?"

No answer was necessary. Bing appeared with it, running proudly toward his master. Then, with Al's help, he found the other two.

How quickly can fortune change! And how quickly with it can spirits soar and fatigue fall off. Thirty seconds before, we had been tired. We had walked six miles and killed two birds. Then, in a fraction of a minute of hurtling bodies and flashing wings, of honest recoil and the sweet smell of burnt powder, we were rejuvenated. The day was once more fresh and crisp. We saw again the low sunlight slanting across the soft, grass-covered ridges, brightening the colors along the stream below them, fading in the blue haze of the distance toward the far canyons.

We swung on sharply. In the bottom, under a steep bank that shielded our approach from their keen ears and sharper eyes, Bing found the other covey. They had sailed on 200 yards farther than we expected, but they had held a straight line.

Bing had come in from the left below them. He was frozen when we saw him, his white and tan now highlighted by a fringe of silver from the sun beyond. We knew he had them; he was transfixed by the scent flowing down the gully. We walked on quickly, though quietly, and when we stepped out on the edge of the bank 10 yards above him, we saw the Huns spring from the grass below us.

Again, the guns swung true. Again gray feathers hung against the sky, then fluttered earthward. Again, Bing brought the result of our efforts to his master.

We had killed ten birds. Our hunt was over. We walked back to the car. Ben and his family were still away. Al penciled a note that said, "You should stay home to protect your property. We have killed ten of your Huns." He hung it on the white door. Then we got into the car and drove homeward slowly. There was no pressure.

Chapter 39

Chukar Tactics

Willard Cravens stopped the car and we let the dogs out, then put on our game vests and uncased our guns. And as we did, the whole mountain, 400 yards away across the basin, started talking to us. It was crawling with chukars, and dozens of them were giving us their derisive *ca-ca-ca-ca-ca-ca*.

We were near a pond made by the Bureau of Land Management by damming a dry streambed to catch spring runoff and provide water for cattle during the summer and fall. This water, where there had been none before between March and November, made it possible for stockmen to utilize the good grass in the area. But it also did something else: It created a great hunting spot. There were hundreds of chukars and several coveys of quail. Before the dam was built there had been no game birds of any kind. Deer also moved in and took up residence. Even migrating ducks used the pond.

In the arid West, water is the key to life. That's why the springs and little streams were all homesteaded a century ago. The early-day stockmen had a saying to the effect that if you control the water, you control the range. Even today, despite the BLM's many water developments, some areas of good grass can't be grazed because they are too far from water. And, of course, there is no game in them, either.

The mountain across the basin was an ideal chukar slope: steep and

This rugged terrain is one kind of chukar country. If you
look carefully, you'll be able to spot Ted and his
dog in the middle of things.

rocky, with several kinds of grass and scattered sagebrush growing on the
patches of soil among the boulders. There was a day when I would have
charged directly up it. No more. I began hunting chukars in 1953 and I
have finally learned that it is futile to start up a mountain after them. They
can loaf along, pausing occasionally to hop up on a rock and insult you,
and no living man can gain on them.

At one end of the mountain a little valley sloped up to a saddle a mile
away. Willard and I started up it and were soon out of sight of the birds on
the south side that faced the car. But we didn't stay in the draw, because we
seldom found birds in the bottom. Instead, we began angling up along the
eastern slope of the mountain, still walking away from the chukars that had
greeted us.

The hillside had several little benches, grassy draws, and rocky points, all
of which chukars like. Each time we topped a rise we would have a chance
to surprise a covey. This is one of the most important points in chukar

From the looks of his surroundings, you might infer that
the chukar loves rocks. You'd be right.

hunting—to pull one little sneak after another. You can seldom get near an
unbroken covey of chukars that see you coming. They habitually run until
they are out of sight, then fly. (We've proved this repeatedly while hunting
in snow.)

Thus, to hunt them successfully, you must not only have chukars; you
must also have the kind of terrain where you can approach them. A long
mountainside with many side ridges is ideal. As you go around each one
you have a new chance to walk into birds.

We did just that when we came up onto the first little bench. Rip and
Queenie began to make game and we saw fresh droppings where the
chukars had been feeding on the velvety cheat grass, newly sprouted by the
first fall rain. Suddenly, before the dogs had a chance to point, a dozen
birds took to the air.

Flushed chukars usually fly downhill, and if you hope to hit them, you've
got to hold low. But sometimes they contour around the mountain. These
did—all but the two we killed—and we knew that as they rounded each
point some were likely to drop out. This is where a dog pays off. If the cover
is halfway decent, singles and pairs often stick as tight as bobwhite quail.
Without a dog, they'll let you walk right past.

So even though we couldn't see any of the covey light, Willard and I continued around the side of the mountain walking about 50 yards apart, on the level at which the chukars had disappeared. Around the very first ridge Queenie pointed and Willard walked in to flush two birds. One flew straight ahead; the other pitched downhill past me. We got them both and the dogs retrieved. We were off to a good start.

We didn't find any more from that covey; they likely curved away downhill somewhere, but after we'd gone another quarter mile we surprised a bunch of birds when we walked over the point of a rocky ridge. We were right on top of them. Willard made a double, but I missed one of mine. The remainder pitched downhill and sailed across the valley.

Climbing steadily but at an easy grade as we continued northward, we eventually came to a saddle over the mountain. There, in open cover, a big covey flushed wild but curved southward along the western edge. This was the direction we would take to return toward the south slope, where the first chukars had greeted our arrival.

The mountaintop was a plateau, sloping gently downward toward the north. It was mostly smooth, but there were outcroppings of rhyolite, some of them 10 feet tall, and chukars often fed and loafed around them. The eastern edge of the plateau was rounded, but along the western side there were cliffs and cuts and the heads of rocky draws, all good spots to surprise chukars. The covey from the saddle would be along this edge somewhere, most likely just under the rim.

It was rough going, steep and rocky, but before long Queenie pointed close below the 20-foot cliff that edged the plateau, and Willard killed a single. I was 50 yards downhill. A bit later, Rip pointed and I walked up a pair. I killed one clean and hit the other, but it set its wings and plunged like a stooping goshawk down into a bowl 200 yards below. The spot was 50 yards across, grassy and comparatively flat, with a few boulders scattered on the bottom.

Rip, retrieving the bird I killed, hadn't seen this one. There was no choice but to go down there, though I dreaded the climb back. Willard, one of the most considerate hunting friends I've ever had, said, "I'll go with you; we might need two dogs. A bird that makes a long flight and drops dead sometimes doesn't put out any scent."

So we scrambled down, the dogs ahead, and before we reached the bowl we saw Rip go on solid point, his nose under the edge of a rock about the size of a bridge table. When we got there we discovered that when the boulder had tumbled down it had come to rest on other, smaller rocks. It was 5 inches off the ground and when I looked under I saw my chukar crouched in the very middle. I told Willard I could reach it, but suggested he stand with Queenie on the opposite side in case I failed to grab it and it ran out. We leaned our guns against the rock.

Lying flat on the ground, I reached under and caught the chukar by the

When you're hunting an area this rough, you especially
appreciate the steps a good dog can save you.

tail. Instead of coming weakly out, however, there was a squawk and a
sudden violent flapping and scratching. The bird shot out past Willard and
Queenie and flew away strongly—if a bit erratically. It flew erratically
because its tail feathers were in my hand!

It wasn't my bird at all. It was a perfectly healthy chukar. We searched
the little basin carefully and the dogs looked everywhere, but we failed to
find my bird. Finally, we gave up and started on, angling up toward the rim
again.

After 100 yards we noticed that Queenie wasn't ahead with Rip as usual. We looked back and here she came, trudging along behind. And that little Brittany, not much bigger than a chukar, was carrying my bird! It must have sailed farther than I thought.

Some hunters say a dog is no help on chukars. They see coveys flush wild in sparse cover and never learn that, once they're scattered, the singles will sit tight and let you walk past unless you have a dog to find them for you. Nor do such hunters remember how many birds they hit and lose. No matter how carefully you may mark them down, no man can find a chukar that lands running in thick sagebrush or plunges down into a hole among the rocks, as they often do.

We were now approaching the south slope, where so many chukars had greeted us when we parked the car. Because we knew from experience that chukars habitually feed uphill, and it had been three hours since we started out, we decided to hunt first across the top of the plateau, 100 yards back from the edge. This was a lovely spot in the eyes of any chukar hunter, with big rocks and low rock ridges and patches of grass and scattered sagebrush, the very kind of place that chukars like the best.

It was, in fact, a lovely spot to anyone who enjoys wide-open country. Before hunting on, we sat down and watered the dogs while I smoked a pipe. (A little plastic bowl for watering your dog weighs next to nothing and a plastic bottle is much lighter than any canteen of the same volume.)

We were on the highest point of the mountain. We could see for endless miles across the rolling ridges and steep canyons with their ragged cliffs of black and red and tan, and everywhere the gray sage lay like a blanket across the land, a blanket deepening into purple far away. Here and there bright patches of fall-blooming rabbit brush specked the desert with flecks of gold. There was not a tree, not a fence, not a house anywhere, and no road, either, save for the dirt tracks on which we had driven in.

After a few minutes, we started eastward and continued until we could look down into the little valley we had first walked up, and from this point we could see the pond and the car nearby, a tiny, glinting speck in the basin far below. We had flown no birds, so decided to hunt back to the west.

At the top of the slope there was a broken cliff, varying from 15 to 40 feet high. Sometimes chukars worked their way to the top but stayed near the edge, while sometimes they stopped at its base. We decided Willard and Queenie would stay near the edge on top while Rip and I would keep abreast below the cliff.

We hadn't gone far when I heard Willard shoot twice, close above me but out of sight. Instantly, I was all but run down by a big mule-deer doe. Rocks clattering and dust flying, she shot out of a shaded cleft in the rock wall, not five feet in front of me. Willard's shots must have given her a dreadful fright, for she bounded away around the mountain in leaps as long as any deer could make. At the same time, half a dozen chukars appeared against the sky above and curved away in front of me. Flustered by the deer, I managed to miss two, but hit a third that had flushed later than his companions.

I called to Willard. He had killed two. The score now stood seven for him, six for me. The limit was eight. I was sure where the six would go—to a saddle between the end of the cliff and a little butte. It had everything: rocks, cheat grass, big sagebrush. Chukars liked it, and it was about the distance they usually fly—a quarter mile from the spot where Willard had put these birds up. (It was a big covey, he told me later, and I had seen only a small part of it.)

I continued along the base of the cliff at approximately the same level as the saddle, while Willard stayed high to come down into it from above. This is always sound strategy; if chukars run after lighting, it is always uphill. And if someone is above, it often confuses them.

Sure enough. Willard met them as he was coming down to the saddle. Queenie pointed a single. Willard killed it. A pair flushed at the shot and came pitching down the mountain, right at me and 30 yards high. A straight incomer is my favorite duck shot and these chukars were coming like a pair of bluebills. I rolled them both and Rip brought them to me.

We sat down on a grassy spot in the saddle to dress our birds, always a good idea, even when the weather is cool. Chukars love wild onions. They scratch up the bulbs and eat them, and if they're left in the crops too long, they give the flesh an unpleasant flavor.

We were half a mile from the car by the shortest route. If we dropped down to the creekbed from the west side of the saddle, we'd have two and a half miles to walk, but we would pass a hidden water hole among the rocks and near it some good quail cover. So after we had rested half an hour we went that way.

Our detour turned out as well as we had hoped and when we got back to the car our game bags were heavy, but our hearts were light. It had been a perfect day. May we see more like it!

Chapter 40

The
Successful Failure

Spring came north to meet us as we drove from Oklahoma City south toward the little Mississippi town of Union Church, east and a bit north of Natchez. The wild plums were blooming in Oklahoma and after a while we began to see redbuds and before we reached the turkey camp the woods were snowy with blooming dogwood.

Dwain Bland, surely one of America's great turkey hunters, had met me at the airport. He is chunky, muscular, brown-haired, brown-eyed, and tan as an Indian. He has hunted gobblers successfully in seven states and he can make turkey talk that must be the envy of many a real turkey.

He and his son-in-law, Tom Preston, took turns at the wheel during the 650-mile drive. I asked questions about turkey hunting. I had never shot a gobbler, and I wanted to very badly.

Tom, twenty-seven years old and with the build of an athlete, said somewhere along the road: "You've never been really tired until you've hunted turkeys."

I smiled. It couldn't be. I remembered how tired I was the night I came down off a mountain in the Alberta Rockies carrying the head of a bighorn ram. I remembered other hunts, especially one day in New Zealand when Peter Barrett and I left camp long before daylight and climbed to perpetual snow, far above timber line, on the steepest mountain either of us had ever seen.

Tom Preston killed this magnificent gobbler.

We hunted there all day and came down off the mountain in the dark and I felt ahead each step with the butt of my rifle, but in spite of that I stepped off a 10-foot bank and we had to crawl around in the dark feeling for the gun until we finally found it. We got to camp long past midnight.

Tom has never been on a hunt like that, I thought. He has only hunted those Oklahoma sandhills. He can't know what it is to be really tired.

Eventually, we turned off the country road and followed a gently climbing, sandy drive to the turkey camp. I liked it. Completely screened by trees from the road, it had a little meadow sloping away in front. The other hunters were not there yet.

Dwain unlocked the door and we carried in our duffel and I found myself getting terribly excited as I changed into my hunting clothes and took my gun out and put it together. I'm really here, I thought, really here! And the season opens in the morning.

It was a delightful spring day. There was not one cloud in the sky and the air was so fresh I stepped outside and sat on the steps to lace my boots and gulp great lungfuls. The eddying breeze was rich with the sweet odor of honeysuckle.

The other hunters came—Ed Norwood and Johnny Nance and Vernon Cade. They brought dinner ready with them and the talk through it and afterward was all of turkeys and turkey hunting. Ed gave me a turkey call and showed me how to use it, but when I tried, some of the others laughed and the remainder shook their heads. So I put it away and knew I would have to depend on one of them to call a gobbler for me.

I listened to the conversation, trying to learn as much as possible, but it was sometimes difficult to separate fact from fiction. An outlandish lie told with a straight face, one of the great American forms of humor, may have been funny to the others, but how was I to know?

They called me to breakfast at 2:30 A.M. I staggered to the table half awake before I heard the sound. It was raining! Big drops were drumming on the roof. It reminded me of the rains that used to hammer on the roof of the old barn when I was a boy. It was a welcome sound then, as I stood just inside the door listening to the rain and watching it and glad because I would not have to work in the fields. It did not sound good this morning and I asked about turkey hunting in the rain.

Johnny Nance answered. "It's about the toughest there is," he said. "The only thing worse is wind."

The others nodded and Vernon Cade added, "We've got some wind this morning, too."

I realized it then by the sweeping of the rain across the roof. It was not steady: It was gusting. You may remember the headlines, almost daily during the spring of 1973, about violent weather in the South—torrential rains, rivers over their banks, violent winds, and tornadoes. We were there just as it got well started.

Everybody put on his camouflage clothing anyway, and smeared his face with green and brown grease paint because nothing looms out in the dim woods like the human face. We left in two pickups. I rode with Dwain and Ed, endlessly it seemed, but we finally pulled into the yard of a wonderful old country couple, Mr. and Mrs. Earl Beasley.

It was still pitch black, but the Beasleys were up and had coffee ready, and while we drank it Mr. Beasley told us where every drove of turkeys on his place was using. (It is always a drove of turkeys, never a flock or covey.) And since it was still raining he told Dwain and Johnny where they could safely drive into his fields without getting stuck in the slick, heavy, reddish soil, and where to leave the pickups, and which way to hunt to find the turkeys.

We were half a mile from the pickups when the graying sky allowed us to turn off the flashlights. Here we separated. Johnny and Tom took one direction; Dwain, Ed, and I, another. (Vernon had to work that day and had gone back to Wesson after breakfast.)

We returned to the pickups at noon. Nobody had seen a turkey and nobody had heard one gobble, and by this time it was *really* raining. Because of some misunderstanding, Dwain, Tom, and Ed drove back to camp. I rode up to the Beasleys' with Johnny and they had dinner ready for everybody—pork chops and black-eyed peas, hot biscuits and red-eye gravy and fluffy, white rice, and I ate until I hurt. Then after a decent interval, we started to camp, and I had never seen it rain harder than it was raining then.

A mile from camp the road went through a little valley, with a trickling branch in the bottom and a 3-foot culvert under the road. When we got there the water was running a foot deep *over* the road. When we got to camp Johnny asked the others if it was over the road when they came by, perhaps two hours earlier. It had not been, they said.

Nobody hunted that afternoon. It would have been like standing under a shower. But the next morning was bright and beautiful, though everything was sopping wet, of course, and every low meadow was covered with water. I hunted with Dwain and Ed once more. After calling several times we walked up an old firebreak to the top of a ridge, the driest spot for miles, and sat down to call again. Dwain said he was a lonely hen, just once. A gobbler answered from behind. Another—closer—gobbled out in front, beyond a little rise.

My hands began to tremble. In a little while I started to shiver, though it was a warm, delightful morning. I doubted whether I could hit the gobbler if he walked straight in and stood there like a post.

I have been hunting a long time and I have called most game that can be called. I thought of a big bull elk I called and how he first ran off his herd of cows, sending them crashing away though the brush for a quarter mile, and how he then came back, blowing and snorting and grunting and making the lodgepole pine forest ring with his bugling—four clear, ascending notes, each time followed by a loud but low-pitched cough or grunt—meanwhile raking the trees with his antlers.

You call elk by imitating the bugle of the bull and this big herd bull was on his way back to run off the intruder. When he was close, just over a little rise, I whacked a log with a dead stick and rubbed it back and forth. He came fast then and Peter Barrett killed him at a range of about 75 feet.

That was exciting. But it was not so exciting as now, with the gobbler 50 yards away, and no way of knowing whether he would come to us gobbling and strutting, dragging his wing tips on the ground, or whether he would slip in as silently as a fox.

I was sitting on the ground, knees up and gun rested over them, pointed at the spot where I hoped the turkey would be when he came into range. My back was against a tree and I was screened by some low bushes.

Thirty-five yards, I reminded myself. Let him come to 35 yards. I hoped I could remember to push the safety off. I hoped I didn't get buck fever so I couldn't shoot at all. And, most of all, I hoped I wouldn't be shaking so much I couldn't hit him.

After five minutes that seemed like an hour, Dwain repeated his seductive call. The gobbler didn't answer, nor did the farther one, behind us. Another wait. Another call. Still no answer. Were the gobblers coming silently?

Afraid to turn my head, I rolled my eyes from side to side, watching for movement, hoping to see a gobbler's head appear above a bush. I saw only a pair of white-throated sparrows searching busily for food among last fall's leaves.

Dwain clucked softly, paused and clucked again, but still there was no sight of a gobbler, nor any sound. Finally, Dwain gobbled with his box call, a gobble as realistic as the bird's. We waited some more. At last Dwain said, "He isn't coming. Sometimes a gobble will bring them when hen talk won't. But neither one of them is going to come. We might as well move."

"Just let me sit here a little while and relax while I smoke my pipe," I begged. "I'm so excited I'm falling apart. I've never been so excited."

"That's why men hunt turkeys," Ed said softly, and we sat there fifteen minutes while I pulled myself together.

The area with the closer gobbler lay in a triangle with fire lanes on all three sides. We had walked up one of them to the top of the ridge. "Maybe he wouldn't come uphill," Ed said. "Let's walk back down the way we came and take the lane across the bottom. We can call a couple of times from it. Then we can come back along the third side and call there."

It didn't work and eventually we were back where the gobblers had answered. Dwain and Ed decided to give up, walk back down the lane we had first climbed, and head for new territory. Halfway down the hill there were turkey tracks in the wet sand—big gobbler tracks! They were fresh. They were in the footprints we had left when we walked down the first time to circle the triangle.

We could walk very quietly. The rain had washed the leaves off long stretches of sandy soil and where there were leaves they were still wet and noiseless. At each bend of the trail Ed and I stopped and Dwain slipped ahead to look. We had done this several times when the turkey tracks, which had been 18 inches apart, suddenly became 3 feet apart. Ed groaned and whispered, "We've scared him. He's running."

But we went on, still quiet and careful, and after 100 yards or so the gobbler's stride resumed its normal length. Dwain eased around a bend. He raised his gun, hesitated, and fired. Instantly, the turkey was flying across the firebreak. Dwain hit him cleanly with the second barrel; I could see the big bird move sidewise with the heavy impact of the No. 4 shot. He crashed into low brush by the trail and Dwain ran to him. Ed and I ran, too, and the magnificent, bronze gobbler was still flopping when we got there, his head bright blue in death.

That was the only turkey for the second day of our hunt. And the third. And the fourth. It rained. Sometimes the wind lashed the forest until I could not hear Dwain's call from 50 feet away. The weather was discouraging.

One evening, Ed Norwood, who is a very funny man as well as a great cook, was getting dinner when he held the following dialogue with himself: "I saw a nice day once," he said. "I wish my boy could see a nice day." Then. "How old is your boy?" he asked. "Forty-five."

Up at 2:30 again the next morning. I couldn't even see until I had downed a mug of coffee. By this time I realized that Tom had spoken nothing but the truth when he said, "You've never been really tired until you've hunted turkeys."

Tom got a great gobbler that field-dressed at nineteen pounds that morning, but Dwain and I neither saw nor heard one. That afternoon they took me to hunt with Frank Davis, another turkey expert, in another area. Next morning again, we were in position and Frank was calling just as it broke day. My first dreadful excitement was gone. I was calm now—maybe because I was so tired—and I felt sure I could kill a gobbler if one came. None did. We moved to a second spot, and a third, and called and waited and called and waited. Nothing answered.

The fourth stand was beside a little patch of clover, which turkeys love, and it was full of fresh sign. If only we had come here first! But *if* bags no game. We went to Frank's camp, which wasn't far, for lunch and while we were eating Frank said, "I think your best chance is to watch that clover patch. A good drove fed there early and they'll probably feed there again before they go to roost."

At 3 P.M. I lay down on my belly near the edge of the clover, in a slight depression so my eyes were level with its tops and only my camouflaged cap showed above it. I put my gun beside me and a little ahead with my right hand over the trigger guard and my thumb on the safety. I was determined to lie without moving until Frank came along the road, 300 yards away, to pick me up at 6 o'clock.

The first hour wasn't bad. I had chosen a smooth spot, free of humps and sticks, and since it looked as though the sky might open up at any minute I had brought my rain gear. I rolled it up and rested my chin on it. Lying down felt so good. It felt like the first rest I had enjoyed in all my life and if I hadn't been so sure the turkeys would come walking into range at any minute I would have gone to sleep. But I didn't dare sleep.

After an hour, I began to hurt. I hurt everywhere. My shoulders ached and my muscles cramped and the earth that felt so smooth and soft at first became a bed of cobblestones. By 5:30 I was in agony. There was no spot from chin to toes that did not ache. But I stuck it out. I finally hobbled up the hill at the appointed time and nothing ever felt so good as the seat of Frank's car.

Frank had spent the afternoon scouting and he had good news. He had heard a gobbler just before roosting time. The big bird would be nearby at daylight.

Frank and I were there early. When it was light enough to shoot, Frank called. Instantly, the gobbler answered loud and clear, from no more than 100 yards.

Frank waited, then called again. Once more the gobbler answered, but he was farther away. Another wait, another call, another gobble—farther yet. "He's with hens," Frank whispered, "he'll never come to us now."

He not only refused to come; he didn't answer the call again. We tried two more spots and went in at 10 o'clock for coffee. Frank had to run an errand, and he suggested I walk down a trail past two good clover patches while he was gone. I visited both of them and in a sandy bottom saw fresh tracks where turkeys had come and gone that morning. I had walked very slowly and very quietly, peering into the open at each bend. I hadn't scared the turkeys. They had fed and left earlier.

On his errand, before he came to the main road, Frank saw a gobbler cross the sandy wheel tracks and stop in open woods. After lunch, we circled this area, not too close, stopping to conceal ourselves and call frequently. No answer. The gobbler had left.

I knew then that I wouldn't kill a gobbler on this trip. It was starting to rain and I had half a day left in which to hunt. Dwain came and took me back to the turkey camp with a plan for morning hunting.

I went, but I had a hopeless feeling and that is no good when you are hunting. You must have hope, always. It had rained all night and there was water everywhere, but Dwain, Vernon Cade, and I were half a mile from the car by daylight. Mist was rising from the lake-like fields when we finally made our first stand.

Call and wait, call and wait, call and wait, and then move on to another spot and do it all again. And all the time I knew it was no use. I wouldn't kill a gobbler.

We went back to the turkey camp at noon and ate and packed up and it was 4 o'clock the next morning when we got to Oklahoma City. By the time Dwain and Tom unloaded me at the motel near the airport so I could sleep until the last possible minute and still catch my plane, I was so tired I could scarcely stand. After eight days with never enough sleep, I had now been up for twenty-six straight hours.

On the long flight home I tried to sleep, but couldn't. I tried to read, but I couldn't do that, either. I was still wound up like a clock spring. Had the trip been a failure? Maybe, but tired as I was, I still felt contented and happy.

In the bright-leafed springtime, the Southern woods are lovely. There were the dark and waxy-leaved magnolias and the deciduous magnolias that bear huge blossoms, oaks of several kinds, hickory, and the smooth-barked, handsome beech, gum trees, probably of two kinds, poplar, short-leaf and loblolly pines, and finally, the sassafras trees. In New England the sassafras is usually a shrub; here a sassafras might be 18 inches through at the butt and 60 feet tall.

And then there were the flowers—the lovely white dogwood everywhere, honeysuckle of two kinds, wisteria, and many others. On the nice days it was wonderful just to sit and look and listen to the birds and everything was lovely, and every minute was good—in retrospect, even suffering on my belly by the clover.

But the best of all were the sweet and generous and gentle people whom I met—Beasleys up at 4 A.M. to serve us coffee and disappointed later because we did not all come back for dinner at noon; and Mr. Beasley on his tractor taking us across the swampy bottoms where the pickups could not go.

Dwain Bland and Frank Davis worked their hearts out to get me a chance at a gobbler. Ed Norwood, the humorist and great cook, did his best. Vernon Cade and Johnny Nance and Tom Preston could have done no more.

So if, indeed, my Mississippi gobbler hunt was a failure in one sense, it was still a great success.

Part X

SOLVING SHOTGUN MYSTERIES

Chapter 41

Shotgun Fit

There was nothing much to buying a shotgun when I was a boy. In those uncomplicated days, everybody knew that the longer the barrel, the harder it shot. It had to be full choke, too.

I had a hunting buddy who saved his money and bought a new pump gun with a 32-inch, full-choke barrel. When he stood beside it, he had to look up at the muzzle! But he was the envy of all his friends. Nobody else had a new gun and none of us had one that so closely approached perfection—what we considered to be perfection, at any rate.

We had never heard of gun fit or balance, and it didn't occur to us that a

The right amount of drop at comb for you depends on
the height of your cheekbone. If your cheekbones
are high, you will shoot best with a
relatively straight gun.

slight boy might actually be handicapping himself by shooting an 8-pound
gun with a stock long enough for a 6-foot man. All we were interested in
was how far it would kill a pheasant.

My gun, which I bought secondhand for $20 when I was thirteen, was the
envy of nobody. I wasn't happy with it, and I got it only because it was a
bargain and the man who had it agreed to let me work and pay for it as I
could. I was dripping with luck and didn't know it.

This gun was a side-by-side 20-gauge double with 26-inch barrels bored
improved cylinder and full choke. It weighed 6 pounds. I still have it.
Unfortunately, I can't give the dimensions of the stock because the original
has long since been replaced, but I realize now that it must have been
nearly perfect for my size and strength and the hunting I did.

Our upland birds were pheasants and quail, though we boys seldom shot
quail because we hated to "waste" a shell on a little, 7-ounce bird. We also
hunted ducks, but it was all jump shooting—slipping up to the bank of a
creek or drainage ditch and surprising any that might be there. Of course,
this was the same as upland shooting, and my little gun was perfect for it,
too.

When I was seventeen I borrowed a real "man's gun," a 12-gauge pump
with a 30-inch, full-choke barrel, and hunted with it for part of the season. I

couldn't hit a thing. Only then did I begin to appreciate my little double. Years later, when my son Jack began hunting, I started him out with one exactly like it. Since he was only twelve, I cut an inch off the standard 14-inch stock; otherwise, it fit him well.

A lot of nonsense has been written about shotgun fit. A noted writer who has now gone to his reward once published an article extolling the virtues of custom-made guns with the stock individually fitted to the owner's measurements. He went all out and wound up by saying, "Since I got my made-to-measure gun, I have never missed a pheasant."

I wonder why he quit hunting pheasants at that particular time!

A good shot can pick up any standard American shotgun and shoot it well because he can adapt himself to the gun. Perhaps the majority of hunters do the same thing without realizing it. Nevertheless, fit is important. Anybody, whether he's a good, mediocre, or poor shot, will do better with a gun that fits. Gun fit is most important for fast, instinctive shooting such as at ruffed grouse in the timber or quail in the brush. It is less important for deliberate shooting—close-rising pheasants in open stubble, for example.

Gun fit is the way the dimensions of the gun conform to the dimensions of the shooter. Choose a mark on the wall, bring the gun to your shoulder, and press your face against the stock. If the gun fits, you will be looking down the rib or along the top of the barrel and parallel to it and the front sight will be either on the mark or close. If the gun is too straight, you will be looking over the muzzle at an angle. This causes high shooting. If the stock is too crooked, you will see only the back of the receiver and will have to raise your cheek off the stock to look down the rib.

Discussions of gun fit are usually limited to the dimensions of the stock, but several other things are important, too—weight, balance, total length, and the depth of the fore end, which (if you are right-handed) you hold in your left hand. The standard American stock, give or take a fraction of an inch in each dimension, in 1½x2½x14. This means a drop of 1½ inches at the comb, 2½ inches at the heel, and a pull of 14 inches.

To check a gun's dimensions, lay the gun upside down on a table or bench. Measure from the front of the stock, just behind the grip, to the surface of the table or bench. That gives you drop at comb. The distance from just in front of the butt plate to the surface is drop at heel. Pull is the distance from the trigger to the center of the butt plate or recoil pad.

Another stock measurement sometimes mentioned is pitch. This is the angle between the butt plate and the barrel; on a gun with zero pitch it would be 90 degrees. To determine pitch, set the gun butt flat on the floor with the receiver touching the wall and measure between wall and muzzle. (This isn't very precise because total gun lengths vary so much, but it's the way to do it.)

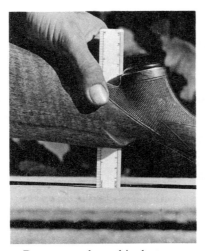

Drop at comb on this shotgun measures 1½ inches.

The drop at heel on this stock is 2⅜ inches.

Most shotguns have a down pitch (muzzle away from wall) of about 2 inches. It is easily increased by putting shims under the butt plate at the heel (top of the stock) or made less by inserting shims under the butt plate at the toe (bottom of the stock). I've tried this sort of adjustment on several guns and couldn't see that it made any difference, one way or the other. But a used gun I bought on which the stock had been altered to zero pitch felt awkward and I soon changed it to give a 2-inch down pitch.

Nobody can tell another man how heavy a gun he should shoot. Although it is now fashionable to recommend light, open-bored guns—just as it once was to extol the virtues of long, full-choke barrels—not everyone will shoot well with a light gun.

I hunted with many shotguns after I outgrew my boyhood 20-gauge and eventually discovered that I shot consistently better with a rather heavy gun of 7½ to 8 pounds or a little more. I once bought a light over-and-under 12-gauge for almost enough to pay off the mortgage and used it several seasons for both upland birds and ducks. Then I decided it was taking a dreadful beating in a duck blind and bought a standard American pump with a ribbed, full-choke barrel for duck hunting. I immediately began to shoot better, so before the next season came along I got a modified barrel for my pump and began using it in the uplands. I shot better there, too.

This gun weighed an even pound more than the over-and-under, which is quite a difference as gun weights go. Besides, it was longer. I think quail flew 5 yards on the average before I could get on them with the pump. But once I was on, I was on. It may be harder to start a long, heavy gun swinging with a fast-moving target, but it's harder to stop, too. And we all know that when we stop the swing, we miss.

So don't let anybody tell you that you should have a light gun or a heavy gun. Choose the one that feels best to you. As my longtime friend and hunting companion Al Miller once said, "A light gun may be nice to carry. But there's not much sense in carrying a 6-pound gun all day only to miss a bird with it at 6 o'clock in the evening."

I like the feel of a gun that balances about 4 inches in front of the trigger. The balance point of various guns varies, depending on the barrel length, the type of action, and the wood in the stock. The more weight forward, the slower a gun is to swing—but the better it sustains that swing once started.

You should try various guns for balance as well as fit because the balance point probably will vary more than the stock dimensions. And the balance has more effect on handling speed than a few ounces' difference in weight.

A double gun of the same barrel length and weight is faster than a magazine gun. The receiver adds about 4 inches to total length—out where it counts, at the muzzle. After I had shot my pump for about twenty years, I realized that I was having trouble catching up with crossing birds; I couldn't swing it as fast as I once did. So I bought a side-by-side double with 26-inch barrels. It was only 8 ounces lighter than the pump, but it was much faster. I could swing it as fast as I did the pump when I was younger. This would have been no advantage in a duck blind, maybe even a handicap, but it immediately improved my upland shooting, particularly on grouse and quail.

The standard stock fits most men—that's the reason it's standard—but it doesn't fit all men. And if I ever saw a woman it fit, I'd be afraid of her. My wife, who is 5 feet 5 inches tall and weighs 132 pounds, is an enthusiastic hunter and good shot. Several years ago she made a grab at a crippled quail among a maze of washed-out willow roots and broke the second finger of her right hand. When it healed, arthritis set in. As the result she suffered every time she fired her light, 12-gauge over-and-under because the trigger guard hit this finger.

I set out to find her a gun with the trigger guard close to the trigger and wound up with a 12-gauge, skeet-grade semi-automatic—26-inch barrel with skeet boring and ventilated rib. The stock was too long for her and I cut it off a little at a time until the pull was 12¾ inches. The drop at comb is 1½ inches and at heel 2⅛.

I can't shoot this gun at all. The stock is too short for me, but it is just right for her. Despite its 7¼-pound weight, which I feared would be too much, she shoots better with it than with any other gun she ever had, including one 12 and two 20's that all weighed a full pound less.

The two critical stock measurements are drop at comb and length. I'm 6 feet 2 inches tall. In view of that, I once got the idea I should have a long stock, so I put a 1-inch recoil pad on the double I had at the time. This gave me a pull of 14¾ inches. Early in the season when I was hunting in shirt sleeves, it wasn't too bad. In the winter when I wore more clothes—half an inch of insulation on your shoulder amounts to lengthening the stock half an inch—it was hopeless. I now know that, despite my height and long arms, I shoot better with a stock somewhat shorter than standard.

I cut ½-inch off the stock of all my guns, giving them a pull of 13½ inches. This is better for me. The gun mounts more easily, the butt never catches on my clothing, and, most important, it swings better to the right. Most right-handed gunners dislike crossing shots to the right. They would discover that a short stock made swinging with these birds much easier.

The comb is sometimes called the shotgun's rear sight, because when you press your cheek against the stock the bottom of your cheekbone rests on the comb. If the gun is too straight, it positions your eye too high; if the gun is too crooked, your eye will be too low.

So the height of your cheekbone determines how much drop at comb your gun should have. If your cheekbones are high, you can shoot a straight gun; if they are low, you need more drop.

This seems obvious, now that I know it. But it wasn't obvious until Al Miller pointed it out to me. Al, in addition to being observant and having hunted with a shotgun for more than fifty years, also has made many stocks for friends who were having trouble with their shooting. The measurement that determines how much drop at comb is necessary is the distance from the bottom of the cheekbone to the pupil of the eye.

Al and I took this measurement on each other. Holding one ruler horizontal and pressing it firmly against the bottom of the cheekbone, we held another on it at a right angle and sighted past the vertical ruler at the pupil. This distance for Al was 1¾ inches; for me, it was 2. We then measured our guns, both of which fit well.

There was the same ¼-inch difference in the drop at comb. His gun had 1¼ inches; mine had 1½. Al's gun is too straight for me. I couldn't shoot it, no matter how hard I might press my cheek down against the stock. Mine has too much drop for him; with his cheekbone on the comb he can see only the back of the receiver.

A fraction of an inch makes a lot of difference here and, fortunately, there is enough variation among the stocks of standard factory shotguns so that most hunters can find a gun that fits. Fit is more important than make.

If you already have a gun with too much drop, you can correct it by attaching a lace-on pad or gluing on a walnut cheekpiece. I did this to a crooked double I once owned and it worked very well. Conversely, if the stock is too straight, you can scrape the comb down, but proceed with caution. It is a lot easier to take wood off than it is to put it back.

Good position for field shooting. With your left foot
forward, you can swing farther to the right,
and swinging to the left is never a problem for
a right-handed shooter.

Sooner or later you are bound to encounter someone who will tell you
you should have a gun with a stock so straight you can't quite get your eye
down into line with the barrel, but will, instead, see about half the rib. This,
he will explain, automatically causes you to shoot a little high so you can hit
rising birds without blotting them out with the muzzle. Trap guns have
straight stocks for this reason, and if all upland birds were rising when you
shot at them it might be all right. But not all birds are rising. Chukars
habitually fly downhill; others level off as soon as they clear the cover. For
most shooting, I find a too-straight gun as much a handicap as one that is
too crooked.

The way to have most fun with a hand trap is to play
"miss and out." You throw claybirds for your buddy till
he misses. Then he throws for you till you miss.
While shooting at clay targets, you learn things
about your shotgun that you wouldn't discover in the
field, because the excitement of the
covey rise is lacking.

Shotgun fit really isn't mysterious. Drop at comb and length of pull are the most important points, and both can be changed. Many other things are involved in good wing shooting—eyesight, coordination, footwork, and whatever may be in the back of your head, to name a few. Forget your problems, relax, and enjoy yourself. You'll shoot better if you don't try too hard.

Chapter 42

The Mysteries
of Lead

Some years ago when I was twelve or thirteen, I read an article in *Field &*
Stream called "Lead on Ducks." When I saw the title I thought it was
strange because I had never heard of "lead" in wing shooting and knew
only the metal, pronounced "led."

I soon discovered my error and I remember one bit of advice to this day:
"Shoot ahead of them. Shoot farther ahead of them. Shoot still farther
ahead of them." The author probably was George Bird Grinnell, who first
put these words into print and was considered the dean of American duck
hunters in his day.

Whatever, I can't dispute his wisdom. Yet I do believe that no two duck
hunters or upland gunners lead passing birds exactly the same, even though
they may be straight crossing shots at identical range and flying at identical
speed. That explains why it is so difficult for one gunner to tell another how
much to lead a passing goose or duck.

One frosty morning years ago, my brother, my wife, and I were pass-
shooting mallards, and Ellen was having trouble. Burtt and I soon killed
our limits—twelve that year—and began telling Ellen how to hit them. (A
great help, I'm sure!)

But the one exchange that impressed me most and that I still remember
as though it happened yesterday was this:

Who can tell another shooter how far to lead a duck?

I told her, "Lead them 10 feet."

Burtt said, "No, lead them 2 feet."

Now, we had each killed our twelve ducks with less than a box of shells, and I must point out for those who have done little waterfowl hunting that one for two is mighty fine duck shooting. I wish I could do as well today!

Aside from youth, there were several reasons for our good shooting. First, there was no wind. Second, the birds were all at approximately the same range, probably none closer than 35 yards or any farther than 40 yards. Third, although they were all sifting right along, they were all flying at about the same speed, and all in the same direction. Fourth, all shots were directly overhead, or nearly so.

You seldom find such an ideal situation on waterfowl, anywhere or at any time. Once we established the proper lead we had it made. Yet, according to our best estimates, my lead was five times as great as Burtt's!

Why? I think I know now, though I didn't then. I established what I thought was the proper lead and then maintained it, the muzzle of my gun apparently moving at the same speed as the duck. Burt swung much faster and continued this fast swing after he pulled the trigger. So the ducks flew into his shot the same as they did mine, even though his apparent lead was much less.

I have since quit the maintained-lead method and for years have used the fast swing-through, partly because my own results were more consistent with it and partly because all the best shots I have ever known used it. My favorite waterfowl shot is a straight-overhead incomer at any reasonable range. I swing fast from behind and pull the trigger as the muzzle blots out the bird. This is one shot I seldom miss.

All of us, I'm sure, have had a bird appear suddenly in an unexpected direction, giving us only a fleeting instant in which to shoot, but have killed it dead as a stone. I recall one such shot in particular.

I was following a covey of chukars around a steep hillside, sure that they were somewhat downhill to my left, when a single flushed above, on my right. It flew only a few yards before disappearing behind a boulder as big as a house. I twisted around, swung with it as fast as I could, and shot. I was so sure I didn't catch up with it before it flew behind the rock that I kept right on walking as I reloaded.

The dog who owned me then, didn't agree. He ran up the hill, around the boulder, and soon appeared carrying a chukar that was limp as a dishrag. A fast swing killed the bird. I actually thought the muzzle was behind it when I pulled the trigger.

Another time, I was shooting trap with my old school-days hunting buddy, Alvin Morrison, and his boys and for some unknown reason I expected a high bird to the right. Instead, the target was a low, fast bird to the left. I swung hard about 90 degrees and powdered it. One of the boys was standing behind me, looking over my shoulder. He said, "You couldn't have hit that blue rock! You were behind it when you shot."

I pointed to the puff of black dust, still hanging in the air. "Yep," he said, "but I still can't believe it."

Admittedly, such shots occur more often in the uplands than in the lowlands, but they happen while duck hunting, too. Surprise shots are not unusual in timber or even with trees on one side of your blind and open water on the other. We've all killed ducks we thought we'd missed when we shot, and a fast swing was usually the reason.

There are few times when all shots are so similar as they were that day Burtt and I did so well. Usually, no two shots are exactly alike. You have birds dropping into the decoys with their flaps down, others flaring from them or the blind, and still others passing at every conceivable angle. To complicate matters further, a duck crossing at 50 yards doesn't seem to be flying so fast as one moving at the same speed at 25 yards. Yet it obviously takes the shot more than twice as long to travel the greater distance.

And still another point: Puddle ducks—mallards, teal, pintails, baldpates, and their kin—flare at the first shot. Varying the angle, but holding generally true, you must allow vertical lead for the second shot, but less apparent horizontal, or forward, lead. Divers—canvasbacks, redheads, bluebills, and the rest—don't flare. Instead, they bore right on through. Maybe they put on a little extra speed. I wouldn't know. It has always seemed to me that, except for setting down or taking off, they travel full bore all the time anyway.

I took a young friend duck hunting one morning and about 9 o'clock I killed a lone mallard drake straight overhead at 40 yards. "Good gosh!" the boy exclaimed. "I never saw such a shot! That greenead must have been 70 yards."

I reloaded while the dog brought the duck. The lad picked up my empty and read the dope on the side. "And with a trap load, yet!" Actually, I was shooting 3¼-1¼-7½ (3¼ drams equivalent of powder behind 1¼ ounces of No. 7½ shot).

This incident illustrates still one more thing that helps to make duck shooting the fascinating and challenging sport it is. Just as the moon looks bigger near the horizon than it does high overhead, so a duck near the water seems closer than one at the same range above. The youngster had been shooting at 40-yard ducks—and killing some of them—all morning. None were overhead, however.

Now we come to wind. How I hate it! Yet I want it to blow when I'm hunting ducks. It drives them off the open water and makes them fly, and we never get any ducks unless they're flying. A duck flying with the wind isn't any more difficult than any other duck shot. Its ground speed is, of course, increased by the velocity of the moving air. This automatically forces you to swing faster and the problem of lead pretty well takes care of itself. A duck flying against the wind is a horse of a different hue.

I have a vivid recollection of a most disheartening experience, the first time I remember shooting at ducks flying into the wind. Jim Clark and I were hunting on the Weiser River. The wind was blowing down it and the ducks were flying up, barely. Their ground speed was about that of the dog that doesn't quite want to catch the cat.

When the first long, wavering line of mallards appeared, we thought they'd never reach us. We waited and waited and waited. At last, they were overhead. I picked a greenhead that was hanging against the sky like an anchored balloon and shot right at him. I heard Jim's gun a fraction of a second later.

Those ducks didn't flare, they bounced! With the help of the wind, they literally bounced about 40 feet. Neither of us was quick enough to fire the second barrel. Jim had aimed at his duck the same as I. We talked it over and decided to give them a little lead next time. We did. Same result.

There was a great flight that morning. We had chance after chance. Foolishly, we had left home with only one box of shells apiece. We kept leading farther and farther and finally, when we were about out of ammunition, we began to hit an occasional duck. We wound up with four or five. Imagine—five for fifty, one for ten!

What we didn't know was this: Once the shot leaves the barrel, you are dealing with air speed, not ground speed. A duck flying into the wind, though apparently barely moving, is actually flying faster because it is working harder than one flying at normal speed through still air. I know those facts now, but it's still hard to swing fast through a duck that seems to be only creeping ahead.

Then you have crosswinds. They drift ducks sideways so they actually are not flying in the direction they appear to be headed. Once I shot at the leader of an angling line of five goldeneyes quartering into a strong wind and killed the last duck in the line!

Though hitting ducks flying into the wind has always been tough for me— I have to force myself to lead them as I know I must—some hunters do it consistently. I once saw Clayton Davidson, the man who taught me most of what I know about duck hunting, make six for six on mallards flying into a wind that seemed to be blowing 40 miles an hour. To make it even tougher, he was lying in a shallow ditch for concealment and had to sit up each time he shot. I suppose I used a box of shells to kill my limit, down to six by then.

With all these variables, not to mention the difficulty of estimating range correctly, how does anyone ever manage to kill a duck? It is somewhat of a minor miracle, I'll confess, but here are four rules that help:

• Rule one—Swing through fast and pull the trigger as the muzzle passes the duck on close shots, progressively farther ahead as the range increases. And *never* stop your swing.

• Rule two—Follow George Bird Grinnell's advice: "Shoot ahead of them. Shoot farther ahead of them. Shoot still farther ahead of them."

• Rule three—Find a load that patterns well in your gun, with recoil that doesn't hurt you, and stick with it. I once had a gun that shot a fantastic full-choke pattern with magnum 4's. I quit shooting them for two reasons: First, I wasn't good enough to realize their potential; the lead on a duck or goose at 60 yards is about ten times as difficult to figure as the lead at 30 yards. Second, the recoil hurt me and when that occurs, regardless of how tough you may be, your percentage slumps. My longtime favorite load, 1¼ ounces of No. 7½ shot pushed by 3¼ drams equivalent, smothers a duck at 40 yards. I don't shoot them farther.

As for geese, you'd be surprised how many big Canadas I've killed with this load. As the immortal Fred Kimble once said, "I can hit a quail; why couldn't I hit a goose in the head?"

• Rule four—Never shoot at a duck if you think, "Maybe I can kill it." If you confine your shots to birds you *know* you can kill, your percentage of hits will improve. Furthermore, you'll be far more likely to kill clean or miss clean.

Chapter 43

You Need A Scapegoat

Rare indeed is the waterfowl or upland hunter who is not familiar with that bogy of the smoothbore gunner, the shooting slump. Sired by uncertainty, born of mystery, nurtured on anxiety, the shooting slump descends on the just and the unjust alike.

It comes without warning, usually at the most unexpected moment. There is no escaping its tenacious grasp. Like the starfish which, once it chooses an oyster, enfolds it in loving arms and sucks out its very marrow before dropping an empty shell, so the shooting slump clings to its victim. He can no more escape before it is through with him than the oyster can elude a starfish.

Experience is no protection. In fact, I am inclined to think that the worst shooting slumps are known only to those veteran gunners who have fired thousands of shots at feathered game and who by logic—if there were logic in such things—should be immune.

There is a vast difference between shooting-slump missing and any kind of explainable missing. To miss is normal. Everyone misses. Some of us miss more frequently than others, of course, but since the days of Bogardus we've all done it. Usually after a few seasons of experience, however, we know why. We fail to lead a crossing bird far enough and so we miss him.

We shoot under a rising bird, possibly realizing it even as we pull the trigger. We stop our swing. We allow too much for a bird curving to left or right and shoot ahead of him.

There are many good, sound reasons for missing, and so long as we can find a reason for our failure to intercept a feathered target with a load of shot, there is no cause to worry. We can correct next time. Nor is a period of more or less routine poor shooting cause for alarm. We all have times when we shoot below our usual average, just as we have others when we shoot over our heads.

A shooting slump is different. When a real shooting slump pulls the rug from under us we don't miss more than usual. We miss everything.

I had a dreadful shooting slump one fall, the worst in years. I started out pretty good. I missed a lot of doves the first day, but I wasn't ashamed of that. We had a violent wind and, friend, if you haven't shot doves in a hard wind you have a treat coming! For the rest of the dove season I shot about as well as I ever do on them.

When the grouse season opened a little later, I was hot. The leaves were still on and I killed five or six grouse that I couldn't see when I pulled the trigger, plus several others that I had no business hitting.

I did all right on pheasants, chukars, and quail, too, when those seasons opened together. I wasn't so hot as I had been on grouse, but at least I was shooting up to average, and maybe a little better. The season went along— too fast, of course, as bird seasons always do—and then one day I suddenly couldn't hit the ground with my hat.

It started with chukars. They were scarce. Maybe that contributed. Maybe I was too anxious. Anyway, my wife and I were driving along a sagebrush road on a ridge when a covey of chukars ran across ahead. There was a pretty good chance they'd stop just under the rim, since they don't like to run downhill. We got out, loaded our guns, and, with dog at heel, walked over to the edge. They flushed just below us, flying straight downhill, and I missed three times. My wife killed one.

Half a mile farther we saw a covey sunning themselves on some rocks on the east side of the ridge, about 50 yards below the crest. I backed up until we were out of sight, then parked. I sent my wife ahead with instructions to stay on the west side of the ridge until she was opposite them, then cross over and start down toward the rocky outcropping on which they were sitting. She was to walk as quietly as if she were stalking a deer.

After giving her a few minutes, I took the dog and started around the east side of the ridge, contouring to hit the base of the rocks on which we had seen the chukars. What I hoped would happen was this: They would hear me coming and run uphill—they always do—but Ellen would be on top waiting for them. She would get an easy shot and they would fly downhill, another chukar characteristic you can bet on. By that time, I'd be at the rocks and get shooting, too, as they came over.

I never made a plan that worked better. Dog at heel, I walked around the sidehill. I didn't see a chukar, of course—I hadn't expected to. I had barely gotten to the rocks, however, when I heard two quick shots above. Then, there they were! Fifteen or twenty of the cackling idiots came sailing off the top, 25 yards high and straight overhead. It would be just like duck shooting.

There is no shot I like better than a straight incomer. You bring the muzzle from behind and when it blots him out you pull and he is dead. It didn't work that way this time, however. I missed. I tried again just after he passed and managed to scratch him down, then missed another.

I watched the covey down while Rip retrieved the cripple, then I climbed the hill to join my wife. The chukars had run right into her and she had made a double.

We worked another good strategy on a third covey a little later, and I missed three easy shots. These birds sailed down into the valley and lit near a patch of heavy sagebrush where the second covey had gone, so we went after them. I killed a single. He sailed 300 yards, then towered and dropped, which meant only one shot in him, in the heart. Then I missed two twice.

The rest of the chukars eluded us somehow, so when we got back to the car I had a magnificent score of two scratch hits and twelve misses. That was only the beginning! I went from bad to worse during the next three or four hunts.

Every old bird hunter knows the feeling. There is nothing else quite like it. I changed guns, but it did no good. The over-and-under shot as crookedly as the pump I had been using when the slump started. I probably went hunting ten times and, thanks to a terrific expenditure of ammunition, I got approximately enough game to put in your eye.

Finally I decided that my hunting coat was to blame. The weather had turned chilly and I'd started wearing it about the time I began missing. I bought it originally to wear duck hunting with a lot of clothes underneath, so in the uplands, over only a wool shirt, it fitted me like a saddle fits a sow. I put it away and started hunting in a light wool jacket and the same game vest I'd worn in warm weather.

The first morning, I killed four pheasants and a quail in five shots. Then I quit.

The next day I killed six quail and two chukars in eleven shots, and on the third day I did as well. For the remainder of the season I was as good as I usually am.

Now the question is, was the big hunting coat to blame? I really doubt it. I doubt that it had any more to do with my poor shooting than the phase of

During one shooting slump, Ted switched from a hunting
coat to this wool jacket and started hitting again.

the moon or the color of my dog's eyes. I had to blame *something,* however.

Once, and only once, I nipped a shooting slump in the bud. It began when Willard Cravens and I were hunting California valley quail and I couldn't hit them.

My trouble started on the first scattered covey rise when I put up seven singles in a row without getting one shot. Two or three birds flew toward some nearby cattle. Others buzzed behind the tall brush so fast I couldn't get on them.

No doubt this made me overanxious. I got to straining, and every old shotgunner knows you never put meat on the table when you try too hard. Finally—but only because there were hundreds of birds and I had enough ammunition to start a war—I managed to bag the ten quail the law permitted. Willard was through long before I finished the shameful exhibition. He walked along and watched me miss, but was kind enough not to offer either sympathy or advice.

The proper thing to do after such an experience is to forget it—and the sooner, the better. I can't seem to do that, however. I keep trying to find a reason and by the time Willard and I went back to quail heaven, three days later, I had come to the conclusion that my eyes were to blame. After all, they're certainly not what they once were, and in dim light valley quail *are* hard to see. They're small and fast and they blend into the usual background like sugar into oatmeal.

I decided to wear my bright-yellow shooting glasses, which increase contrast and would, I hoped, enable me to pick up the flying quail more quickly. I'd previously found them a real help in seeing big game under poor light conditions, but somehow had never tried them bird hunting.

We left the car about 4 o'clock. By 6 I was explaining to Willard just what my trouble had been for all these recent years. I had killed ten quail in eleven shots and a lot of them were in heavy cover. That's about as good as I ever hope to do. The glasses were the answer!

It's too bad wing shooting is never so simple. The next three or four times out I shot my usual average. The glasses had nothing to do with it. In the long run I shot just the same with them as I did without them. The trouble lay in me. But at least the glasses did give me a fresh start after a horrid day and probably averted a prolonged shooting slump.

I think a shooting slump, like an ulcer, starts in your head. And, also like an ulcer, you can cure it right there—if you have the gumption. As every ulcer sufferer and bedeviled smoothbore man knows, however, that isn't easy. Your doctor may tell you to stop worrying and get over your stomachache. Your better sense may tell you to loosen up and shoot for fun, rather than as if your life depended on it. But unless your mind has a lot better control over your nerves than most minds do, either thing is much easier said than done.

Shotgun shooting is about half mental. One of the surest ways to miss—and probably the most common—is to try too hard. I consistently shoot better when I am alone, or with a friend who doesn't shoot as well as I do, than when I am hunting with a superior shot. This is a common failing. We try hard to shoot as well as our friend who seldom misses and as a result we shoot worse than usual.

Trying too hard, however, is only one of many things that can cause us to tighten up and shoot poorly. Seeing a bird on the ground before it flies causes many of us to miss, especially if it sits there a long time. Inexperienced hunters nearly always get tense as they walk up to a point. Poor shooting on opening day is common, simply because we are overanxious.

There can be no question that our general health has a bearing on coordination and so on our shooting. If we feel badly, or are worried about something, or are nervous, or even too tired, our shooting will suffer. The most consistently bad shooting I ever did was one fall when I had a seven-days-a-week job. I worked five days and five evenings in order to have two days to hunt and I couldn't hit a barn with a ball bat.

This was not a slump, though. It was a permanent condition as long as I had that job. The typical slump doesn't last long, but while we're suffering with it we wonder if it will last forever. If it is caused by some physical thing, such as the flu, we are almost sure to figure out the reason. Correct this and the slump ends.

The mental causes are the tricky ones to spot. Yet because our minds and nerves can have such a devastating effect on our shooting, we have to correct the cause—at least we have to *think* we've corrected it.

That is the reason why we must have a scapegoat. We have to find something to blame. Many a hunter has laid aside a perfectly good gun, convinced that he couldn't hit anything with it, then shot well with a different one. I've done it myself, then gone back to the first gun after a while only to discover that I could shoot it as well as I ever did. Many a new gun has been bought because some poor devil found himself unable to hit anything and had to have a scapegoat.

Whatever we do, the important thing is to find a cause and then correct it. This will give us confidence again. So closely is the mental related to the physical in wing shooting, however, that we may never know for sure.

Come to think of it I wonder if that loose hunting coat was catching the butt of my gun—or something?

Chapter 44

Covey Birds

A bobwhite quail weighs between 6 and 7 ounces. A California valley quail weighs maybe an ounce less, and a mountain quail about 3 ounces more. Hungarian partridge run an ounce or two less than a pound. Chukars vary more than the others, but they average about a pound and a quarter.

Compared to the 2½ or 3 pounds of a mature cock pheasant, none of these popular covey birds is very big. Yet all of them possess a strange power to demoralize the man behind a gun. Young hunters, particularly, are subject to it, but even old-timers occasionally suffer an acute attack of the awkwards at the explosive rise of a big covey. I know; I've had 'em.

I once got right smack into the middle of the world's biggest covey of valley quail. That's taking in a lot of territory, because in good quail years, coveys of fifty to a hundred birds aren't uncommon, but this was the biggest. Quail were running and flying everywhere. I got excited. My companion got excited. The dogs got so excited they were out of their minds. They were running around snapping at quail on the ground. They even gave tongue.

It was wonderful. I'll never forget. But before long I reached the state where I couldn't have hit a balloon tied to a stake, much less a quail buzzing through the brush.

There was only one thing to do. We got hold of the dogs and made them

When a covey gets up, pick one bird and concentrate on
it. Don't even *think* about another until the first is falling.

lie down. Then we sat down and smoked a pipe and tried to forget all about
quail hunting for ten minutes. After that we were able to resume operations
somewhat more sanely.

Things like this seldom happen to a man who's been shooting quail for
years. It takes something pretty unusual to unnerve him. But to the
beginner or to the man who's shot only birds that usually rise singly, such as
grouse or pheasants, *any* covey rise is a trying experience. If he shoots well
from scratch he's a phenomenon.

When chukars conquered the West, they quickly gained the reputation of
being hard to hit and hard to kill. Some of the boys took to shooting
magnum 4's at them. An acquaintance, admittedly not the best hunter in
the country, told me proudly after the first open season, "I killed a chukar!"

Chukars nearly always fly downhill. Unless you hold under a bird flying
downhill you're sure to miss him, but this doesn't prove he's hard to hit; it
only proves you don't know how to shoot birds flying downhill.

Second, unless you know how to hunt chukars—and obviously nobody did at first—they'll run and then flush wild. This always makes birds seem faster than they actually are, harder to hit and harder to kill.

Third and, I think, most to blame, few of our neophyte chukar hunters had ever shot anything but pheasants, one at a time. The covey rise was confusing. They did all right on the singles, but a dozen birds in the air at one time was too much.

Shortly after the chukars moved in, a lot of pheasant hunters discovered quail. They'd never been hunted much before; they were too little. As Al Miller said, "If ostriches were legal game, most of these guys wouldn't waste a shell on a pheasant."

But the chukars got the boys out into the desert, and they ran into the valley and mountain quail and started shooting at them. Scads of quail were killed on the ground, mostly by hunters standing in the back of pickup trucks, but some of them did have the decency to shoot only at birds on the wing, and this made even worse problems than the chukars had.

Anybody can tell you how to shoot covey birds: Concentrate on one. Forget all the others. When your first bird is falling, swing to another and kill it. If you're fast enough and shooting a magazine gun, you can then pick a third bird and shoot it.

But this last is strictly brag talk. Very, very few hunters can kill three mountain quail on a simultaneous covey rise, fewer yet can do it on bobwhites, and I've yet to see the feat accomplished on California valley quail, in my opinion the fastest upland bird we have.

The advice to choose one bird and ignore the others is all right as far as it goes, but it doesn't go far enough. Which bird? How do you pick out one target when the air is full of them, all making a thundering racket and leaving at better than a thousand miles per hour?

As in practically everything else, doing what comes naturally is wrong. If you do what comes naturally you'll shoot at the easiest bird first. It's usually the last off the ground; sometimes it's the one that flies at the best angle. Do this, and even if you hit it, it will nearly always be the only bird you get.

The photo accompanying this compendium of wisdom shows me doing what came naturally. I was about to shoot at the last chukar off the ground, the one at the extreme right, just below the skyline. I killed the bird, all right, but by the time I could swing to another, it was too late. They had all pitched down over the crest of the ridge. I should have shot one of the others first; then this slow riser would still have been in sight, and I probably could have made a double.

There are quail hunters who shoot open-bored magazine guns and spend the first shot on the thick part of the covey the instant it clears the cover. Next, they pick an individual bird and shoot at it, and if they have time or if there's a sleeper they get off a third shot. Most of the hunters who claim three quail on the covey rise do it this way.

I suppose it's a little better than shooting them on the ground or out of a tree, but as far as I'm concerned it's on a par with netting fish. One No. 8 shot will kill a quail if it gets into its lungs or intestines, but it won't kill it immediately. That bird will fly away, usually without any sign of being hit, and die later. Flock shooting is unsportsmanlike and wasteful of game, and when I speak of killing two or three on a covey rise I mean picking individual birds and killing them cleanly.

Of course, a good shot occasionally catches two birds crossing and kills them both intentionally. That isn't what I meant by flock shooting, nor did I mean those times when we shoot at one bird and accidentally kill a second that flies into the pattern. Everybody who's shot many covey birds has had that happen, usually when he was completely unaware of the second bird.

Once, years ago, I was hunting sage hens with my brother. On a scattered covey rise he killed a bird flying to the right at a range of about 25 yards. I was too far away to get a shot but in a good position to see what happened, and a second bird, flying in the *opposite* direction, fell when he fired. When he picked up the one he'd shot at and started on I said, "Don't you want your other bird?"

"What other bird?"

I told him he had another down, about 20 yards farther out. He wouldn't believe me, and I had to show him where it was. Then when I told him which direction it had been flying he was literally dumfounded. That sage hen obviously had walked under a ladder.

Unless you're alone, the first rule of hunting all covey birds is to shoot at those on your side. If you and a companion walk in on a point and he is to your left, you can shoot only at birds on the right side of the covey. And if they curve too sharply to the left, you can't shoot at all. Swinging through and shooting across in front of your gunning partner are unpardonable sins.

When hunters ignore the rule to shoot only at birds on their own sides, frequently they both hit the same one. This results from doing what comes naturally. On any flush one bird always looks easiest. The eye automatically selects it, and an untrained shooter will always send his first load in its direction.

This is the wrong thing to do, even if you're alone. Try to pick one of the first birds off the ground for your first shot. Your second shot will be much closer than if you had shot the easiest bird first.

Once the new gunner learns for sure that the holes are bigger than the birds and masters the knack of picking out a single bird and killing it, he'll encounter a new handicap to good shooting—greed. Determined to make a double, he'll find himself selecting the second target before he hits the first. As a result, he'll miss both. Whether there are five birds in a covey or fifty, forget all but one until you've hit it. Then look for another. If you miss the first time, it's better to shoot again at the same bird anyway.

Old quail hunters will tell you that bobwhites know where they're going before they leave the ground. This is true, to some degree at least, of all covey birds. The man who thinks he can make them fly the way *he* wants them to is due for some tough shooting. Ducks overhead at 30 yards are one thing; quail buzzing over so close you can almost hit them with your gun barrel are something else again.

Learning to anticipate which way birds will fly and then approaching your dog's point from the proper direction to get the best shooting the terrain permits is an important part of successful hunting. Eventually, you learn to do it almost instinctively, but logic is a good substitute for experience. Quail usually head for the nearest heavy cover; Huns are more likely to fly away from brush than toward it.

Unless you have a dog that's good on down game, finding the birds you hit is somewhat of an art. If you hope to make a double, you can't watch your first bird to the ground. Instead, the instant he's hit you're looking for another. And, of course, you're swinging and looking simultaneously, so the gun is almost on your target as soon as you choose it.

A good system is to mark down the last bird carefully and hurry to it. If you see it at once, fine. If not, put your hat or handkerchief on a bush and go look for the first one you hit. It will be harder to find. Mark the spot where it should be too, so you can come back and start over if necessary, then cover the area systematically. Unless you watch a bird clear to the ground, it will almost always be farther away than you thought. And if it was flying downhill when hit, it will be much farther.

One help is that a dying bird flutters. Cripples never do, but cripples are easier to find. Pause and listen where you think a bird should be. This is an old grouse-hunting trick, but it often helps to find all other upland birds.

All the Western quail, Huns, and chukars run like jackrabbits. Never try to save ammunition when you have a running cripple; you'll probably never see it again if you don't stop it while you have the chance.

Part XI

THE MANIA CALLED DUCK HUNTING

Chapter 45

Laws of Duck Hunting

After hunting ducks with varying success but with unflagging enthusiasm for more than thirty years, I have finally come to the conclusion that certain inflexible laws govern the sport of wildfowling. They are not man-made laws. They have nothing to do with the number of times your gun will shoot without reloading, whether you can have a motor on your skiff, or the kind of decoys you must use.

In fact, the laws to which I refer are much more rigid than these. A man-made law can be broken. Doing so might not be a good idea, but it is possible. It is not possible to violate the laws to which I refer. They are laws of nature, as inexorable as the law of gravity. Every old duck hunter will recognize them. Let the newcomer read and beware.

There is a law to fit each situation, and each situation has its law. For example: You have been sitting in the blind for hours and not a duck has come near. The only thing to fly across the area of sky that you can watch has been an occasional dickeybird. You are cramped and stiff, and you decide to walk around (or take the skiff) and see if you can jump a few ducks.

The law: As soon as you are too far away to get back in time, they will start pouring in like bees to honey.

Young hunter, do you doubt this law? Let me tell you. One New Year's Day, Clare Conley and I went duck hunting. We made our setup before daylight on a bar in the Snake River. When the water is low, the gravel is exposed in a narrow strip about 50 yards long, and it is a great spot for mallards to loaf and rest. Right in the middle of the bar is a tiny, brushy island, just big enough to conceal a couple of hunters.

For some reason, however, the ducks didn't like our bar that day. We got four or five right after shooting time and then for the next three hours we might as well have been in the middle of a desert. What few ducks were flying knew exactly where they were going—and it wasn't to our bar, either. Our decoys, on the bar and in the water, looked good to us, but they obviously didn't look good to the ducks.

Conley, at that time, was fairly new to duck hunting. About 10 o'clock, he said, "Nuts! I've had enough of this. I'm going down the river and try to jump-shoot a few."

Although I did advise him not to leave the blind, I was wicked enough to be secretly glad that he was going. I knew what would happen.

Sure enough, he had been gone scarcely ten minutes when a little wad of mallards saw the decoys and came in like long-lost friends. I managed to drop a couple on the bar. A flock of bluebills whisked over almost low enough to knock my cap off, but I didn't see them in time to shoot. One greenwing teal lit among the decoys. I didn't disturb him.

When Conley had been gone thirty minutes, I saw a flock of Canada geese flying up the middle of the river. They were low and apparently looking for a place to sit down. I waited until they were opposite the blind, then gave them just a little soft, confidential mallard talk on the call. They turned, set their wings, and came straight in, and I killed two.

Conley had seen the geese, and he came back upstream in time to pick mine up. He was disgusted. He tied the boat under the overhanging brush that concealed it and got into the blind without a word. Then we sat until 1 P.M. without breaking another cap and finally went home.

There are laws that govern various other aspects of the sport of duck hunting, too. Take the matter of weather. Everybody knows that good shooting depends on the weather. I never miss a forecast during the duck season, but the problem is more involved than that. If I plan a trip far in advance I am certain to draw a bluebird day; if I wait until the last minute, the boss piles on more work or relatives come to visit and I can't go at all. In the spring when I am trying to fish the wind blows all the time; in the fall when I need it to make the ducks fly, it never blows at all. Therefore, I have arrived at this law: No matter what you do, the weather will be wrong 95 percent of the time.

Once I had discovered the law of weather, the solution was fairly simple. I just went duck hunting as often as I could, and approximately one day out of twenty was perfect. Knowing this, I was spared a great deal of fretting.

Then there is the law of arrival. It is so simple that it requires no explanation. It states: If you arrive at the chosen spot early and get your decoys out well in advance of shooting time, the flight will be late. If, however, you arrive a little late and are still putting out decoys when shooting time comes, the flight will be early.

There are two minor laws that might well be grouped together, though in the aggregate they save a great many ducks. The first is the law of smoking: If, after a long dry period, you set down your gun to light a smoke, a flock of ducks will immediately whip over the blind and be out of range before you can recover. The second is the law of coffee: If, likewise after a long dry spell, you decide to have a cup of coffee, a flock will swing over while you have vacuum bottle in one hand and a half-filled cup in the other.

Normally during the duck season, I carry lunch, coffee bottle, dry gloves, camera, shells, and various useful odds and ends in a waterproof box. I take it home each evening to be restocked and return it to the boat next morning. One bleak day several years ago, my wife and I set out our decoys in a likely spot, and since we both had quite a few shells left in our coat pockets from the last hunt, we didn't attempt to get more out of the box at first.

The flight was slow, but we eventually began to run low on ammunition. A few snowflakes began to curl down about this time and, judging from past experience, I decided that I'd better get more shells. I walked along the shore to the boat, which was hidden 50 yards away, and opened the box. There was not one shell in it! I had forgotten to put more in the night before.

When I returned to the blind with the bad news, we counted up and discovered that we had just six shells between us—and we still had six ducks to go. Judging from the way we had been shooting so far, this was definitely too many ducks to go. Sure enough. We did the best we could, but we ran out of shells when we were still short of our limit by three birds.

Meanwhile, the snow fell harder and harder. When it snows, mallards feed in the fields all day, but every time they get a neckful of corn or wheat they have to make a trip for water. They also need gravel, and if you are in a convenient spot that offers both you will see shooting out of this world. We were in such a spot, and an hour after the first snowflakes fell the ducks came.

We could no longer shoot, of course, but we could look. The air soon was full of ducks as far as we could see. The water was black with them. Mostly, they were mallards, a few pintails and green-wing teal and some baldpates.

They plummeted down so close that we could have hit them with a stick. They splashed and gabbled among our decoys with no concern whatever and walked out on the bar, almost at our feet. For two solid hours they came and went in a steady procession. Very likely they continued all day. It was something I'll never forget, but two hours of it with empty guns was all we could endure.

This experience, coupled with similar ones in the days when limits were bigger and running out of shells not so unusual, led to my discovery of the law of ammunition: The one sure way to bring on a spectacular duck flight is to run out of shells.

No doubt all duck hunters are familiar with the law of lunch—the quickest way to bring a flurry of activity on a dull day is to start eating your lunch—but I question whether most duck hunters know about the equally infallible law of decoy moving. It was one of the most difficult to discover, but after getting the hang of it, I have profited many times.

It works best on a dull day—a time when only a few ducks are flying and all of them are going somewhere else. About the middle of the morning, you decide your decoys aren't placed right. You will move some of them. As soon as you are up to your boot tops in the water with a bundle of blocks in each arm, you hear a cautious "Pssst" from your partner, who is still in the blind. You look up, and there is a big flock coming straight at you, wings cupped for a landing. Of course, it is too late then and the first willing ducks in two hours flare off out of range.

This happened to me so often that I finally began to get wise. I kept an eye cocked skyward at all times. Sometimes I saw the approaching birds in time to rush back into the blind. Once I flopped face down on a gravel bar and my partner dropped mallards on both sides of me. I felt quite clever about this maneuver until I discovered that I had somehow broken my pipe in the process.

At any rate, the law is this: When things are desperate, go out to move your decoys. It will bring ducks nine times out of ten.

I shouldn't have to mention the law of sleep. Every old-time member of the clan has discovered it to his mortification. But for the benefit of the younger generation, this is how it works. The situation calls for a flat-calm, sunny, warm, bluebird day. No ducks are stirring. You are sleepy because you were up late getting ready and up early getting where you are now, and you finally give in to Morpheus. The law: As soon as you are sound asleep, a big flock of ducks will light among the decoys. They will remain until you wake up. Then they will fly safely away before you are able to collect your senses, pick up your gun, and get ready to shoot.

There are two laws concerning friends. The first is the law of special friends: If you have a special friend that you are particularly anxious to show good shooting, and you take him to the best spot you know during the best part of the season in the best kind of weather, the shooting will be miserable.

I took a special friend duck hunting twice one year. One day we got one duck and the other day we didn't get any. I am sure he is now convinced that I never do kill one and that all my duck killing is purely imaginary.

The other friend law concerns conversational friends. If—as all duck hunters are forever hoping to do—you discover a new and wonderful place to shoot and make the mistake of telling a talking-to (as distinguished from a hunting-with) friend, there will be a hunter behind every reed when you go back. Furthermore, each hunter will have a nervous dog, a loud call, and an inexhaustible supply of ammunition.

Although I consider it inexcusable, people do have parties during the hunting season. This led to my discovery of the law of society, which follows: If you offend your friends by not attending their party so that you can go duck hunting early the next morning, the shooting will be terrible; if, however, you do go and give up hunting you will learn later that you missed the best day of the year.

Consider, too, the law of the upwind ducks. The situation is this: You are pass-shooting at ducks that are beating their way into the wind. It is a hard wind. Some of them seem to be hanging almost still in it as they slowly approach and others are drifting back and forth. You burn up a scandalous amount of ammunition. Finally, after leading them farther and farther out of sheer desperation, you connect twice in a row. You have it made! Law: The flight will stop immediately.

My last law is one that no experienced duck hunter will challenge. It has been a miserable day. Only a handful of ducks flew early and still fewer later on. Those that did pass by were both high and far, and if they saw your decoys they failed to give them a second look. After hours of waiting, during which your feeling of hopelessness steadily increased, you decide to pick up and go. Law: As soon as the last decoy is in the bag a great flight will commence.

Thus we see that the lot of the duck hunter is not a happy one. He is the child of frustration, the collector of mishap, the victim of misfortune. He suffers from cold and wet and lack of sleep. He is punished more often than he is rewarded. Yet he continues. Why? Because one great day—and great days do come, days when the ducks are willing and the gun swings true—repays him manyfold for all the others.

That is why there are so many of us. We are all waiting for the next great day—whenever that may be.

Chapter 46

Make the Ducks Come to You

Anybody can kill ducks early in the season and again, later, on those days when unusual weather makes the birds forget all caution. But normally by late season some ducks in every flock have been shot at. Then they are blind-shy, call-shy, decoy-shy, and always suspicious. This is the kind of duck hunting that separates the men from the boys. It sometimes makes me appear downright juvenile. But during many years of trying I've picked up some tricks from older and smarter duck hunters, and I'm going to pass them on.

The most important thing, always, is to find the right location. Not being a duck, I don't know why they like some spots and don't like others that look similar to me, but that's the way they are. Careful observation is your best guide here, though sometimes luck can help.

One day four of us put out two dozen decoys on a little puddle at noon and crouched in the reeds around it. About the same time, a fellow who has the reputation of being one of the finest duck callers in this part of the country put out his stool 250 yards away.

We had shot twenty-four mallards and four or five pintails and baldpates and were picking up by 2 o'clock. We did no calling. Meanwhile the other hunter blew his heart out and killed one duck.

Unfortunately, you can't always be in the one best spot. There may be a

Clare Conley can tell you that nothing helps your duck
hunting the way ducks do. Where I live, they fly on
snowy days—out to the fields to feed, back to the river
for gravel and water. At a time like that, you'll have
shooting if you're where the ducks want to go.

dozen equally good, with ducks willing to light in any of them, and plenty
of competition. It's then that a good stool, a suitable blind, the ability to
talk duck language, and attention to details can bring them in to the man
who knows how.

Let's consider decoys first. The most important thing is the overall
impression created by the stool. Even the best decoy, taken by itself,
resembles a real duck about as much as an artificial fly looks like a natural
insect. But the entire spread can create the illusion of a flock of feeding,
loafing, or resting birds, and the more successfully it does that, the more

birds it will bring within range. A few little touches can make a big difference.

You need only a few decoys on a pond or a small stream. Ducks trading among such places are usually in small flocks, and a little bunch of decoys will bring them in. A dozen is frequently enough, and I can't recall when I needed more than twice that number.

On big water, however, I like a big stool. I use about five dozen most of the time, and I'd probably use more if setting them out and picking them up didn't run into so much work. A big flock of ducks ordinarily won't pay any attention to a little wad of blocks.

About fifty of these decoys are mallards and the rest are pintails. Their purpose is not to bring in sprigs, which, like all other shallow-water ducks, will come to a mallard stool. They provide eye-catching splashes of white and help to attract the attention of passing birds.

There is another eye-catcher that works well when some of the decoys are set on the shore of a pond or on a river bar. I save a few duck wings early in the season and lean them against four or five decoys, with the white underside out. In any flock of loafing ducks, one or two always have a wing up, stretching or searching for bugs. The white wings are perfectly natural as well as attention-getting.

A few drakes usually have their necks erect, looking around. On a bar, you can add one more detail to your illusion by propping up a few ducks—after you shoot them, of course—among your stool. I think real ducks set in a natural position, their heads held up by 15-inch wires, are the best decoys. The trouble is, with the current limits, by the time you have enough decoys out you're through shooting.

I skin out the necks of the first half dozen I kill each year. Then I pour borax into them and work it well up into the head, and they stay in the freezer until hunting begins to get tough. With a little care they last the season.

I carry my heads, wings, and a dozen pieces of No. 6 wire, 15 inches long, in a little bag with my decoys. When I set up, I put a wire inside each skinned-out neck and stick it into the head. I shove the other end into the ground. Then I set a decoy close against it so that the decoy head won't show, and the deception is complete.

It is amazing what the heads and wings do for a decoy spread, even when you know what they are. I discover hopeful hunters stalking my stool every season. When I make the setup in a stubble, I can hardly resist stalking it myself.

About three dozen of my decoys have strings a little less than 2 feet long. There are three reasons for the short strings: First, puddle ducks don't like deep water; so this usually is long enough. Second, short strings don't tangle so badly as long ones. Third, and most important, decoys on short strings are far more active in a breeze. They swing steadily back and forth.

Most of my remaining decoys have strings 4 feet long. In some places where I hunt there's no choice but to set out in deep water and then, of course, I need the longer cords. Fortunately these places are small pockets surrounded by willows where I don't need so many decoys.

Five of my decoys are rigged with heavy anchors and strings 6 feet long. On the big river where I do most of my hunting, I set them way out in the current, as much as 50 yards from the remainder of the stool. Their purpose is to catch the attention of high, passing ducks. They're supposed to be taken for a little bunch swimming in to those already clustered along the bar. Apparently they are, because they seem to help.

Loafing, resting, or feeding mallards are always tightly bunched. Therefore, I group my decoys tight—as close together as they can be without touching. Ducks never attempt to light among them, just as they never pitch into the middle of a raft of their fellows. They always light on open water nearby and swim in. So I divide the bulk of my decoys into two bunches with a patch of open water 25 or 30 feet wide between. All the ducks that decoy head for that.

A lot of factors enter into the arrangement of decoys: the wind, the current (if you're on a stream), their relation to the spot from which you have to shoot, and the direction the ducks are flying. Usually it's impossible to have everything just right, and what is a good stool one day may not work the next.

The ideal, of course, is to have the wind coming from behind the blind with the decoys in front of it. This gives you one shot as they're coming in and a second as they flare up toward you. With a wind from right or left, you get crossing shots; I find it helps to locate the blind toward the downwind end of the decoys, if possible. A wind blowing from the decoys toward the blind means tough shooting with your back toward the stool. If there's room, I move a little farther away and take the ducks as they come to me, just before they're directly overhead. With this one exception, I like to have the blind as close to the decoys as I can.

All of these things, from the pintail blocks to the location of the stool in relation to the blind, help to bring ducks into range. There is one remaining thing that helps more than any of them—possibly more than all the others together—when the going is tough. This is what Clayton Davidson called his "worker decoy," "jumper duck," or "diver". He "invented" it, as he did many other tricks of duck hunting.

Everybody knows how lifeless a spread of decoys looks on a flat-calm day, and they look even more artificial to ducks in the air than they do to the hunter in his blind. Clayton's jumper duck animates all of the other decoys within 10 yards by sending waves among them. It also provides movement that attracts the attention of ducks overhead.

Notice the rings around the decoy in the center of the
spread. That's the working decoy, and it helps keep
the rest of the decoys moving slightly.

He simply attaches a 2-foot strip of rubber—six or eight heavy rubber
bands looped together will do—to the keel of a decoy. He ties a piece of
cord to the end of the rubber and a second cord, about 50 feet long, to the
keel. The short cord is tied to a stake; the long one goes to the blind. When
the water is flat, he begins working the cord while approaching ducks are
still mere specks in the sky. Each time he pulls and releases it, the rubber
jerks the decoy back toward the stake. This makes the jumper tip up, bob,
splash, and dart back and forth.

Here's the way to rig a "jumper duck." The rubber and
short cord go to the spike that's pushed into the
waterway bottom. The long cord, shown here wrapped
around the board, leads to you in the blind.

Clayton believed that the jumper was worth more than a call for bringing in skeptical ducks. I think he was right, but it's a wonderful help with a call, too. Everybody who uses one has seen ducks overhead looking for the old girl that's talking to them. The jumper attracts their attention and keeps it away from the blind.

The cord from the worker to the blind should be an inconspicuous color. It should be kept fairly tight, so that you need move only your hand to make the worker bob around. This hand, of course, will be down in the corner of the blind where the ducks can't see it.

The thing that makes the jumper so valuable should be the tipoff for the hunter in his blind. Nothing catches a duck's eye like movement. One day last winter I had a single mallard coming to the decoys. She made a couple of passes and finally was satisfied, dropping in against the wind with wings cupped and feet down.

I had been chuckling to her through the call, which was in my left hand, and I was watching her through a hole in the reeds. When she was about 60 yards away, I dropped the call and lowered my left hand to the fore end of my gun. She flared off and bounced 30 feet with the aid of the breeze, and I never did get a shot at her. Just the movement of my hand was enough!

You don't need much cover if you can hold still. If you can't hold still, you can hardly build a blind that will hide you. Every winter I see blinds that might pass for two-car garages. They're probably necessary for men who can't hold still. But I've seen good duck hunters kill limits while crouching in a few sparse reeds or lying flat in open stubble.

There is nothing to be gained by turning your head to follow circling ducks. If they're going to come in, they'll come into the wind and you'll be looking right at them. A white face surrounded by the dark shadows of a blind looms up like a neon sign. And if you twist around the chances are they'll see you and won't come in at all.

I like to get all set, with my back to the wind, while approaching ducks are still a long way off. My call is in position in my left hand, and my gun across my lap with my right hand on the grip. I lower my face so that I can barely peek under my cap over the edge of the blind. Then I don't move a muscle until the ducks are in range. When they're close enough, I drop the call and come up ready to shoot.

Since my hunting covers quite a stretch of country as I follow the ducks in their feeding and loafing, the advantages of a portable blind are obvious. A good many years ago, Sam Davis showed me his. It was the best I had ever seen, and I made one like it. Later I made another. They weigh only nine pounds apiece and roll up into bundles 10 inches in diameter. I can carry both under one arm and set them up in five minutes. They can be used separately, with a hunter in each, or together, in which case they will conceal two men side by side.

Best of all, there is no place they can't be used. They are practically invisible in typical marsh surroundings or along the reed-bordered edge of a slough or a pond. I have used one successfully by setting it up in front of a cut bank or beside a puddle on a mud flat. They can even be used in an open stubble field or on a bare river bar. A little tuft of cattails is inconspicuous anywhere.

Sam made his blind—and I copied him—by stretching two ropes tight on the ground, 26 inches apart, fastened to stakes at each end. The ropes were 7½ feet long, including the loops at the ends through which the stakes were driven. Next we tied to the ropes cattails cut 44 to 48 inches long, keeping them parallel, like the pickets of a fence. The butts must be kept even, but the tops should be irregular. Tan cord and ¼-inch hemp rope are best. The leaves on each stem are tied in, but the fuzzy tops are cut off. The whole job can be done in about an hour.

Each blind is complete with four 48-inch stakes made from old broom handles or the like. One stake stays in the loop at each end. The other two stakes are rolled up inside.

To set up a blind for one person, I drive the loose stakes a few inches into the ground about 30 inches apart, pull the blind around them with the rope inside, and drive the two end stakes, pulling the blind tight as I do. This makes a U-shaped shelter. You sit with your back to the open, upwind end on an empty shell box, or kneel, and lean forward, hiding your face.

There is only one blind less likely to flare ducks than a little clump of cattails, and that is none at all. If your setup is close to brush or reeds, you're better off to kneel or sit on a low box in them than to make a blind of any kind. Camouflage clothing, especially a face net, helps.

I suppose every duck hunter in grain- or corn-raising country has a sheet to hide under when there's snow and the ducks are feeding in the fields. The trouble with a sheet is that it's so awkward. Cover yourself well enough and you can't get out from under the thing to shoot. Remain partly exposed, and the ducks see you long before they get near enough for shooting.

Another old duck hunter showed me the obvious solution: A pair of white coveralls, such as dairy workers wear, big enough to go on over your other duck-hunting clothes. Crawl into them, pin a piece of white cloth to your hunting cap with some hanging down in the back like a bobtailed burnoose, put on white cotton gloves, hide your gun with another strip of cloth, and you're practically invisible when there's snow on the ground.

This getup is perfect in stubble. It works well even on open mud flats when there's snow. You don't need any blind at all. Just tip your face down. And hold still!

Chapter 47

Mysterious Journey

It was 10 o'clock of a bright October morning. The frost had melted off the mountain meadow and wisps of steam were rising from it, the sunlit wraiths luminous against the black shadows of the pines beyond. I had been hunting elk since daylight. When I came to a convenient log I decided to sit down and smoke my pipe.

I was on a ridge 8,000 feet above the level of the sea. Nearly a mile below I could see the silvery ribbon of the Salmon River, still shaded in its narrow canyon. Rugged mountains, separated by other deep canyons, stretched away endlessly in all directions.

On the slope below, a pine squirrel was chattering excitedly. Far away, I heard the odd, half-musical croaking of a raven and, farther yet, the wild, thrilling bugle of a bull elk. Then came still another sound, thin, clear, flutelike, repeated steadily—the calling of a flock of snow geese. For some time I searched the sky in vain. Then, almost out of sight above, I finally found the wavering V of their formation, minute specks of brilliant white against the deep-blue sky. They were so high that even with my 6X binoculars, I couldn't see the black tips of their wings.

But snow geese they were, on their annual fall migration from the Arctic Coast to the valleys of central and northern California. What a mysterious and wonderful sight! For thousands of years, these little geese with the

Few sights are more thrilling than a V of Canada geese
passing overhead. In this formation, a mallard—no
doubt a social climber—is flying in the No. 2 position.
A lone mallard often flies with a flock of big Canadas.
The third goose in the left line is a lesser Canada,
also not too unusual.

poetic name, *hyperborea* (from beyond the north wind), have followed this route over mountains and across deserts, impelled by we know not what, guided we know not how.

What started birds migrating in the first place? How do they find their way? And what triggers their migrations in spring and fall—food, temperature, light, or something else?

In the valley where I live, most of the mourning doves head south after the first cool nights in September, yet a few remain the year around, occasionally enduring zero weather in January with no apparent ill effects. Similarly, most of the mallards and Canada geese that winter in the valley go north in the spring, but some remain all summer to nest and rear their broods. If food or temperature or light provides the stimulus to migrate, why doesn't it affect all birds of the same species in the same way?

The snow geese soon passed from sight, their sweet calling gradually growing fainter and fainter until it, too, was gone. Probably because the inhospitable country over which they were passing provided no opportunity to rest or feed, they crossed high above it. How high? I think they were a mile above the ridge, which would put them in the neighborhood of 13,000 feet, or nearly three miles above sea level.

Yet this height is modest by comparison to that reached by graylag geese crossing the Himalayas. Buffeted by fierce winds, often half blinded by swirling snow, they fly through their ancestral passes at an altitude of 26,000 feet.

Despite man's conceit, a bird remains the most efficient flying machine there is. The tiny ruby-throated hummingbird makes a 500-mile, nonstop flight across the Gulf of Mexico. The golden plover consumes less than 2 ounces of fuel, in the form of body fat, while flying 2,400 miles nonstop in 48 hours.

The migration of birds is one of nature's most thrilling and mysterious phenomena. It has intrigued the imagination of man and invited his speculation for thousands of years. Aristotle commented on the migration of cranes, geese, and other birds, but apparently he also originated the myth that swallows hibernate in hollow trees, in caves, or in the mud of marshes—a misconception that persisted for some two thousand years.

Probably the most quoted statement on migration is Jeremiah (8:7): "Yea, the stork in the heaven knoweth her appointed times; and the turtle (dove) and the crane and the swallow observe the time of their coming. . . ."

But while it was long assumed that many birds of the northern hemisphere went south for the winter and then returned the following spring, the course, speed, and extent of their journeys were unknown. Then, in 1899, H. C. C. Mortensen, a Danish schoolmaster, had an idea that was eventually to answer many of the questions that had plagued naturalists and laymen alike for centuries. "Why not," he asked, "capture birds, attach a numbered band inscribed with a return address to one leg of each, and then release them?"

He began banding storks, teal, and starlings. Three years later, in 1902, Dr. Paul Bartsch, of the Smithsonian Institution, started banding birds, thus initiating a long-continuing research program, carried on largely by volunteers, in North America.

The American Bird Banding Association was organized in 1909 and it conducted the program until the U.S. Biological Survey took over in 1920. Its successor, the Fish and Wildlife Service, still carries on an intensive banding program in cooperation with the Dominion Wildlife Service of Canada. To date millions of birds have been banded in North America, England, and Europe, and each time a band is returned it adds to our knowledge of birds and their movements.

It was the banding of waterfowl, for example, that enabled Frederick C. Lincoln, of the Fish and Wildlife Service, to discover the four great flyway systems used by North American ducks and geese. His findings, since confirmed by additional band returns, established the flyway concept that has been used since 1948 as the basis for setting waterfowl hunting regulations.

Not only did banding show that ducks and geese visit the same wintering areas year after year and return to the same breeding marshes in the spring, it also proved that these flights are not all the simple north and south movements we had previously thought them to be.

In his *Migration of Birds,* published by the Fish and Wildlife Service, Dr. Lincoln gives this example: "The redhead duck is one of the common breeding ducks of the Bear River Marshes of Utah, where a great many have been banded each summer. The recovery records of banded redheads show that while many travel westward to California, others start their fall migration in the opposite direction and, flying eastward across the Rocky Mountains, either turn southeast across the plains to the Gulf of Mexico, or deliberately proceed in a northeasterly direction to join the flocks of this species moving toward the Atlantic Coast from the prairie regions of southern Canada."

The return of the waterfowl bands has been greater than for other kinds of birds because ducks and geese are hunted. Most hunters, either from a desire to be helpful or merely from curiosity, send in the bands they find on the waterfowl they kill. But enough bands have been returned from other migratory birds to establish some utterly incredible flights, to disprove many once-commonly held beliefs, and to confirm others as true.

Thus banding has shown that a robin may indeed return to the exact tree where it built its nest twelve months before—a feat many of us suspected but were unable to prove. Banding has also shown that some of the birds spending the summer in North America don't stop in the tropics for the winter as we had assumed. Instead, they continue flying south almost to the tip of South America.

But the most startling discoveries made possible by banding have had to do with the length of bird migrations and the accuracy of their navigation. Arctic terns, some of which breed within 10 degrees of the North Pole, winter on the Antarctic ice pack, 11,000 miles away. Further, these terns apparently arrive there by crossing the North Atlantic and flying down the west coast of Europe and Africa. Ornithologists estimate that they travel 25,000 miles per year.

The golden plover makes an incredible 2,400-mile, nonstop flight on its southward migration from northern Canada and Alaska to the pampas of Argentina. And the Pacific golden plover makes an over-water, nonstop flight from Alaska to the Hawaiian islands.

That calls for pretty accurate navigation, yet the great shearwater performs an even more amazing feat. Ranging over the Atlantic Ocean up to 60 degrees north, these birds breed on the tiny Tristan da Cunha Islands at 40 degrees south. The islands spread across only 30 miles of ocean and are 1,500 miles from the nearest land mass.

Naturally, there have been many theories on how birds find their way. One had them flying by known landmarks, the old migrants teaching the route to the young. Another held that they possessed a magnetic sense and were responsive to the magnetic field of the earth. A third merely credited them with a "sense of direction," whatever that might be.

Banding, thousands of experiments, both in the laboratory and in the field, and the use of radar and tiny radio transmitters that can be attached to the birds have found flaws in many of the older theories. In a recent book, *Bird Navigation* (Cambridge University Press), G. V. T. Matthews makes a strong case for the perfectly logical explanation that birds, like men, navigate by the sun and stars.

Countless experiments have been performed with homing pigeons because of their availability and recognized ability. Many migratory birds have been transported far from familiar territory and their ancestral migration route and released to find their winter homes. But to me the most amazing flights reported by Matthews were these:

He took a Manx shearwater from its burrow on a Welsh island and sent it to Boston, more than 3,000 miles away, where it was released. It was back in its own home burrow 12½ days later!

Reversing the process, he released seven tiny Leach's petrels on the Sussex Coast. In less than a fortnight he received a cable announcing the return of the first two to their nests on an island off the coast of Maine, again more than 3,000 miles.

But, he reports, "The longest successful homing flights to date have been those of Laysan albatrosses taken from Midway Island in the Central Pacific. Two birds released in Washington State, a great circle distance of 3,200 miles, returned in 10 and 12 days. Another actually returned from the Philippine Islands, 4,000 miles away, although taking 32 days to do so."

Matthews' book is fascinating reading to anyone intrigued by the wonders of migration. So is *The Great Migrations* (Macmillan) by Georges Blond. Nontechnical but factually accurate, Blond's book describes the migration of the graylag geese of Europe, salmon, eels, American bison, locusts, and lemmings.

We will surely learn more about avian migration as time goes on— provided we don't exterminate ourselves and the birds, too—but the day will never come when it ceases to fascinate all of us who enjoy nature and the outdoors.

Nor is aerial migration limited to birds. On another hunt, I once paused to rest on a high, rocky ridge and was soon amazed by the appearance of hundreds of handsome butterflies with black-lined wings of rusty-orange. Drifting with a gentle breeze, they came fluttering past by twos and threes and sometimes a dozen were in sight at once. And they didn't follow the steep slope down into the valley below, either, but continued on at approximately the same level as far as I could see them.

I was puzzled. There were no flowers blooming now in this high country and, in early October, the grass was painted white by frost each night. I later learned that they were monarchs, one of the migratory butterflies. And if the nonstop flight of the golden plover from Nova Scotia to South America seemed incredible, consider the journey of this defenseless insect.

Many monarchs have been tagged by gluing a slip of tissue paper to one wing, and a surprising number of tagged butterflies have been recovered. One of them, tagged in Ontario, was captured in San Luis Potosí, Mexico. It had traveled 1,870 miles in four months and seven days. And the next spring, barring some misfortune, it would return to Ontario!

Chapter 48

Other Values

One evening, while Ray and Dan Holland and I were watching the ducks leave a big lake on their way out to feed, Dan made a remark to remember. The sun had set and the western sky was washed with every hue of red and orange. Against this background, great rafts of ducks, mostly mallards but also a few pintails and an occasional little bunch of greenwing teal, were stringing out toward the stubble fields.

We were not duck hunting. In fact, the thought of hunting ducks didn't even enter our minds. We had enjoyed a good day with quail and were on our way home when the arresting sight of thousands of ducks against the fiery sunset compelled us to stop and watch.

We sat there in the car quietly for some time. When twelve or fifteen mallards came by fairly close, I broke the silence to say, "Look, what an artistic formation!"

Dan paused a few seconds, then replied, "Any flight of ducks is an artistic formation."

How right he was! This truth, which should have been obvious, had not occurred to me before, but I have recalled it every time I've seen a flock of ducks since, and it is always true.

Simply watching ducks is fascinating; it would be a dull clod indeed who failed to thrill to their magnificent flight. But there is more to it than meets

What do you do after you've put out the decoys in the
dark, watched the sun come up, and discover
the ducks aren't arriving?

the eye. Al Miller and I were watching ducks one morning—it was a good
day and we were through shooting—when he said something that, like
Dan's remark, has heightened my appreciation of waterfowl greatly.

It was a wild day. The dull sky lay close above leaden water. Wind hissed
through the reeds and pushed up whitecaps on the open reaches of the
river. And ducks were moving. High overhead long, wavering strings of
them fought their way against the wind. Goldeneyes in singles, pairs, and
widely scattered flocks beat past with the high pitched *wh-wh-wh-wh-wh-wh*
of wing that has earned them the name "whistlers." Occasionally a tightly
packed raft of bluebills swept past us with a roar. But our attention was
mostly riveted on the mallards that swung by in flocks of from ten to fifty,
saw the decoys, and turned back.

These ducks were looking for a sheltered spot where they could rest. Our
decoys, in the lee of an island, occupied such a place, and every flock was
eager to join them. The same mallard that would circle warily out of range
on a calm day now broke all holds and pitched in like pets. Once down, the
low, contented rasping of the drakes and the satisfied gabbling of the ducks
made it perfectly clear that this was exactly where they wanted to be.

We had crouched fascinated for an hour, motionless and silent in the
blind, when Al nudged me and whispered, "It must sound wonderful!"

Here was a new thought and a shocking one. I was so taken aback by it that I asked aloud—thereby putting a great raft of mallards to flight with the attendant alarm calls and roar of wings—"Can't you hear them at all?"

"Not a sound. But I've heard it before. I know what it is. You listen for me."

Al had gone completely deaf about ten years earlier. Although he wore a hearing aid, if I wanted him to catch my words I had to speak to him face-to-face and from no more than six or eight feet away. In spite of this, it hadn't occurred to me that he couldn't hear the wonderful sounds I had been enjoying. Nor had I ever before appreciated how great a part the roar of pinion and rasp of voice play in the drama that is waterfowl.

Watching ducks and listening to them are two of what I call the "other values" of duck hunting—the things entirely apart from shooting that make this sport one of the most rewarding of all—but there are many others. It isn't worth going hunting for two or three ducks. Maybe it wasn't worth going for ten—and it has been a long time since the limit was that high. Yet the other values are as great today as they were when nobody could possibly have foreseen a limit on waterfowl.

It is a well-established fact that the more you know about a subject, the more interesting it becomes. Most of us can remember when looking at the heavens revealed only stars, and how, upon learning to recognize a few of the brighter ones and some of the constellations, and where to expect the planets, we saw with new eyes. As the night sky became familiar, it grew more fascinating.

So it is with waterfowl. No birds are more inspiring, none have more intriguing life stories or reward the keen observer and student more richly. Learning to identify ducks in flight and on the water is the first step in this fine hobby. And the best time to make progress is after you have killed your limit—a short task these days.

One day when I was hunting alone I quickly killed the six we were allowed that year. Instead of picking up and going in at once, I sat in the blind, calling judiciously, until there must have been at least three hundred ducks almost within spitting distance. Most of them were mallards. There were a few pintails and baldpates, and occasionally a little wad of restless greenwing teal would buzz in, stay a few minutes, and buzz away again.

Identification was no problem here; I knew all the ducks that joined the convention. But it was a grand opportunity to bone up on calling. In fact, after the first fifty or so made themselves at home I laid my call aside and listened. The old virtuosos, the hen mallards themselves, could do a far better job than I in tolling in passing flocks.

What a clamor they set up! Did you know that no two ducks have exactly the same tone of voice or use exactly the same "words" to attract potential visitors? You would know this beyond the shadow of a doubt if you had been with me that morning. And did you know that decoys—even old, battered ones, with most of the paint rubbed off—are not at all alarming to ducks on the water? These wary mallards that had been shot at for two months swam among my decoys unconcerned. Ducks even waded out onto the gravel bar, where I had other decoys stationed, and settled down to nap beside them.

It is an excellent idea to take binoculars along. I've done it, and profited thereby. Six-power glasses bring a 100-yard duck in to 17 yards. At that distance, plumage, the color of bills and feet, and other helpful features are perfectly clear. And you need a duck book—not a bird book, because most bird books are hopelessly inadequate when it comes to waterfowl.

Eventually you will want many duck books, but as a start I recommend *The Ducks, Geese and Swans of North America*, by Francis H. Kortright, published by Stackpole, Cameron and Keller Streets, Harrisburg, Pa. 17105. It shows summer, autumn, and winter plumage, which can be extremely confusing. The little ruddy drake, for example, wears his bright feathers in the summer and his drab ones in the winter, just reversing the sartorial habit of the more familiar mallard.

Neither color nor size is much help at the times when the most ducks usually are flying. Dull, overcast days and the first hour after dawn, even on clear days, tend to make all ducks drab gray. And a big duck at 40 yards looks little different from a smaller one at 30, provided their outlines are similar.

Silhouette, flight habit, and wingbeat are helpful; one can't mistake the silhouette of a canvasback, pintail, or wood duck, and many of the other species appear equally distinctive with practice. The fast wingbeat of the divers, of course, makes it easy to distinguish them from all the puddle ducks, and after you can do this you will begin to notice flight characteristics peculiar to each species.

Try to identify ducks when you can barely see them, then check your determination as they get closer. It's both fun and good training.

Photography also enhances appreciation of waterfowl and adds enjoyment to those times when we aren't shooting. It isn't easy. In fact, it is far less difficult to make a good shot with a gun than with a camera, but the camera has two advantages: We can shoot a thousand ducks with it in one day if we want to, and the result is more lasting. The quick eye of the camera also reveals secrets previously unsuspected. I never knew, for example, that mallards come in with wings cupped and tails spread and use their feet like skis to scoot along on the surface before their bodies touch the water, but the camera revealed all this.

Not all of the "other values" of duck hunting are provided by the ducks themselves. It is good for man occasionally to come close to the raw elements from which he is now almost completely shielded. There are sights, sounds, and smells known only to duck hunters—cold spray; rain or snow and driving wind; the rustling of reeds; the pale, pink streak of dawn beneath a leaden sky; the unforgettable odor of a marsh. These things are not hardship; they constitute a privilege. For those who have never known them, and, even worse, for those who may never know them, I have only sympathy.

Finally, I am a bird watcher. This may shock you because a bird watcher is commonly thought of as a gentle person with book and binoculars who strolls slowly through a park intently identifying as many of the little tweeters and twitterers as possible. In fact, all sportsmen, which excludes the unappreciative few who shouldn't be out with rod or gun at all, are bird watchers.

I have a friend who is a purist bird watcher. He loves birds, but he neither hunts nor fishes. I am quite sure that he doesn't spend a tenth the time actually watching birds that I do for the simple reason that I am outdoors in all seasons a great deal more than he is. There are many times

A killdeer hunting for midges along the edge of the water provides some diversion. This bird supposedly should have gone south in October.

when a sportsman has to watch birds. My last long session of uninterrupted bird watching is a good example.

We had enjoyed several days of good duck shooting during a period of cold, stormy weather. But this particular morning was clear and unusually warm for December, and the ducks left the river before sunrise. We stayed on. It was foolish and we knew it, but the season was nearly over and you can always hope.

About 9 o'clock a great flock of evening grosbeaks descended on a clump of Russian olive trees near the blind and greedily attacked the dried fruit hanging there. We watched the birds, sometimes only 5 or 6 feet away, for several hours, interrupting this mild Audubonian pleasure frequently, of course, to scan the vacant sky for ducks that never came.

At noon, our attention was diverted from the grosbeaks by a flock of—no, not ducks!—Western bluebirds. About twenty of them came fluttering and hopping along the shore and soon were all around the blind. They ran on the ice and perched on the reeds, sometimes so close that we could have touched them with a gun barrel. They were feeding on little gray midges that hatch out on sunny days all winter. Hundreds of midges were drifting onto the edge of the ice immediately in front of the blind and the bluebirds were picking them off.

I doubt that any bird watcher of the purest strain ever watched bluebirds so long, so intently, so close, and with so little interruption as my companion and I did that afternoon. I know we appreciated as never before the literal interpretation of "bluebird day" when we left, duckless, at 5 o'clock.

Chapter 49

From Blind to Table

I know duck hunters who never eat a duck. They like ducks in the air but not on the table—so they say. These hunters all like steak, they tell me. I like steak too, and the only thing I like better is a corn-fed mallard duck, properly prepared.

I wonder sometimes if duck hunters' appetites are not influenced by laziness—because giving ducks the proper care is work. Or possibly their birds have been improperly cooked. There is as much difference between correctly and incorrectly cooked ducks as there is between a charcoal-broiled steak and one simmered in grease for an hour.

The flavor of ducks is largely determined by their diet and since this varies in different areas there is little point in saying which duck is best. Where I live, the mallard heads the list, with the green-winged teal second, and the pintail third. Diving ducks usually are good if we get them within a few days of their arrival, but after that our local aquatic food has its effect.

Of course, there are establishments in duck-hunting country that pick and dress ducks commercially. You just take in your wildfowl and the next day you come back and get them, minus feathers and guts.

That is all right, but I prefer to take care of my own. There are several reasons. First, I believe I do a better job. Second, we save the down. My wife has made four sleeping bags and countless pillows out of it. Third,

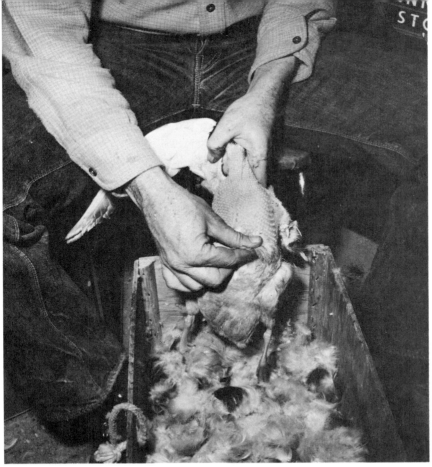

If you hope to get done before next Christmas, you don't
pluck the feathers out of a duck. You roll them off
with your thumb, cleaning as you go, down and all.

while there aren't many things at which I'm good, I am a good duck
picker—at least for an amateur. I can prepare a limit for the oven faster
than I can make two trips to the pickery. So can you if you have a mind to.

Here's how:

Start by jerking out the big feathers from the tail, along the flanks and
out to the first joint of the wing. If you intend to save the down, put these
rough feathers into a separate container to be disposed of with the wings,
feet, and heads.

You need a box to pick into, a stool to sit on, and a saucer of water to
moisten your thumb, unless your ducks are damp. Hold your bird by the
neck and let it hang over the inside edge of the box. Start picking on the
back near the base of the neck.

Now, the secret of fast duck picking is to pick clean as you go. There is only one way to do this. Pick in the direction in which the feathers lie and bear down hard with your thumb. You should push the feathers off, not pluck them out. This technique will leave the skin clean. Let the feathers roll off your hand into the box and work down the back. Moisten your thumb occasionally if necessary and keep working from front to rear. You will be amazed at how quickly the back is finished.

As soon as it is, turn the duck slightly and work down the shoulder, flank, and leg. Then turn the duck breast up. The spot where you are most likely to tear the skin is around the base of the neck on the underside. Be careful here. Otherwise you can strip the breast just as fast as you did the back. When you have worked down the second shoulder, flank, and around that leg, the body of your duck is done.

I pick the wings to the first joint, but the sensible thing is to cut them off an inch from the body. The same with the neck. Pick an inch of it and cut it off. But don't cut off the wings, head, and feet at this point. You need them as handles for the next operation.

Light your camp stove—the two-burner type will work, although a one-burner is handier—and singe your ducks over it. The hot, blue flame will almost instantly take off all the fuzz and down and the feathers that you missed.

Now, with the aid of a block of wood and a cleaver or a hatchet, cut off the heads, feet, and wings. At this point I switch the scene of operations from the furnace room to the kitchen sink.

The quickest way to dress a batch of ducks is to do most of the knife work on all of them first. To start, you should make two incisions on each duck. One is at the base of the neck, on the underside, through the skin and fatty tissues under it. It should be about an inch long and crosswise. The other is across the abdomen half an inch back of the end of the breastbone. Pinch up a little skin and cut it, then slip the knife inside and cut toward both sides, thereby avoiding puncturing the intestines. This cut should be between 2 and 2½ inches long on a big duck, such as a mallard.

After you have performed this surgery on all your ducks, reach into the forward slit of each and loosen everything you can reach with your index finger. Pull out the windpipe and esophagus.

Now turn the bird around and, reaching up inside next to the breast with two or three fingers, pull out the heart, lungs, and intestines, but don't break them. As you remove them from each duck, let them hang down over the sink and pick up your knife. Make a longitudinal cut from the lateral cut back of the breast down to and around the vent.

After all your ducks are drawn, turn them breast down and cut out the oil glands. There is a pair on the back, about an inch ahead of the tail. They provide the oil with which a duck waterproofs his feathers and impart an unpleasant flavor when the fowl is cooked.

These five ducks are ready for the oven; or they could be frozen in water.

The last step is to wash the carcasses thoroughly, inside and out. I hold them neck up to the cold-water faucet and run a good stream through the body cavity. At the same time, reaching in from the rear, I dig out everything that will come. After washing, I set them on end in the dish drainer for a few minutes before putting them in the refrigerator.

This is as good a spot as any to bring up the subject of hanging ducks to age. Some hunters hang them by the heads; others hang them by the feet. Some leave them hanging for three or four days; others for a week or more in cool weather. This, of course, is before they are picked and drawn. There is no agreement on the subject and I will simply tell you what I think; nobody has to follow my system unless he wants to.

I prefer to pick and dress all feathered game, including ducks, as soon as convenient after I return from hunting. Then I like to age them four or five days in the refrigerator before cooking them.

Follow the same procedure if they are to be frozen. Frozen meat doesn't age, and should be cooked immediately after thawing; so you can't age it then. If you want to preserve the moisture and flavor of your ducks or upland birds in the freezer, put them into suitable containers and cover them with water. Then quick-freeze them. They will keep perfectly for a long time if each of them is locked in ice.

In my opinion, there is only one way to cook a duck. That is *fast*. I prefer ducks roasted, but I want the job done in a hurry, with intense heat, in either case.

We make a stuffing by chopping—not grinding—green onion, green pepper, and celery, and season it with salt, pepper, and sage. Make your stuffing and put it in the body cavity of each duck while the oven is heating. Our electric range is set at 550 degrees—as hot as it will go.

The ducks are placed breast up on the broiler rack, and when the oven is hot we slide the rack in. Then we watch the clock. We give mallards twenty minutes; green-winged teal, twelve. The others receive varying periods between these two extremes, depending on their size.

When they come out of the oven, we empty the stuffing into a salad bowl. It is still crisp after such a short period in the oven.

I never got tired of eating duck but once. That was before World War II. I put in a fall and winter trying to write cowboy stories and, since nobody would buy them, my wife and I didn't have any money. My brother was with us, and he didn't have any either.

We were living on the farm, which was only a mile from good duck shooting; so we went hunting every morning. We ate ducks every day from the middle of November, when the pheasant season ended, until the conclusion of the duck season on January 15.

The daily limit was twelve and the possession limit was twice that number. When the season closed, each of us had twenty-four mallards—a total of seventy-two big ducks hanging on the back of the house. Considering that we had warmed up to the job by eating duck every day for two months, I think we did pretty well to polish them all off in about thirty days. My wife didn't eat any for the last week or so and, I must admit, I was beginning to get a little weary of them.

But I'm sure I wouldn't have, even then, if we had been able to cook them right. Unfortunately, we had a coal-burning stove and couldn't get the oven hot enough. We couldn't simultaneously brown the outside and keep the inside pink; consequently they always came out too well done.

If there is anything that will make a man tired of ducks in a hurry, it is cooking them too long.

Part XII

WHITHER HUNTING AND THE HUNTER?

Chapter 50

Days on Bunny Mountain

The dismal month of February came that year as it always does, unwanted but inevitable. Something went amiss, however. While the rest of the country was suffering the worst weather of the winter as usual, we enjoyed a succession of delightful sunny days and frosty nights. Save for the fact that the lawns were brown and the leaves lay dull and weathered on the ground, it would have been easy to mistake the season for October. It was hunting weather.

So we went hunting. Willard Cravens parked his car facing Bunny

Willard Cravens has one bunny in hand as he makes his
way up Bunny Mountain.

Mountain and we sat looking at it as we drank a cup of coffee. What a
strange place for cottontails! There were no briar patches, no brush heaps,
no cornfields, no stone walls. I mentioned to Willard that when I moved to
North Carolina back in 1941 one of my first ambitions was to kill a
cottontail in a cotton patch—which I did. Bunny Mountain was a far cry
indeed from that Tarheel countryside.

Steep, sandy, with little pockets and benches here and there, it was half
covered with boulders and outcroppings of weathered granite. The open
spaces among the rocks were sparsely vegetated with sagebrush, bitterbrush, and grass. In many spots the earth was bare.

Yet cottontails were here. We had seen them when we were hunting
chukars—more than we saw anywhere else—and so we had named this
nameless hill in the southern Idaho desert Bunny Mountain. In fact, Clare
Conley and I hunted them here for a few hours one afternoon in October
while Willard went on shooting chukars. I used a scope-sighted pistol and
Clare his pellet gun—and thereby hangs a tale.

Before Clare became the Editor of *Field & Stream,* he wrote articles for it.
Our houses were only a block apart and we hunted and fished together and
helped each other with pictures, and I was sorry when he moved to New
York. One time he wrote an article on hunting cottontails with a pellet gun.

I read it, and it was good. He had good pictures to go with it, too. But it was rejected by the editors on the grounds that hunting rabbits with a pellet gun wasn't sporting. Like shooting deer with a .22, they said.

Clare was indignant. He told me—I was too important to hunt rabbits in those days—that he stalked them until he was close, 25 to 40 feet, and shot them in the head. Certainly, if that isn't sporting, nothing is. But you can't sell stories by arguing with editors, so Clare laid his article away and I forgot about it.

But I remembered it that afternoon. Clare left the car before I did and disappeared over the bank of a deep wash that ran down between it and Bunny Mountain. When I topped the bank and saw him, he was sitting on a big rock in the bottom of the wash dressing a bunny. He hadn't been hunting three minutes!

I scrambled down the steep, 30-foot slope. Just as I reached the bottom of the wash a cottontail popped out of a sagebrush almost underfoot, dashed past Clare, and disappeared around a bend. Clare started after it and I followed with my camera.

Moving very slowly and quietly, Clare eased down the wash, watching carefully ahead. Before long, he saw the bunny. It was crouched behind, and partially concealed by, a thick sagebrush. Stepping even more slowly and softly, Clare shifted to one side until he had an open shot. He raised the gun without any sudden movements, sighted, and I heard the pop as the .22-caliber pellet started on its way.

There was nothing slow about the ten or twelve quick steps that followed. Clare hurried to his bunny, picked it up, and we walked back to the spot where we had left the first. They were both shot through the head.

That afternoon, I killed two cottontails. Clare killed five, all with head shots. I wished the editors who turned down his story had been there.

Willard and I had left home after lunch. Now the sun was warm at 2 P.M. and we left our jackets in the car. We were dressed just as we had dressed in late September, yet my cap was moist with sweat before we had climbed the first slope. Oh, that all February days could be so fair!

Separated by 50 yards, we started around the end of Bunny Mountain. Willard dropped down below the rim of the bench out of sight, and shortly afterward I heard him shoot. Just once. I assumed, correctly I learned when we met again, that he had killed a rabbit.

Minutes later, a little gray bundle of fur shot out of a bush I was approaching and sped away, twisting and dodging and bouncing up the hill. I wonder if a cottontail could run straight if it wanted to. Maybe—if a woodcock could fly straight!

Confidently, I cocked my rifle and waited for the bunny to stop. I whistled. If anything, it ran faster. Among the scattered brush, around big boulders, it ran as though its life depended on reaching a barn-sized granite

The bunnies live in snug retreats among the rocks.

outcrop 150 yards away. The granite was weathered and slabs of it lay around the base. There were cavities under the slabs. Without even pausing to look back, the cottontail shot into one of them.

Willard and I hunted on around the edge of the bench, climbing over or slipping around each big boulder cautiously in hopes of surprising a bunny on the other side. I flushed two more that also ran until they were out of sight. They flattered me; I'm not that dangerous.

Willard put up a black-tailed jackrabbit that ran past me. We didn't shoot at it. We were hunting bunnies, not jacks.

When the sportsmen in our area say they're going rabbit hunting they mean jackrabbit hunting as surely as a Southerner means quail hunting when he says bird hunting. So we say we're hunting bunnies when we hunt cottontails. And, actually, our cottontail really is a bunny, though Hugh Hefner might not agree.

Our little cottontail occurs only in a rather narrow band of arid country that extends from southeastern Washington down along western Idaho and eastern Oregon, then curves westward to include a corner of both Nevada and California. Like most desert animals, it is predominantly gray. It has white-tipped black fur, buff fur, tan fur, white fur, and yellowish fur, like a coyote. But at 20 yards it is just a little gray bundle with a ball of cotton for a tail. And it is small. Five mature bunnies, weighed on February 11, came to 7½ pounds, an average of 1½ pounds apiece. They were fat as pigs, too. If my treacherous memory serves me right, cottontails in the Midwest and East average a good pound heavier.

My rabbit book lists twenty-seven different cottontails in the United States, not counting the swamp rabbits, which belong to the same genus, nor the unique Idaho pygmy rabbit, which does not. This pygmy rabbit is very dark, sometimes appearing almost black, and the underside of its tail is dark gray.

Its range is far more restricted than our cottontail's, and even within this restricted range the pygmy rabbit is scarce. I see but few each hunting season and I am out in the desert country it inhabits several times a week from the first of October until the middle of February. It is included with cottontails in the Idaho seasons and bag limits, but I have never shot one. Newcomers from the Midwest, remembering their big cottontails at home, often think they have bagged a pygmy rabbit when they kill one of our little bunnies, but no one who has seen both could confuse them.

Willard and I still had only one bunny when we were halfway around the east end of Bunny Mountain and decided to sit down, take five in the warm sunshine, and compare notes. We had seen nine cottontails. I had missed one. It was sitting on a rock a foot from a crack between two bigger rocks and it was only 50 feet away when I saw it. I tried to shoot it in the head and missed. It made two hops, one to turn around, the other into the crack between the rocks.

"Dumb bunnies!" Willard exclaimed. "The guy who first said that should be here."

I agreed and observed that the rabbits now were much, much wilder than they had been in October. "Nobody has been hunting them, either," I added.

"No human hunters," Willard said, "but the hawks and owls and coyotes and bobcats have been working on them for three months since then. The dumb bunnies are all gone."

It was pleasant. Velvety cheat grass, sprouted by the fall rains and stimulated by the recent warmth, was 2 inches tall. A few ants, ignoring the calendar, were creeping over the top of their mound 10 feet away. We noticed where bunnies had nibbled the tender tips off young sagebrush, eating some and leaving others on the ground. A pair of ravens sailed past, caught an updraft, and soared, circling, in it. We were high and the air was clear, but we could look down into the valley from which we had come and it was gray with smog. I was grateful to be out of it. In fact, I was grateful, period. To be far from noise and confusion, on a delightful day, with a good companion, and a rifle within reach . . . Good night!

There was a bunny! It was sitting on a foot-wide ledge at the base of a big rock, 40 feet away. Had it been there all the time or had it come out after we sat down? It didn't matter. Lucky my rifle *was* in reach! I felt for it slowly, rested my elbows on my knees, cocked the hammer, aimed, and squeezed the trigger. I made a good head shot. The cottontail tumbled over and didn't move.

We had now seen ten rabbits and had shot at three, the only ones that had stopped within range. We decided we might as well start shooting at them on the run. We couldn't hope for head shots, of course, and maybe they'd *never* stop running. But you can't bag bunnies if you don't shoot.

Shortly after we went on we jumped a rabbit we could both see and we opened fire. It sounded like a TV war. And to our absolute amazement, after we had fired three or four shots apiece the bunny stopped on top of a rock within inches of a crevice in a still-bigger rock where it would have been safe. Willard killed it. After that we started shooting at every rabbit as quickly as we could, and more of them stopped to give us sitting shots than when we had quietly waited.

When we left the car, Willard had handed me a wire loop about 6 inches in diameter, obviously made from a coat hanger. The ends were doubled back an inch or so and hooked together, but these hooks were not pressed shut. He said, "That's the way I used to carry rabbits when I was a boy in Kansas. Hook them under the tendon above one hind foot."

I said I expected to carry mine in my hunting vest, but Willard said the wire loop was better so I took it along. I soon learned why it was better. I shot a bunny and picked it up by the hind feet to carry it over to Willard, who was about 50 yards away. A few seconds later I felt something on my hand. I glanced at it. Half a dozen fleas were hurrying for my shirt cuff!

I dropped the rabbit and brushed them off. Evidently fleas desert their host as soon as it dies, like rats leaving a sinking ship. Perhaps a change in temperature, however slight, warns them their happy days are over.

With the rabbit lying on the ground, I poked the loop through the leg, shut the hooks, and picked it up. At least a dozen fleas were clutching the ends of the hair on the bunny's hind feet. By the time I got to Willard they were gone, and they weren't on me, either. Whether they jumped off or fell off I don't know, but they couldn't climb the wire.

Strangely, out of about forty rabbits we killed last February, only two had fleas, and we got both of them that first day. Rabbit fleas don't stay on people—I didn't always know about the wire loop!—but it's nicer not to have them for even a short visit.

About the time I was fourteen, I was deadly with my .22. I grew up on a farm and shot it almost every day, and I'll never forget my finest Saturday. I was out of shotgun shells and had only twelve .22 long rifles. Right after lunch—it was dinner then and I had to work in the morning—I took my .22 and started for the river. On the way, I surprised a rabbit. I killed it on the run. A little later I saw a pheasant, also running and about 50 yards away, and killed it, too.

Slipping along the riverbank, I spotted a flock of mallards a quarter mile ahead. Marking the spot carefully, I made a stalk and came out on the bank above them. They didn't suspect a thing. I tried to shoot one through the head and missed. But when they jumped I killed two on the wing. Of course, I missed some. I had one cartridge left when I was checking up while I shivered dry and dressed on the bank after retrieving my ducks. (Shooting upland birds and ducks with a rifle was legal in those days.)

A few minutes later, I saw a hawk sitting on a post and killed it. (All hawks were bad in those days; I don't shoot any now.) I had hit five times out of twelve and four of my targets were either running or flying. To cap it off, as I was walking home I met a couple of hunters from the little town where I went to school. They were armed with shotguns, but they didn't have a thing.

I told Willard about that day and he admitted that when he was a boy he was deadly with his .22, too. The squirrels and rabbits didn't have a chance. Not so in the 1970s. We had been shooting shotguns and big-game rifles for years. Now we discovered that shooting a .22 at a twisting, dodging, bobbing bunny, or even at one crouched in half-concealing brush, was an art in its own right. Our marksmanship was rotten.

Of course, we might have used our shotguns, but we had no desire to do so. In the first place, we weren't hunting in self-defense; even if we didn't kill *any* rabbits we wouldn't starve. Our .22's were more difficult, hence more fun. Second, many of the cottontails we saw were already out of shotgun range when we saw them. And finally, a bunny killed by a load of shot is sometimes pretty messy; killed by a solid-point long-rifle bullet, its meat is clean. A head shot is best, of course, though we couldn't always make head shots.

The afternoon sped by. About 4:30 we began to see more bunnies. We were out on the west end of Bunny Mountain when the sun went down and then there were rabbits everywhere. I hit one on the run. It tumbled head over heels and got up and I quickly shot it through the head. I was proud of that shot because it wasn't close.

It was dark when we got to the car with ten bunnies. The law permitted eight apiece, but we had no complaint. If the day ever comes when I have to kill the limit to be happy, I'll quit hunting.

Before Willard dropped me off at home, we made a date to start early the next time. If half a day was good, a full day should be better.

We started in a fog so thick it was like driving through a tunnel, but as we expected, we were above it on Bunny Mountain. The sky was clear and the sun was bright and the valley was a sea of silver fog. Arms of it stretched up like bays among the nearby ridges.

The bunnies were out and hunting was good. Then a breeze came up and drifted the fog over Bunny Mountain. Immediately, it was colder—damp and raw in the wind. The cottontails retreated to their safe cubbies beneath the big rocks and in cracks among the outcroppings. It was too cold to sit still so we continued hunting, but we saw no more until the breeze changed and the fog drifted away.

Twice during the day the fog swept over Bunny Mountain and both times we saw no rabbits while it was there. Fortunately, it didn't stay more than an hour either time and we had a good day.

Another time, when we also started early, a cold wind came up just as we arrived. We hunted anyway, hard and long, and it was our poorest day. We only saw thirteen and Willard killed one with a long, long shot, and it made up the sum total of our bag at dark.

Wind makes all game alert and nervous because the animals realize they can't hear an approaching enemy when the wind is blowing. The rabbits reacted just as deer or grouse or chukars do on a windy day. They jumped wild and never quit running.

We did have a few unpleasant days that February, and we soon realized that when the weather was nasty the cottontails vanished. And why not? They can bundle up in their snug, safe retreats under the big boulders and watch the weather. Maybe they hop out a few yards to feed occasionally when it's bad, but they don't stay. When it's warm they like to sit on a rock and bask in the sunshine, and if I lived in a cave I'm sure I'd do the same.

So Willard and I got to watching the weather in the morning and going hunting after lunch if it was nice.

We learned things about how to hunt, as well as when to hunt. For one, it paid to hunt together, walking slowly along between 25 and 75 yards apart, depending on the terrain.

One afternoon Willard jumped a bunny that went dodging and bouncing down through a rocky basin and stopped in some sagebrush where we couldn't see it. Since I was farther back, but in the direction it had run, I made a half circle. The brush in which the rabbit had disappeared was about 100 yards from Willard. He stood still, watching it. Just above the brush there was a big, dome-shaped boulder, a good landmark. I pussyfooted up it, my crepe-soled shoes noiseless on the rock, and looked down into the sage.

At first, I couldn't see anything. Finally, I made out the rabbit, crouching half screened by brush, watching Willard. It was only 30 feet away and I shot it through the head.

We did this often, sometimes one making the sneak and sometimes the other, depending on which was in a better position to do it, and we usually got the bunny. With one alone, it was more difficult, but by walking slowly and never directly toward the rabbit it sometimes worked.

Near the end of a good day when we had both shot well, I killed four rabbits in short order. I hit two on the run and shot two, which were foolish enough to stop at 50 feet, through the head. Back at the car, I said to

Ted and Willard take a five-minute break on
Bunny Mountain.

Willard, "My shooting is getting better. What I needed was practice. I had hardly shot a .22 for twenty years."

He replied, "Me too. It's a lot easier to hit a deer at 200 yards with a scope-sighted '06 than it is to hit a bunny dodging through the brush at 50 feet—or sitting at 100."

We felt so good. Maybe that was our undoing; you should never feel expert. The last day was a debacle. We started hunting at 2 P.M. and we counted nine rabbits in the first forty-five minutes. It was dead calm, sunny, and too warm for comfort. We shot enough ammunition to make John Olin shout for joy. And we got *one* bunny.

"Well," we said, "if the game is here we can't complain." So we didn't complain. But we felt like it.

Then a bitter wind sprang up and whistled among the rocks on Bunny Mountain and through our summer shirts, and dirty-looking clouds streaked in from Oregon and quickly blotted out the sun. And the "dumb" bunnies hopped into their snug nests beneath the rocks. In an area equally as good as the one we had just hunted we went for two solid, shivering hours without firing a shot.

Then the wind stopped as suddenly as it had sprung up. In minutes the rabbits began to show up again. They were thicker than ever. We had an hour of daylight left and, fortunately, plenty of ammunition.

Willard is a good shot normally. He couldn't have hit a barn that afternoon if he had been locked inside. I shot worse than he did. I shot at a bunny under a big rock not 30 feet away and I knew it was dead. But when I went to pick it up I found only a little rock under the big one. The hole went on through. The bunny had hopped out the other end.

When we got back to the car we had two. Both of them were pregnant. Maybe it was a good thing we did shoot poor. It was February 18 and the season lasted through the 28, but that was our last hunt. The pleasant days on Bunny Mountain were over.

There was one comforting thought. On that final day, by some strange coincidence and despite the wind, we counted exactly as many bunnies as we had the first time we hunted it. We counted fifty-one. There were plenty left for seed.

Chapter 51

Must This Be?

My Beloved Readers: You have been kind to me. You have praised me when I wrote well of true things, and when I was wrong you have been tolerant. Now I ask you to read the following letter:

"Dear Mr. Trueblood: I read your article 'Days on Bunny Mountain' in the December *Field & Stream* and I couldn't help thinking how different it must be from the place where I hunt. My friend Tom and I call it 'The Gully.'

"My name is Charles Thompson. I live in Cleveland, Ohio. I have been a city boy for all of my 25 years, here in Cleveland. My father never took me hunting, and seldom fishing. I love fishing and went every chance I could get after I was old enough to use my mother's car. I was about 17 then.

"My father had died the year before. He left me an old 12-gauge, single-barrel shotgun. It was made in 1913 and had been abused. I decided to try hunting now that I could get the car once in a while if I was good.

"My friend Jack and I went to a public hunting area some 30 miles from home. The first day I shot a pheasant and I was hooked on hunting. We hunted together there once the next year and that was the last time. When we got afield we were scared of all the hunters in that small area shooting at what seemed to be their own shadows. We left promptly. I hunted there again this year for the first time since that episode with another friend, Tom. The situation was the same.

"Tom hunted the Gully and he had known about it for a long time before I met him, which was two years ago. He told me about this place and what it looked like some fifteen years before—how families used to go there and picnic and camp, and the beauty of it, with pine trees and apple orchards.

"But now it is a fill project, with cans and garbage and the acid-filled stream an open sewer separating Cleveland from Cuyahoga Heights. Only a very small area on the Cuyahoga Heights side is halfway decent now. It is about two miles long and maybe a little more than an eighth of a mile wide. There is garbage on the hillside, scattered among the trees and brush.

"In this small area in the middle of the city there are rabbits, a few pheasants, skunks, owls, and who knows what else—besides rats. This is where I hunt, a place just down the street from home. Tom lives near the other side of the Gully.

"The place is hunted by others, but the pressure is light. The rabbits are fat and fast. As you shoot your bunnies from under rocks and boulders, I shoot mine from under garbage piles, down in the Gully. This is now my place to hunt, where few go and there are enough rabbits to go around. Where I can get away—that is, almost, except for background road noise. And maybe if the wind is right we won't get the smell of the garbage, which comes from the Cleveland side of the stream.

"I don't know of any other place here in Ohio to hunt in peace. The only countryside I know is near Burton, where my cousins live, and where I fish. Farmers out there are fussy about hunters and 'most all the land is posted by them or owned by the City of Akron, and also posted. So where can a city boy go to hunt? In the city, I guess, down in the Gully where the rats and rabbits play.

"As I said, I have lived in Cleveland all of my 25 years. I am married and have two small children. I own my own home and I work in a smelly factory, drilling holes. I recently enrolled in the North American School of Conservation and I am looking forward someday to being a game warden—I hope!

"I love nature and love to be out, just out in the woods or fields or anything, just to be away from manmade things and noises.

"I hope I didn't bother you with this nonsense, but I felt I had to tell it to someone and I picked you. I feel that you may understand what sports-minded city boys must feel when trapped in the city boundaries.

"I read your articles and enjoy what you say. And I hope someday that I could live some of the things you write about. I wrote to you because I couldn't say these things to just anybody. I feel if I could have a dad again it would be you because I admire you.

"There is so much I'd like to say to you, but I'm afraid I have used up too much of your time. So with this I bid you 'so long' for now. Maybe someday, by some great fortune of fate, we may cross paths. Who knows? Maybe in the Gully or even on Bunny Mountain.—Sincerely yours, Charles W. Thompson."

When I finished this letter I was close to crying. I took it to my wife and asked her to read it, and when she brought it back her eyes were brimming. After a long pause she said, "He speaks for many others." And I thought, "There, but for luck, am I."

Must this be? Must this be the quality of life for millions of Americans who "love nature and love to be out, just out in the woods or fields or anything?" Must our factories and houses be jammed together without woods or fields or a patch of clear, blue sky? Is this the best we can do?

In "Days on Bunny Mountain," to which Chuck Thompson referred, I talked about blue skies and a landscape with no works of man in sight, save the trail by which we got there. I talked about air that was good to breathe, solitude, and silence.

After reading his letter I sat at my desk, closed my eyes, and was again on Bunny Mountain. I felt guilty. Chuck Thompson and millions of other Americans will never see a place like that.

They will never feel the exultation that follows the sudden realization you are alone, truly alone, with not a single other human being for miles around. They will never know an hour, probably not even a minute, of absolute silence. They will never breathe clean air. They will never see a sky that is truly blue. They will never dip their faces into a sparkling brook to drink deeply—and safely. Must this be?

Had this letter been written by a ne'er-do-well, an agitator, or an adult cry baby it would not have hit me so. But when you read between the lines you know that Chuck Thompson is a self-respecting, decent American, working at a job he hates to support his wife and family. He owns his home. He is taking a correspondence course, hoping to improve his lot. He is not complaining.

But unless America quits trying to force its political philosophy—and dole—on half the world, and diverts that energy to doing something for Americans, Chuck Thompson and millions like him will still be right there in "a smelly factory drilling holes" when the day comes that they are, finally, too old to work.

Must this be? The answer to that and to all my other questions should be a thundering, "No!" It need not be. We have the wealth, the ability, and the know-how. All we need is the determination and the good sense to put first things first.

I can envision a clean factory—factories need not be dirty, you know— with the homes of its workers within walking distance. There would be a school and a shopping center. And beyond the homes would be woods and fields with a clean brook running through, or perhaps a clean pond in which the kids could swim and fish.

This could be. It would require planning and work and money, maybe a lot of money. But how could money be better spent? By putting another man on the moon? I don't fault the space program. Much good has come from it, but it's time to knock it off. All we may learn in space will be valueless if there are no more sane, healthy, happy Americans to benefit from it.

Many capable scientists believe that we are in danger of smothering the very world with smoke, smog, waste, and pollution. But so far our steps toward a clean, healthful, happy America have been faltering. In his State of the Union Message President Nixon promised "new initiatives" to fight pollution. Yet when the budget came along a few days later it listed fourteen functional categories for funding purposes. Natural Resources and Environment showed up fourteenth and dead last.

The budget request for the Environmental Protection Agency was $439.3 million, not counting what it is obliged to spend abroad. The new Space Shuttle Program came in for $5.5 *billion,* more that 1,000 times as much. American taxpayers are subsidizing farmers to take land *out* of production; yet the Bureau of Reclamation, whose chief function is to put new land *into* production, took a cool $516 million from the 1973 budget, nearly a million more than it drew to finance its boondoggles the year before.

Americans who love their country above personal gain have made progress since the first Earth Week in April, 1970. For one thing, the politicians are now aware that they exist. But they are handed the short end of the stick at every turn. Logging, manufacturing, mining, oil and gas production—with a sinful tax writeoff (did you get any?)—still dominate the Washington scene.

Deadly pollution still pours into the air and water. People still pour into the big cities, where most of them will be doomed forever to live in slums. We are still robbing the future by using up our nonrenewable natural resources such as iron, copper, tin, oil, coal, and natural gas with reckless abandon. And, to make it worse, running the whole show on a deficit budget so that future generations will be stuck for our transgressions.

I once knew an old man who was very poor. He lived in a log cabin beside a rushing river. He could safely drink from it. There were plump, colorful trout to strike his fly. And across the river was a mountain. From his window, the old man could watch the deer and elk that wandered on it. Chipmunks played around his doorstep. Squirrels scolded from the pine trees that shaded the cabin. Grouse would frequently wander into his yard.

When the old man needed groceries, he rode his horse six miles to town to buy them. His purchases were always modest; this was before the days of

Social Security. He had to make his pennies last. But he had his cabin and his horse and his dog and his garden and the trout in the river and he didn't really know that he was poor. If he could no longer roam the mountains and collect a rich harvest of furs from his traps, as he once had done, that was to be expected.

But his friends at last convinced him that he was too old to live alone in his cabin, six miles from the nearest road. So he went to the city, where he had a daughter, and moved in with her.

I knew him there as I had known him earlier in the mountains, where he had given me freely the hospitality of his humble cabin. And I saw him fail—day by day, week by week, and month by month. He lived less than a year in the city.

America today is in grave danger of losing all of those intangibles that give life quality. When it does, I fear, it will die—like the old man.

Chapter 52

Gifts That
Last a Lifetime

One summer evening I was riding home from fishing with Franklin Jones and Don Orcutt when Don said, "What's your next project?"

"I've got to write my *Field & Stream* column for December," I answered, "and I wish one of you would come up with an idea because so far I haven't thought of a thing. I'd like to work in a little Christmas."

My friends mulled this over. After a few minutes Frank said, "You might discuss Christmas gifts that influence the lives of boys and girls."

I asked him what he meant.

"Well, for example," he answered, "the gift that had the most profound effect on my entire life was my first gun. It stimulated my interest in the outdoors more than anything else ever did. I probably never would have become so fascinated by all forms of nature if it hadn't been for that first gun of my own. And I think it was responsible, indirectly at least, for all the years of work I have devoted to conservation.

"I grew up on a farm. There were always guns in the house. We treated them as matter-of-factly as the furniture or tools or anything else. We used them when there was occasion, and they sat in the corner when there wasn't.

"Among others, my father had a 16-gauge Model 12 Winchester. He taught me how to handle it when I was just a little shaver—six or seven, I

Jack Trueblood, Ted's son, when he was twelve years old.
The dove is his first game bird.

suppose. I remember taking it down to the pond one morning and killing six big, fat mallards. They were almost more than I could carry back to the house.

"But the Christmas I was twelve my father gave me a gun of my own. A single-barrel Stevens. I was never so thrilled by any other gift, before or since. And it did something to me. It gave me a feeling of responsibility. There is a world of difference between using somebody else's gun and owning a gun of your own.

"This gun was *mine*. What it did was up to me. There wasn't much law enforcement in those days, but at twelve I was old enough to have a hunting license. I've never intentionally violated a game law."

I said, "You weren't exactly a menace to society, like the current crop of antigun bigots would have us view any boy with a firearm."

"I should say not! A gun was a serious thing. I became an adult when I walked out of the house with my own gun."

The headlights picked up a cottontail crouched beside the road and we were all silent for a while. Then Orcutt said, "The story of my first gun is a lot like Frank's, but it goes a little farther. My dad gave it to me when I was twelve, too, and it had the same effect on me that Frank's gun had on him. I was as serious as a judge when I took it out, especially when Dad wasn't with me.

"But when I was going to college my mother sold it. I've never forgiven her, though I shouldn't hold a grudge, really. My dad had died by then and the depression was on. We were desperately hard up, and I suppose to her it was just a gun that nobody used, sitting around the house. Maybe she didn't even remember it was mine. Though there were other, more expensive, guns she could have sold. Mine was a Lefever Trap and Field, a single-barrel 12-gauge.

"Anyway, last summer I went back to my old home town and hunted up the neighbor she sold it to. He's an old guy, eighty-six now. I never was so thrilled in my life as when he said he still had it. I was determined to buy it back at any price. I asked him what he'd take and he said, 'Well, I don't have much use for it any more. You can have it for just what I paid your mother—$14.'

"I brought it home and restored it to its original condition, inside and out. There is one gun I wouldn't sell, no matter what you might offer!"

I remembered my own first shotgun. I still have it, too. Then I thought of something else. America is no longer a rural country. Most of the readers of *Field & Stream* live in cities. I said, "What good would it do to give a boy a gun if he lived in Los Angeles or Chicago—maybe got to make one hunting trip a year with his dad?"

"It would be a lot tougher than what we had when we were boys," Don agreed. "We could walk out the back door and we were hunting. But there are organized target ranges, many of them owned by local clubs affiliated with the National Rifle Association. And most clubs conduct training courses especially for boys and girls. A youngster could learn to handle his gun safely—and become a good shot, too—at one of them. And even if he only got to go hunting once a year, I think owning a gun does something for a boy. I've seen it in my own kids."

"There are other gifts that can lead to a lifetime interest in nature and the out-of-doors," Frank added. "Suppose when you were twelve or fourteen your folks had given you a modern single-lens reflex camera? With a closeup attachment and a telephoto lens so you could take pictures of everything from bugs and flowers to birds and animals."

"And there isn't a place an outdoor-minded kid couldn't use a camera," I added. "Even in a city park or zoo. There are subjects everywhere. I'd like to have time to take a series of pictures of a spider spinning its web. I had that kind of time when I was a boy."

"Sure," Frank agreed. "And then the next Christmas, if his folks gave him some darkroom equipment so he could begin doing his own processing, a boy would be started on a lifelong hobby. And one of the best."

The remainder of the ride home went quickly. I remembered many of the boyhood gifts that undoubtedly influenced my later life. Very likely, those with the most profound influence of all were books. Who, with even the slightest interest in the outdoors, could fail to respond to Ernest Thompson Seton's story of *Lobo, the King of Currumpaw?*

There are thousands of gripping outdoor books, from Vilhjalmur Stefansson's *The Friendly Arctic* to *The Great Migrations,* by Georges Blond, to Durward L. Allen's *Our Wildlife Legacy.* A father who loved the outdoors and hoped to instill an appreciation of it in his son could do far worse than to give him books about it.

Countless fathers who grew up on farms or in small towns and lived a boyhood of easy outdoor freedom have been forced by the necessity of making a living to rear their families in some great city or its suburbs. These men can't give their sons a boyhood such as they enjoyed themselves. But even in urban America there are opportunities for boys with an interest in the wonders of the out-of-doors. I could walk down to the river and go fishing any evening when I was a boy, but I couldn't visit the American Museum of Natural History.

A microscope and a book on fresh-water biology should be a thrilling gift for any youngster with an interest in nature. It would introduce him to the world of unseen things that are all around us and it could be used anywhere. Every summer pond is teeming with life, most of which is too small to be visible to the naked eye. This, again, is a gift that could influence his entire life.

The same thing might be said of binoculars and a bird book. They could be enjoyed wherever a city park or green trees or an ocean beach or a fresh-water pond provide a habitat in which birds can live, even though there might be millions of people within a dozen miles. And I am sure that any adult group, such as the various local Audubon Societies, would take to its heart a boy or girl who showed an interest in birds.

There are other gifts that stimulate interest in the out-of-doors. Various items of camping equipment, such as a knife, hatchet, sleeping bag, or cooking kit, all qualify. Even if a boy doesn't get to use them often, he still has them—and he also has the sure knowledge that they are *his.* This is worth more than an adult might think.

But the greatest gift of all is a gun. Owning a gun does something for a boy. And second to a gun I think a fishing rod, or a complete fishing outfit, might go farthest toward instilling in him an enduring appreciation of nature. This, I know, was true in my own experience.

My grandfather gave me my first fly rod worthy of the name. By today's standards it really wasn't up to much. Yet with an enameled line that was like wire when it got cold and a single-action reel that I earned as a reward for selling magazine subscriptions, I learned to cast a fly. Furthermore, I caught fish on flies. Lots of fish, as I recall, though memory has a way of making any boyhood exploit greater than it no doubt was.

And here I must digress to state that fishing tackle is one thing inflation somehow overlooked. Of course, there is expensive tackle—there always was. But you can buy better equipment today for the same amount of money than you could twenty years ago, or forty.

One spring when my rod-and-gun club was putting on its annual fly-casting class, I asked the manager of one of the local sporting goods stores to bring down two complete outfits—the cheapest he could assemble and one that cost approximately twice as much.

At our first outdoor practice session I demonstrated the principles of fly casting, using the less expensive outfit. I made some long casts, too, and got some "Oh's" and "Ah's." When I told my pupils that the rod, reel, and line together cost not quite $16, they were shocked. So a perfectly good, usable fly-fishing outfit for a boy needn't drain the family sock. The same is true, of course, with other kinds of tackle. If you buy fly-fishing equipment, just make sure the line fits the rod. This is no problem with today's numbered lines and manufacturers putting the correct line number on each rod.

But back to the fly rod my grandfather gave me. There came a day when I was standing in a mountain stream. Blue sky, cotton-ball clouds, spruce along the shore. There was a pool, bubbling at the upstream end, smooth-flowing and mysterious at the lower. My dry fly, one of the first I'd tied, lit softly among the rising bubbles. It floated toward me. Beneath it, a shadow rose. It hung suspended beneath my floating fly. Nearer and nearer the shadow and the fly approached. At the last possible moment the shadow rose, there was a little splash, and my fly vanished. I set the hook.

Centuries later, I slid an 18-inch rainbow gently onto a miniature beach. I had no landing net. I fell on the lovely fish and clutched it to my bosom. There was no question, I was hooked for life.

Index